Risk Appraisal and Venture Capital in High Technology New Ventures

This book is a 'crossover' treatment of quantitative and qualitative risk analysis within the setting of new high-technology ventures in the UK. Reid and Smith have based their research on extensive fieldwork in patent-intensive, high-technology firms. This has included face-to-face interviews with leading investors, and is illustrated by two chapters of case studies. Their aim is to advance the understanding of methods of risk assessment and to illuminate current policy concerns about stimulating innovative output and securing intellectual property.

This book is unique in being academic in intent and purpose, yet strongly grounded in practice, without becoming merely a practitioner volume. Reid and Smith find a considerable consensus in the venture capital industry on the spectrum of investments by risk, and on key commercial factors affecting risk. This book offers a useful and interdisciplinary approach to an increasingly popular field of study. It provides novel insights into valuing high-technology investments, and managing their risks.

This book will be of considerable interest to students of financial and industrial economics, and financial and management accounting, as well as practitioners in banking, private equity and business and management consultancies.

Gavin C. Reid is Director of CRIEFF and Professor in Economics and Finance at the University of St Andrews. **Julia A. Smith** is Reader in Accounting and Finance at Strathclyde Business School.

Routledge studies in global competition

Edited by John Cantwell
University of Reading, UK
and
David Mowery
University of California, Berkeley, USA

1 **Japanese Firms in Europe**
Edited by Frédérique Sachwald

2 **Technological Innovation, Multinational Corporations and New International Competitiveness**
The case of intermediate countries
Edited by José Molero

3 **Global Competition and the Labour Market**
Nigel Driffield

4 **The Source of Capital Goods Innovation**
The role of user firms in Japan and Korea
Kong-Rae Lee

5 **Climates of Global Competition**
Maria Bengtsson

6 **Multinational Enterprises and Technological Spillovers**
Tommaso Perez

7 **Governance of International Strategic Alliances**
Technology and transaction costs
Joanne E. Oxley

8 **Strategy in Emerging Markets**
Telecommunications establishments in Europe
Anders Pehrsson

9 **Going Multinational**
The Korean experience of direct investment
Edited by Frédérique Sachwald

10 **Multinational Firms and Impacts on Employment, Trade and Technology**
New perspectives for a new century
Edited by Robert E. Lipsey and Jean-Louis Mucchielli

11 **Multinational Firms**
The global–local dilemma
Edited by John H. Dunning and Jean-Louis Mucchielli

12 **MIT and the Rise of Entrepreneurial Science**
Henry Etzkowitz

13 **Technological Resources and the Logic of Corporate Diversification**
Brian Silverman

14 **The Economics of Innovation,
New Technologies and
Structural Change**
Cristiano Antonelli

15 **European Union Direct
Investment in China**
Characteristics, challenges and
perspectives
*Daniel Van Den Bulcke,
Haiyan Zhang and
Maria do Céu Esteves*

16 **Biotechnology in Comparative
Perspective**
Edited by Gerhard Fuchs

17 **Technological Change and
Economic Performance**
*Albert L. Link and
Donald S. Siegel*

18 **Multinational Corporations and
European Regional Systems of
Innovation**
*John Cantwell and
Simona Iammarino*

19 **Knowledge and Innovation in
Regional Industry**
An entrepreneurial coalition
Roel Rutten

20 **Local Industrial Clusters**
Existence, emergence and
evolution
Thomas Brenner

21 **The Emerging Industrial
Structure of the Wider Europe**
*Edited by Francis McGowen,
Slavo Radosevic and
Nick Von Tunzelmann*

22 **Entrepreneurship**
A new perspective
Thomas Grebel

23 **Evaluating Public Research
Institutions**
The U.S. advanced technology
program's intramural research
initiative
Albert N. Link and John T. Scott

24 **Location and Competition**
*Edited by Steven Brakman and
Harry Garretsen*

25 **Entrepreneurship and Dynamics
in the Knowledge Economy**
*Edited by Charlie Karlsson,
Börje Johansson and
Roger R. Stough*

26 **Evolution and Design of
Institutions**
*Edited by Christian Schubert and
Georg von Wangenheim*

27 **The Changing Economic
Geography of Globalization**
Reinventing space
Edited by Giovanna Vertova

28 **Economics of the Firm**
Analysis, evolution and history
Edited by Michael Dietrich

29 **Innovation, Technology and
Hypercompetition**
Hans Gottinger

30 **Mergers and Acquisitions in
Asia**
A global perspective
*Roger Y.W. Tang and
Ali M. Metwalli*

31 **Competitiveness of New Industries**
Institutional framework and learning in information technology in Japan, the U.S. and Germany
Edited Cornelia Storz and Andreas Moerke

32 **Entry and Post-Entry Performance of Newborn Firms**
Marco Vivarelli

33 **Changes in Regional Firm Founding Activities**
A theoretical explanation and empirical evidence
Dirk Fornahl

34 **Risk Appraisal and Venture Capital in High Technology New Ventures**
Gavin C. Reid and Julia A. Smith

Risk Appraisal and Venture Capital in High Technology New Ventures

Gavin C. Reid and Julia A. Smith

LONDON AND NEW YORK

First published 2008
by Routledge
2 Park Square, Milton Park, Abingdon, Oxon OX14 4RN

Simultaneously published in the USA and Canada
by Routledge
270 Madison Ave, New York, NY 10016

Routledge is an imprint of the Taylor & Francis Group, an informa business

© 2008 Gavin C. Reid and Julia A. Smith

Typeset in Times by Wearset Ltd, Boldon, Tyne and Wear
Printed and bound in Great Britain by TJI Digital, Padstow, Cornwall

British Library Cataloguing in Publication Data
A catalogue record for this book is available from the British Library

Library of Congress Cataloging in Publication Data
A catalog record for this book has been requested

ISBN10: 0-415-37351-4 (hbk)
ISBN10: 0-203-94038-5 (ebk)

ISBN13: 978-0-415-37351-7 (hbk)
ISBN13: 978-0-203-94038-9 (ebk)

GCR:
To my children Neil, Eilidh, Annabel and Kenneth

JAS:
To my parents John and Eileen

Contents

List of figures   xiii
List of tables   xiv
Preface   xv
Acknowledgements   xviii
List of abbreviations   xix

PART I
Conceptual framework   1

1 Background   3

Introduction 3
Risk appraisal in high-technology ventures 5
The UK venture capital market 7
The policy context 8
Research methodology 9
Outline of this book 14
Conclusion 16

2 Risk and uncertainty   18

Introduction 18
Qualitative and quantitative uncertainty 19
Agency, innovation and business risk 22
Uncertainty and risk assessment 27
Risk and uncertainty in high-technology ventures 29
Intellectual property 32
Conclusion 33

PART II
Sampling and evidence   35

  3 Sampling, fieldwork and instrumentation   37

   Introduction 37
   Unstructured preliminary fieldwork 38
   Samples of investors and entrepreneurs 40
   Instrumentation design 43
   Exploring the interview agenda 44
   Interviewing in the field 47
   Database construction 48
   Analysis of database 49
   Conclusion 50

  4 Venture capitalists' and entrepreneurs' conduct   52

   Introduction 52
   Assessing risk 53
   Attitudes to risk 53
   Factors in risk appraisal 56
   Features of innovation risk 59
   Non-financial factors 61
   Conclusion 63

PART III
Statistical analysis   65

  5 Investor and entrepreneur: statistical analysis   67

   Introduction 67
   Attitudes to risk 67
   Statistical analysis 69
   Concordance of investors' and entrepreneurs' opinion: an
   *   alternative approach 71*
   Factors in risk appraisal 72
   Conclusion 78

  6 Risk appraisal by investors   79

   Introduction 79
   General statistical analysis 80
   Detailed statistical analysis 87
   Conclusion 94

PART IV
Case study analysis 97

7 **Case study analysis of risk appraisal by entrepreneurs** 99

Introduction 99
Case A – Drug development 99
Case B – Thermal imaging 101
Case C – Copy protection 103
Case D – E-commerce acceleration 105
Case E – Light emitting polymer (LEP) displays 107
Conclusion 109

8 **Further illustrative case studies** 112

Introduction 112
Case F – Laser and infrared detectors 112
Case G – Animal robotics 115
Case H – Electronic micro-displays 118
Case I – Automated baggage security inspection 121
Case J – E-commerce retailing 123
Conclusion 126

PART V
Reporting and investment 129

9 **Reporting, risk and intangibles** 131

Introduction 131
Methodology 132
Evidence 138
Intangible assets 143
Conclusion 145

10 **Behavioural variables and investment** 146

Introduction 146
Statistical analysis 146
Econometric analysis 150
Conclusion 153

PART VI
Concluding material   155

11   Conclusion   157

Overview 157
The contents of this book 158
Discussion of main findings 160
Some neglected areas 162
Conclusion 164

Appendices   166

Appendix 1: Pre-letter 166
Appendix 2: Administered questionnaire 167
Appendix 3: Basic data sheet for entrepreneurs 197
Appendix 4: Postal questionnaire 198

Notes   206
References   207
Index   217

Figures

2.1	The principal–agent setting for investor and entrepreneur	23
2.2	The implications of effort for efficient contracting	26
4.1	Venture capitalists' attitudes to risk	54
4.2	Entrepreneurs' attitudes to risk	54
4.3	Most important factors in risk appraisal (venture capitalists)	56
4.4	Most important factors in risk appraisal (entrepreneurs)	57
4.5	Importance of features of innovation (venture capitalists)	60
4.6	Importance of features of innovation (entrepreneurs)	61
4.7	Importance of non-financial factors (venture capitalists)	62
4.8	Importance of non-financial factors (entrepreneurs)	63
5.1	Venture capitalists' rankings of risk of investment stage, by mean rank	68
5.2	Entrepreneurs' ranking of risk of investment stage, by mean rank	69
5.3	Investors' and entrepreneurs' mean rank scores of riskiness, by investment types	73
5.4	Investors' most important factors in risk appraisal	74
5.5	Entrepreneurs' most important factors in risk appraisal	75
5.6	Investors' and entrepreneurs' mean ranks of importance of factors for risk appraisal	76
7.1	Risk and return	110
9.1	Investment preference by technology	134
9.2	Investment preference by stage	135
9.3	Preference for investment by market extent	137
9.4	Usefulness of financial reports in assessing the value of high-technology firms	140
9.5	Risk reporting in financial accounts	141
9.6	Importance of disclosure in financial reports	142
9.7	Requirement for valuation information	144
11.1	Determinants of total company risk	161
11.2	Risk and impact categories	165

Tables

3.1   Venture capitalists participating in fieldwork   41
3.2   Entrepreneurs participating in fieldwork   43
3.3   Eight-point agenda for administered questionnaire (AQ)   44
6.1   Individual investors' rankings of risk of investment types   89
6.2   Individual investors' rankings of importance of factors for risk
      appraisal   91
8.1   Cross-site analysis of all case studies   127
9.1   Summary statistics on investor conduct   137
9.2   Outline of postal questionnaire   139
10.1 Correlations with the usefulness of financial accounts   147
10.2 Correlations with investment in technopoles   148
10.3 Correlations with influence over management accounting   149
10.4 Regressions explaining levels of investment   152

Preface

This book examines how risk is handled in new high-technology ventures in the UK. Both investors (those allocating funds to ventures), typically venture capitalists, and investees or entrepreneurs (those receiving equity funding support for their ventures) are considered. The main evidence reported upon was gathered by face-to-face semi-structured interviews with key UK investors in high technology firms, and in addition by postal questionnaires. That is, our study is unique in being largely based on primary source data. The venture capital investors we examined have included those who have accounted for most of the funds allocated in this industry segment over the period of analysis of our research. The interview evidence covered risk premiums, investment time horizons, sensitivity analysis, expected values, cash flow, financial modelling, decision making, and qualitative appraisal. A set of ten case studies of patent-intensive, high-technology, investee firms has also been constructed, using evidence from face-to-face interviews supplemented by additional company evidence. The firms examined were operating in new technological areas like encrypting and enciphering for digital technologies, light emitting polymers for flexible screen displays, thermal imaging for security applications, and biopharmaceuticals for cancer therapies.

From the evidence gathered on venture capital investors and entrepreneurs, our principal findings are as follows:

- Standard determinants of company risk are a poor guide to an overall risk assessment of the high-technology firm.
- Business risk, agency risk, and innovation risk are crucial categories in high-technology contexts.
- Venture capital investors emphasise agency risk; investees emphasise business risk.
- Investors focus most on novelty in the marketplace and sales; while entrepreneurs focus most on getting to market and meeting innovation milestones.
- There is considerable consensus in the venture capital industry on the spectrum of investments by risk, and on key commercial factors affecting risk.
- There is little industry consensus on innovation risk.

- Investors prefer to rely on their own procedures and processes (rather than on those of entrepreneurs) when evaluating potential investments.
- Financial accounts seem to offer little to investors, in terms of risk disclosure, or the valuation of intangible assets like intellectual property.
- Investors generally would *not* welcome compulsory risk disclosure, as this would provide too much information to rival investors.
- Statistical models can explain levels of investment allocated by venture capitalists, using risk-based behavioural variables.

The authors should acknowledge, with gratitude, the support and advice about various aspects of this research which they have received from various quarters. We are especially grateful to the Research Foundation of the Chartered Institute of Management Accountants (CIMA), for providing funding for undertaking the first phase of the fieldwork, involving the venture capital investors. The Carnegie Trust for the Universities of Scotland subsequently provided valuable top-up funding, which allowed us to extend further our fieldwork on investees in high-technology areas. Further, funding by the Economic and Social Research Council (ESRC) has enabled us to develop the inter-disciplinary approach espoused in this book, which involves a synthesis of accounting, finance and economics methodologies. We have created a new ESRC research network arrangement, called Seminars in Accounting, Finance and Economics (SAFE) to promote further exactly this kind of approach. Finally, the dissemination of our principal results was facilitated by a travel grant from the British Academy. All of our sponsors have played a crucial role in facilitating the execution, development and dissemination of our research, and we record here our especial thanks for their involvement and support.

Continuous development of our work has also been assisted by its exposure to the welcome intellectual feedback received from participants at numerous seminars, workshops and conferences. The latter have included the British Accounting Association (BAA), the European Accounting Association (EAA), the Financial Reporting and Business Communication (FRBC) conference (at Cardiff Business School), the Babson/Kauffman Entrepreneurship Research Conference (both in Europe and the USA) and the annual meeting of the Academy of Management, USA. We have benefited enormously from that feedback down the years. It is hard to single out specific individuals, and there are many more that we have no space to acknowledge (for which apologies), but the following should be specifically mentioned: Zoltan Acs, John Ashworth, David Audretsch, Andrew Burke, John Butler, Bill Bygrave, Gavin Cassar, Robert Cressy, Marc Epstein, Lynne Evans, Sharon Gifford, Paul Gompers, Graham Hall, Richard Harrison, Peter Johnson, Tom Jones, Josh Lerner, Graham Loomes, Sophie Manigart, Neil Marriott, Colin Mason, Falconer Mitchell, Gordon Murray, Mike Nolan, Paul Pacter, Simon Parker, Werner Ploberger, Paul Reynolds, Steve Spinelli, Andy Stark, David Storey, Nicholas Terry, Roy Thurik, Martin Walker, Mike Wright.

A presentation of our preliminary results to a specialist gathering (the EIASM

Workshop on Performance Measurement and Management Control, EDHEC, Nice) was made possible by travel grants from the British Academy. When our work was close to completion, it was useful to have its full range of ideas, as developed in this book, set out and 'bench tested' before members of the Faculty of Economic Science, Development and Business Administration, and of the CNRS research unit MRSH, of the University of Caen. Our particular thanks go to Jean Bonnet and Vincent Merlin, for their creating the sponsorship that made possible this invigorating research engagement.

We should also extend our warmest gratitude to the venture capital investors and the entrepreneurs who gave so willingly of their time, often within the context of extreme commercial pressure, to answer our questions, and also provided us with additional material from which we could construct our ten case studies. Without their active and enthusiastic participation, the completion of this book would not have been possible. The initial contacts we made with key players in the UK venture capital industry were greatly facilitated by introductions from two past Chairmen of the British Venture Capital Association (BVCA), Michael Denny and Robert Drummond, for which our thanks, for opening up to us a persistently fascinating field of enquiry.

A number of academic and practitioner referees have provided valuable critical feedback on several earlier drafts of this book, from which we have learnt much, and to which the text has been adapted, to the best of our powers. The authors remain responsible for the views expressed within this monograph, including any such errors of omission or commission that it may contain, despite our most assiduous efforts to obtain perfection in drafting.

As regards the final product that you see before your eyes, we should particularly thank Terry Clague of Routledge, who has been a most positive force in encouraging us to bring this project to conclusion, and Rob Langham, also of Routledge, who played a vital early role in the commissioning of this volume. Thanks too, on the production side, to Tom Sutton, also of Routledge.

St Andrews, 2007

Acknowledgements

In writing this book, the authors have been able to draw on their published works with permission of the following publishers.

With kind permission of Elsevier Science and JAI Press:

How do venture capitalists handle risk in high-technology ventures?, in Epstein, M.J. and Manzoni, J.-F. (eds) *Performance Measurement and Management Control*, Vol. 12. Series of 'Studies in Managerial and Financial Accounting', 2002, Elsevier Science and JAI Press, 361–79. ISBN: 0-7623-0867-2.

And with kind permission of the *International Journal of Business and Economics*:

Reid, G.C. and Smith, J.A. (2003) Venture capital and risk in high-technology enterprises, *International Journal of Business and Economics*, 2(3), pp. 227–44.

Abbreviations

AIS   accounting information system
BVCA   British Venture Capital Association
DCF   discounted cash flow
DTI   Department of Trade and Industry
EV   expected value
ICFC   Industrial and Commercial Finance Corporation
IP   intellectual property
IRR   internal rate of return
IS   information system
LCD   liquid crystal display
LEP   light emitting polymer
MAS   management accounting system
MBI   management buy-in
MBO   management buy-out
NPV   net present value
R&D   research and development
ROCE   return of capital employed
ROSF   return of shareholders' funds
SME   small- to medium-sized enterprise
SPSS   statistical package for the social sciences
SWOT   strengths, weaknesses, opportunities and threats: a form of company
         evaluation
VaR   value at risk
VC   venture capital
VCR   venture capital report

Part I
Conceptual framework

1 Background

Introduction

The aim of this book is to analyse methods of risk appraisal in new high-technology ventures (compare Reid and Smith, 2001; Norman, 2004). The objectives of the research upon which this book reports were threefold. First, to advance best practice in supporting high-technology ventures (compare Hsu and Kenny, 2005). Second, to suggest new methodologies, drawing on accounting, finance and economics, for risk handling (compare Cumming *et al.*, 2005). Third, to increase awareness of the utility of accounting, finance and economics methods in a combined sense, for improving our understanding and management of uncertainty. Such methods are explored from both the venture capitalist's (investor's) and the entrepreneur's (investee's) perspective.

A principal tool of this book is the notion of a risk class. Three classes of risk are considered: agency risk, arising from incomplete alignment of the interests of investor and investee (Hyytinen and Toivanen, 2003); innovation risk, arising from the use of an entirely new technology (Lerner. 2002; Moore and Wüstenhagen, 2004; Cumming *et al.*, 2005); and business risk, arising from unpredictable competitor and customer reactions (Goodman, 2003; Frigo and Sweeny, 2005). The research project on which this book reports sought to enquire into attitudes to risk and skills at risk management, in the relationship between high-technology firms and their venture capital backers. The basic idea, building on earlier work by the authors and various co-workers (Reid, 1996; Reid *et al.*, 1997), and related developments (e.g. Fiet, 1995a, 1995b), is as follows. It is that as the venture capital industry matures, so should the techniques which high-technology firms and their venture capital backers use for risk management (compare Dauterive and Fok (2004) in a Chinese context; Liu and Chen (2006) in a Taiwanese context; Robnik (2006) in a Slovenian context; Smolarski *et al.* (2005) in an Indian context; and Salehizadeh (2005) for a general emerging economies context).

Finally, the book explores the usefulness of financial reporting, risk reporting and disclosure in the context of high-technology firms (Hand, 2005). This lays the basis for an analysis of how investors' attitudes to risk affect the level of funding they are willing to provide to entrepreneurs who have started (and run) high-technology firms (compare Cumming, 2006).

If total risk is split up into innovation risk, business risk and agency risk, we note that the main category of risk which the venture capitalist seems to have sought to attenuate is agency risk. They have done this by improved management accounting systems, post-investment, and by pre-commitment to the installation of such systems, pre-investment. However, success in this area has been incomplete, and attention to business and innovation risk has been severely limited. Lack of overall success in risk handling has, as a consequence, been a major cause of failure to provide adequate levels of outside finance for high-technology ventures, compared to appropriate yardstick comparisons in the USA. This book reports on research which aims to investigate the spectrum of methods used for managing innovation, business and agency risks in investors and investees. It thereby seeks routes to better practice in risk handling.

The investigation was fieldwork based (Glaser and Strauss, 1967; Sekaran, 1992, Ch. 4). It drew on our extensive experience in the application of this methodology, both in the venture-capital area (Reid, 1998), and in the investigation of information (e.g. management accounting) system implementation and development (Mitchell *et al.*, 2000). In coping with the high-technology dimension of the study, our previous experience in the intellectual property area, especially as applied to patent-intensive regimes, was also drawn upon. This extended to detailed knowledge of patenting protocols, including the generation of patent 'families' (Reid *et al.*, 1994, 1996; Reid and Roberts, 1996).

In this book, we provide a detailed account of our recent and current research into risk appraisal in UK based high-technology ventures. A comparative US component has also been incorporated into our work, as reflected in fieldwork and two case studies (see Case I and Case J of Chapter 8). As our work is fieldwork based (compare Fried and Hisrich, 1995), it is sharply focused on the reality, and efficacy, of contemporary methods of risk assessment. Over a period of a year we engaged in face-to-face interviews (Oppenheim, 2000) with venture capital investors, and with entrepreneurs in whose firms venture capital had been committed (compare Sapienza, 1989). Our sample consisted of twenty leading UK investors who had engaged in the support of high-technology ventures, and ten entrepreneurs (investees), who were involved in bringing to market some of the most exciting high-technology products being developed in the world today (e.g. encrypting and enciphering, quantum cascade lasers, animal robotics, light emitting polymers, thermal imaging). The meetings with venture capital investors and entrepreneurs were conducted using a administered questionnaire schedule (Sekaran, 1992, Ch. 7) (see Appendix 2). This schedule was constructed in a slightly different variant for the investor and investee case, but each used a standardised approach to the following eight-point agenda: risk premia, investment time horizon, sensitivity analysis, expected values, predicted cash flows, financial modelling, decision making, and qualitative risk appraisal. A specimen interview schedule (which contains this eight-point agenda) is contained in Appendix 2. Further sample data were obtained by a postal questionnaire, as reflected in the analysis of Chapters 9 and 10, which is based on the instrumentation detailed in Appendix 4.

This chapter proceeds as follows. First, we deal briefly with general problems of risk appraisal in high-technology ventures. Second, a background sketch of the UK venture capital context is provided. Third, the policy context is briefly considered. Fourth, the research plan behind the work on which we report is laid out. Finally, the structure of the book is outlined.

Risk appraisal in high-technology ventures

Considered as a business proposition, the high-technology venture can be perplexing. It can seem unstructured, distant from exit, highly risky, and difficult to control. In its development company form, the high-technology venture from an investor perspective, can sometimes seem too like a research project, which is largely justified by its pursuit of scientific enquiry, without any plausible justification on commercial grounds. The problem of cost overrun on projects is endemic (Perez-Castrillo and Riedinger, 1999). It is as though the investor feels he or she is being invited by the entrepreneur to bear all the downside risk, without any clear indication of the prospective rewards, except that it might, with a small probability, be 'large'. Without doubt, such an investment involvement embodies considerable risk of the sort familiar from other areas of enterprise.

One kind of risk that immediately comes to mind is 'business risk'. This is caused by the complex, competitive environment in which high-technology firms function (compare Goodman, 2003; Frigo and Sweeney, 2005). In a sense, firms are 'racing' to be first to get an entitlement to the intellectual property (IP) embodied in a new technology (Brouwer and Kleinknecht, 1999). There are so-called 'action-reaction' effects at work. Thus firms will redouble effort, if they are very close to rivals,; but will quickly give up, if they seem outstripped in the race. Reading how other firms will behave in such situations, and crafting one's strategy appropriately, are all aspects of a form of competition in which firms are in significant interaction (namely, oligopoly). In this industrial setting, conjectures have to be made by firms about rivals' conjectures. There is no safe guide as to how this should be done, as the proliferation of varied and different solutions from game theory suggests (Dixit and Skeath, 1999).

Another important category of risk is agency risk. This arises, in general, from an incomplete alignment of incentives between economic agents (compare Hyytinen and Toivanen, 2003). In our case, the economic agents involved are: (a) the venture capital investor; and (b) the entrepreneur of a high-technology firm. Briefly, investors are risk specialists, who know a little about technology, and a lot about monitoring and control. They are willing to back their judgements with large injections of equity finance. Typically, entrepreneurs are immersed in technological developments, and are risk averse and starved of cash. They would prefer a less risky life and more financial backing (compare Repullo and Suarez, 2004). They also need advice and guidance on commercial imperatives. In theory, a kind of 'contract' should be struck, in which the entrepreneur gives the investor access to potentially valuable intellectual property (i.e. 'property' based on new ideas), and the management skill to create it. In exchange for this, the investor bears some of the risk, and provides an infusion of equity finance (Reid, 1998). In practice, it may be hard for the investor to evaluate the entrepreneur's claim to be able to produce valuable intellectual property; and the mere fact of backing an entrepreneur tends to diminish his incentive to continue to be creative in this respect, unless activity is tightly monitored.

Finally, and most importantly, there are 'innovation risks' (compare Lerner, 2002; Moore and Wüstenhagen, 2004; Cumming *et al.*, 2005). Even the entrepreneur (and certainly the investor) is uncertain about what a development programme might produce. The final form an innovation takes and, just as important, both the point in time at which it is proved, and the potential market place value it might have, are subject to high degrees of uncertainty.

Arguably, 'business risk' and 'agency risk' are in some measure amenable to standard methods of risk analysis. For example, the agency approach has been successful in the insurance industry, and elements of this approach can be carried over into the investor-investee context. However, 'innovation risk' is harder to handle in this way. Essentially, the 'frequency limit principle', widely used in standard risk analysis, cannot be applied to this category of risk. In this approach, one considers the frequency with which a known event occurs in a large number of trials, conducted under essentially unchanged conditions. However, the conditions necessary for the standard estimation of the probability of an event as a 'frequency limit' (implying the number of trials becomes indefinitely large) are never satisfied with innovative events. They are essentially a 'one-off'. By their very nature, innovations have not happened before. There is no continuous record of evidence on which one can base estimates of their probability of occurring. This is especially true of radical innovation (see Rice *et al.*, 2000). Therefore one cannot estimate the relevant risk on an actuarial basis, as one needs to, for example, in using Value at Risk (VaR) methods of risk assessment (Jorion, 2000).

The assigning of risk in such cases has to be subjective (Moesel and Fiet, 2001; Moesel *et al.*, 2001). This need not occur in a vacuum. For example, there may be technologies which are related to the innovation being attempted which provide useful yardstick comparisons, concerning matters like development costs, and time to discovery. Technology foresight specialists may use a variety of methods (e.g. the polling of opinion of top technologists in a specialist area) to estimate the chances of an innovation occurring. However, the assigning of a numerical probability to an innovative event is perhaps too stringent a requirement. For many purposes, it may be satisfactory to think in terms of 'risk classes' rather than in terms of point estimates of probability. Simple classifications of risk like 'high', 'medium' and 'low' may be adequate, if not perfect, substitutes for statistical estimates of probability.

It has been suggested that UK investors have tended to overlook good potential prospects in new high-technology firms. For example, Murray and Lott (1995) have maintained that high-technology firms are not comfortably accommodated within existing frames of reference for risk assessment by investors. Therefore, they tend to be excessively cautious in their risk appraisal, and set risk-adjusted hurdle internal rates of return (IRRs) that are excessive (see Manigart *et al.*, 2002). It would not be unusual to see hurdle IRRs of 45 per cent being set, and rates as high as 90 per cent (or more) are not unknown (Murray, 1995). One interpretation of this evidence is that UK investors invoke different, and usually more stringent, investment criteria, than do their US counterparts. This interpretation finds favour, in the light of the evidence that venture capital investors in the UK allocated (proportionately) about one third of the funding to new high-technology firms that US investors did (Lockett *et al.*, 2002).

The UK venture capital market

Our research was largely conducted in the UK venture capital industry. Though often perceived as a relatively new activity, it had earlier roots in colonial merchant adventuring. It then mutated into merchant banking, and, finally was given formal institutional expression in the post-Second World War Industrial and Commercial Finance Corporation (ICFC). The latter was subsequently revamped and modernised into 'Investors In Industry' (3i) when the UK venture capital industry emerged in the 1980s. It remains the biggest 'player' in the UK industry today and is, indeed, the largest single allocator of venture capital funding in the world (Coopey and Clarke, 1995). As befits European practice, we adopt a broad definition of 'venture capital' (see *Venture Capital Report (VCR) Guide*, 2000, p. 80). The narrower US definition would refer to the outside equity funding of the seed-corn, inception, early growth and expansion stages of the entrepreneurial firm's life cycle.

Here, our definition is closer to what is broadly referred to as 'private equity'. It includes the equity financing of management buy-out (MBO) and management buy-in activity (MBI). Such activity has been central to the early development of the UK venture capital market, although the situation is changing rapidly.

In an earlier analysis of venture capital, one of the authors, Reid (1998), reported on the UK venture capital market as it approached maturity (see Terry, 1994; Murray, 1995). It was asked of investors what it felt like to be at the 'leading edge' of technology. The reply, a common joke in the industry at the time, was that they avoided what was humorously called 'the bleeding edge'. Investment involvement of this sort was perceived to be too risky, compared to the abundant, more attractive (and relatively safe) MBO and MBI activity, which arose from the radical restructuring of UK industry, often far from the leading edge. Today, the scene has changed considerably, with UK activity in MBOs still rising, and much more action in the MBO and MBI area in mainland Europe, where it has been strongly supported by UK venture capital investors for some time (Wright and Robbie, 1996b). Within the UK itself, investors are now more keen to be involved in higher risk investments, both in terms of stage (e.g. seed-corn, inception, early growth) and of sector (e.g. high-technology, leisure industry).

The UK venture capital industry ranks second in the world to the USA (compare Gompers *et al.*, 1998). In Europe it is the dominant 'player', and accounted for 38 per cent of private equity investment in 2000. In that year, a record total of £8.3 billion was invested, in over 1,500 companies, of which 76 per cent was invested in the UK. Over half of the private equity funding committed to firms in the UK was for expansion purposes. This is generally perceived to be the low risk end of the investment spectrum. It probably explains the US perception that UK investors steer clear of high risk. However, this perception is increasingly inaccurate. In the year 2000, when our fieldwork on investors was started, over £1.6 billion (over a quarter of total UK funds committed) was invested in backing UK high-technology companies (British Venture Capital Association (BVCA), 2001; www.bvca.co.uk). As history records, that investment was certainly prudent, if not buccaneering, and the UK high-technology sector largely avoided the 'high-tech meltdown' that occurred in the US at that time.

In investigating the UK venture capital market, we initially used unstructured fieldwork (Oppenheim, 2000). In this first stage of fieldwork, entry into the field must be undertaken with an open mind. The purpose is simply to explore the universe within which the actors under investigation (here, investors and entre-preneurs) normally function. Our starting point was to seek meetings with two key 'gatekeepers' to the venture capital world. The role of the gatekeeper is to legitimise the enquiry of the field worker, and to facilitate ports of entry to 'pivotal points' or 'high communicators' in the field. We selected a Director of 3i in London, and the then Chairman of the BVCA. At that time, the latter insti-tution had about 120 members, who were responsible for almost all of the venture capital finance invested in the UK.

We have already observed that the 1990s saw great changes in the UK venture capital scene. An aspect of this is that the old aversion to high-technology involvement was disappearing. At the time of our study, up to a third of new funds were being allocated in this area. A good illustration of this is the Cambridge high-technology agglomeration, centred on its science park, where part of our fieldwork was conducted. This area alone had over 1,500 small, new, high-technology firms, most of them energetically seeking venture capital. The 'M4 corridor' of England, especially the stretch extending from Reading to Bristol, provides a similar illustration. At the same time as firms in high-technology areas such as these have been enjoying increased access to venture capital, so too have the methods used by venture capitalists for risk appraisal, in high-technology investment contexts, been improving. The broader purpose of our work is to investigate this phenomenon.

The policy context

It is important to establish that part of the motivation behind our work has been its potential relevance to the policy arena. When we started our fieldwork, pub-lished output by Government Departments and accounting bodies illustrated their interest in high- technology investments.

For example, in July 1999, a UK Government Department – the Department of Trade and Industry (DTI) – issued a consultative document on equity gaps in small and medium sized enterprises (SMEs), and advanced the argument for venture capital funding at the regional level. It specifically referred to problems of 'market weaknesses' of the sort we address under our business risk category, where we look at market opportunities, quality of proposal, etc. Further, its interest in venture capital arose from their expressed desire 'to support early-stage, high technology businesses' (DTI, 1999) of the sort we are concerned with in our research. This commitment was reinforced by statements made at the same time by Lord Sainsbury, Minister of Science, to the effect that steps would be taken to diminish business risk in the UK's biotechnology sector, by creating conditions which stimulated 'clusters' of biotechnology firms and their support-ing firms and markets.

Accounting bodies were pressing for reforming the treatment of intellectual property of the sort that the high-technology companies of our research gener-ated (e.g. leading to patented products). They favoured reducing the complexity of the taxation of intellectual property, with a view to encouraging a climate of innovation in the UK. Further, for quoted high-technology companies, they favoured an improvement in risk management by company directors, to secure a low cost of capital and to increase shareholder value (Carey and Turnbull, 2000). Thus an important goal of our research was both to achieve a better understanding of how to value intellectual property, and to help to identify emerging best practice in risk management (e.g. in a management accounting context).

Research methodology

The three initial stages of our research (set against the background described above) involved: (a) determining appropriate sampling frames for both venture capitalists (investors) and high-technology companies (investees); (b) designing an administered questionnaire schedule, in two variants, for face-to-face inter-views with venture capital investors and entrepreneurs of high-technology com-panies; and (c) designing a postal questionnaire to investigate risk, information and fund allocation in high-technology companies. The interview aspect (points (a) and (b) above) involved working through an eight-point agenda, covering matters like the risk premium, time horizon and cash flow. Consideration of how these stages were undertaken would extend the discussion beyond the methodo-logical scope of this chapter, but for detail of design see Appendix 2. Chapter 3 provides a compact treatment of this aspect of our work. For the moment, suffice it to say that a variety of sources exist for obtaining random samples of investors and investees, and that it is desirable that some form of stratified random sam-pling should be utilised, to ensure that a representative sample of high-techno-logy firms is obtained. As an operational issue, much of the active problem solving of our research arose not through sampling per se, but through the need to deal with problems of access to the field. The solution to these problems was found to be complex, and not susceptible to a formulaic approach. Suffice it to say that it called for flexibility, imagination and determination.

The investigative side of the fieldwork had to be responsive to 'time and place' circumstances. In seeking 'ports of access', the authors benefited from their past acquaintance with major players in the UK venture capital world, and previous success in both making contact with target individuals and in eliciting their co-operation. The initial concern was with getting inductive evidence that would help in the design of the proposed methods with which the investor and investee were to be investigated. We concluded that an administered questionnaire would be appropriate for face-to-face interviewing, and a postal questionnaire (Appendix 4) would be appropriate for investigating risk management and fund allocation. The administered questionnaire (Appendix 2) was designed to explore innovation, agency and business risks. James Fiet (1995a) has used a postal questionnaire to acquire data in the US. This method is certainly convenient and economical, but a lot is lost in neglecting the opportunity to have face-to-face meetings with investors and investees. For example, face-to-face interviews allow a more thorough and deep investigation of contractual arrangements between investors and investees to be pursued (compare Fried and Hisrich, 1994). It also increases response rates markedly, and thereby largely averts problems of non-response bias. Certainly, we found it to be an extraordinarily effective way of exploring the fine detail of how risk was handled in high-technology investments.

It allowed us to pursue a more refined and detailed approach to the investigation of risk appraisal. With time to develop ideas simply in the face-to-face interviews, we were not tempted to take short cuts, which (falsely) assume more knowledge on the respondents' part than is reasonable (e.g. as regards risk classes, like 'innovation risk'). Our investigation did not require that any of the respondents, be they investors or entrepreneurs, should be familiar with the disciplinary basis of our research work.

A further article of faith in our designing of the investigation instruments was that concrete data on risk handling should be referred to, wherever possible. For example, a possible approach to business risk, as regards competition, is to ask venture capital investors whether they agree or disagree, mildly or strongly, with the statement that 'the existence of many competitors, if not dealt with in some way, could cause a venture which they had backed to lose money. The approach has many weaknesses. The most obvious is that the researcher should be interested in calibrating the effect of risk management on performance using a scale of performance, rather than reducing it to a binary outcome (e.g. do you or don't you run at a loss?). Further, the researcher is interested in the specifics of risk handling methods. To illustrate with the same example, he or she might enquire into ways in which competitors' actions can be detected, diverted, forestalled, and so on in terms of concrete actions (e.g. use of a trade intelligence database; protection of intellectual property by patents, trade-marks, etc. and aggressive strategies like acquisition or take-over).

The above are merely illustrative, but they serve to show that a significant aspect of the research work accomplished, in terms of its claim to novelty, was embodied in the fieldwork methods used and the design of new instruments of investigation (specifically as in Appendix 2 and Appendix 4). Our research goal was that our work should reflect the best of the extant literature, as we went into the field, yet should be free of any assumption that the respondent was familiar with the terms of reference of our enquiry (e.g. its hypotheses, or its technical vocabulary). In approaching the problem of designing new instrumentation, the authors drew on considerable prior experience in prototyping, piloting and con-structing successful instrumentation for administered and postal questionnaires, and for semi-structured interview schedules (e.g. Reid, 1993, 1998, 2007).

Naturally, part of the intellectual background we brought to this research was work on risk and uncertainty, arising from a variety of fields, including accoun-tancy, finance and economics, but also extending to information systems, philo-sophy and cognitive science. Risk and uncertainty may sometimes be distinguished by saying that both refer to future outcomes of which one is unsure, but whilst in the former case this can be quantified, in the latter case it cannot be. Another way of putting the point is to say that we are distinguishing between 'hard' and 'soft' analysis. However, it is possible that this goes too far, at least when viewed from the perspective of Frank Knight's (1921) influential framework. Knight thought of uncertain situations as being those in which one could not appeal to a frequency limit principle in assigning probabilities. However, this does not rule out assigning probabilities by judgement, made, for example, in the light of reasoning in relation to similar, if not identical, instances. Certainly, in complex, novel, uncertain situations, subjective evalu-ation (possibly involving some process of pattern recognition) must replace the assigning of a probability, by using frequency data.

One reaction to risk and uncertainty may be conservatism in estimating out-comes. The apparently benign intention here is to make the business well-protected or safe. The attitude which one investor adopts could be 'It can't get any worse than X'. This might be regarded as no more than prudential manage-ment. It fits in well with the primacy often given to attenuating the downside risk by investors. However, it may lead to a systematic bias in decision making. One is ignoring the average or typical outcome, which, over time, may lead to forgoing potentially profitable possibilities. This conservatism may extend beyond merely being systematically pessimistic about outcomes, to a foreshort-ening of the time horizon of decision making. If a future situation is highly uncertain, there may be a tendency to argue that nothing can be said about it at all, in which case, less is said about the future than is really possible. Short-termism in decision making can be the consequence of this frame of mind. Potential for profit may be overlooked because of an unwillingness to look into the eye of the storm of uncertainty.

The above are the sorts of issues we had in mind when we investigated the extent to which formal and informal methods of appraising risk and uncertainty were used by investors and investees. So far, we have been highlighting key points and central issues. In practice, a catalogue of approaches, embracing all levels of formality, was investigated. These included: using conservative estimates; looking at best and worst estimates; applying sensitivity analysis; assessing probabilities; and assessing evidence. It is useful to make a broad distinction between *quantitative risk assessment* and *qualitative risk assessment*. Under these two headings, we indicate below what governed our thoughts in going about designing our instruments (see Appendices 2 and 4 for their form). We consider first the administered questionnaire.

Quantitative risk assessment

Our key concerns were:

- What effect does risk have on investment decisions? For example, does it influence the discount rate used, or does it lead to thinking in terms of risk classes?
- What effect does risk have on the conduct of investment appraisal? For example, does it influence the time horizon, the payback period and the target rate of return?
- Do risk considerations enter into investment sensitivity analysis? For example, are probabilities attached to cost and revenue flows and, if so, how are they determined, and how widely might they be varied in a sensitivity analysis?
- How is risk analysis used to reduce uncertain values to 'certainty equivalents'? Does the form this method might take differ, depending on the variable in question (e.g. cost, revenue) or the year in question?
- How does risk affect the willingness to accept or reject a decision in the firm, like a new high-technology product launch? For example, is a positive (i.e. greater than zero) net present value (NPV) the key consideration, or is a more qualitative approach to risk to be taken?
- How does risk influence the financial modelling of the firm? For example, would simulation methods (e.g. of the Monte Carlo variety) be used (Brigham, 1992, Ch. 10)?
- How is decision analysis affected by risk? For example, are probabilities or estimates of values used in 'decision trees' (Arnold and Turley, 1996)?

These indicate the key lines along which our research agenda was developed, in the context of designing an administered questionnaire schedule for interviews. The explicit implementation of questions asked above, in interview instruments (namely, semi-structured interview schedules) is a matter of detailed design and testing, which is beyond the scope of this chapter. Additional detail is given in Chapters 3 and 9, and in the Appendices to this book. Thus, the above bullet points are only indicative of the sorts of issues that were addressed, so far as quantitative risk assessment was concerned.

The postal questionnaire (Appendix 4) examined background information (e.g. location, sector, funds), financial accounting, management accounting and performance. It too enquired into attitudes to risk (e.g. risk disclosure) and information (e.g. extent and type).

Both instrument designs (see Appendices 2 and 4) also made enquires about qualitative assessments of risk. Some of the conceptual thinking behind that is mapped out below.

Qualitative risk assessment

As regards qualitative risk assessment, some hints at the significant issues have already been made. For example, qualitative risk appraisal tends to take over once the limits of quantitative risk appraisal have been reached (compare fifth bullet point above (p. 12), which, when translated into questionnaire format, suggests seeking a further judgement on probability after the quantitative risk appraisal has been completed). A fuller development of qualitative risk appraisal issues in investor-entrepreneur venture capital contexts has already been undertaken elsewhere, by one of the authors (Reid, 1998). That treatment is extensive, and not readily encapsulated in a few sentences here. However, it may be useful to illustrate, by way of one example, how the approach to qualitative risk appraisal, used in the semi-structured interviews, was inspired.

The inspiration for this goes back to a decision methodology first developed for personal use by Benjamin Franklin (American statesman and inventor, 1706–90). It has since been adapted and modernised by specialists in the design of expert systems for decision support purposes (see Hardman and Ayton, 1997). Franklin suggested adapting a score-carding method for evaluating the chances of an event occurring. Examples of this might be the outcome of a political process, like a candidate being elected or a vote going in favour of a proposition; or the outcome of an economic process, like a company failing, or a business achieving main market listing. Inspired by this, we have used score-carding question design extensively in creating our structured interview schedule, though in a broader sense than the balanced score-card method (see for example, Kaplan and Norton, 1992).

In creating his score-card, Franklin simply enumerated arguments for or against an event occurring. To illustrate, an argument for a company failing might be that it was too highly geared, and an argument for it succeeding might be that it had a new product for which there was a buoyant market demand. If these were the only arguments on either side, then whether the company would succeed or fail would be regarded as 'equivocal'. If one wanted to move from a qualitative appraisal (i.e. 'equivocal') to a quantitative appraisal, a probability or chance of failure of 0.5 is naturally suggested.

It may seem that arguments for or against an event occurring are rather fragile guides to probabilities. However, evidence on real-time decisions taking by human subjects suggests that probability judgements based on explicit reassessing are considerably more reliable that those based on hunch or intuition, gut reaction, judgement and so on (Hardman and Ayton, 1997). This holds true, irrespective of the specific context of the arguments per se, whether they be in favour or against an event occurring. Thus the construction of expert decision systems to assist in risk assessment takes *an argument* as a basic building block. An argument has a known logical syntax, and only statements conforming to this are accepted. However, the context of an argument need not be explored.

The translation from arguments for or against an event occurring into a qualitative (or even quantitative) risk assessment may be carried out in a variety of ways. Very often, a focus of interest in risky situations is on whether there is a 'more than even chance' of an event occurring. This judgement might be made whenever the balance of arguments *for* the event occurring exceeds those *against* it occurring. More contentious, but still probably superior to acting on a hunch, would be to use the proportion of arguments for an event occurring as a quantitative estimate of its probability. The application of these new techniques for risk appraisal in high-technology ventures is as yet untested, but they promise to cast new light on a hitherto darkened corner, which, until now, appeared difficult to illuminate with currently available techniques.

Outline of this book

The basic framework of this book is as follows: Part I introduces the venture capital industry and basic notions of risk and uncertainty; Part II, explains the fieldwork methods adopted, and sampling methods used and provides summary evidence on risk appraisal from respondents; Part III uses inferential techniques on the data gathered to explore hypotheses about industry consensus and factors which impact on risk appraisal; Part IV presents ten illustrative case studies in a common framework; Part V introduces another sample, examines the evidence on financial and risk reporting, and estimates a behaviourally-based model of investment fund allocation; Part VI reviews and discusses the main findings, and is followed by appendices on instrumentation.

We have already established in this chapter the essential elements of the research upon which we are reporting. Our focus is on how risk is managed in investor/entrepreneur relations when the setting is a high-technology new venture (compare Lefley, 1997). We take a broad view of what is meant by risk, extending to what experts might distinguish from risk as being (uninsurable) uncertainty. The investigation is fieldwork based. It involved personal visits to meet investors and investees, who were then interviewed using an administered questionnaire. This guided the interviewer and respondent through an eight-point semi-structured interview agenda.

Chapter 2 extends our discussion of risk and uncertainty. In doing so, it makes explicit reference to principal–agent analysis, as a suitable way of model-ling investor/entrepreneur relations. Algebraic and geometrical formalisations are presented. Particular reference is then made to the three risk classes we use extensively, namely agency, innovation and business risk. It enlarges the narrow focus of risk to wider issues of uncertainty and risk assessment. Specific features of risk and uncertainty that are germane to high-technology ventures are considered next. This leads on to a discussion of methods of securing intellectual property rights, with a view to attenuating exposure to the innovation risk.

Chapter 3 looks in detail at the research methodology. This considers the research plan, fieldwork entry, unstructured fieldwork, instrument design, sampling, site visits and interviewing, debriefing, data recording and storing, and fieldwork exit. In summary, it provides a kind of 'route map' of how the underlying projects were devised, launched, and executed.

Chapter 4 looks at the responses of investors and entrepreneurs in a comparative sense. The focus is on: attitudes to risk, over investment types (compare Lipe, 1998); the most important factors in risk appraisal; the importance of features of innovation; and the importance of non-financial factors. These responses are related to the overarching theme of the book, that risk can be broken down into three principal classes in our high-technology context – agency, business and innovation risk. The approach adopted is both descriptive and analytical.

Chapter 5 reinforces the treatment of Chapter 4, by re-examining the evidence, asking not what the evidence tell us, but rather, what can we infer from the evidence. In doing so, it introduces techniques from the statistical analysis of rankings, using such tools to examine concordance of opinion amongst investors and entrepreneurs, and key factors in risk appraisal.

Chapter 6 looks at the quantitative evidence on investors from a statistical standpoint. The emphasis is not so much on 'what does the evidence suggest?' (the concern of Chapter 4), as on 'how confident are we about this bit of evidence?' and 'what can we infer about investors in general from this evidence?'. In short, the approach adopted is inferential.

Chapters 7 and 8 look at evidence from the investee (rather than investor) standpoint, and uses both quantitative and qualitative evidence to construct ten case studies. Five case studies are considered in Chapter 7, looking at the following forms of high-technology: thermal imaging (security and safety devices); copyright protection and rights management; biopharmaceuticals for cancer therapies; light-emitting polymers for colour display devices; and enciphering to expedite e-commerce. Chapter 8 provides a further set of illustrative case studies, looking at: laser and infrared detection; animal robotics; electronic micro-displays; automated baggage security inspection; and e-commerce retailing. Cases I and J arose from US fieldwork, and help to provide some triangulation on the evidence. All the cases are brief, in vignette form, following the pattern of the interview agenda. They serve as illustrative case studies, to animate the more formal and technical discussion of risk management elsewhere.

Chapter 9 is concerned with further empirical work, based on a postal questionnaire (see Appendix 4) focusing on financial reporting, risk disclosure and intangible assets. The sampling frame was based on UK investors in diverse sectors, ranging from biotechnology, through software/computer services, to communications and medical services. This evidence is used to examine the usefulness of financial accounts, reporting and disclosure, and the benefits (or otherwise) of publishing financial accounts. It concludes by asking how much public information should be made available on key intangible assets.

Chapter 10 builds on the evidence set out in Chapter 9. First, it engages in a statistical analysis of the usefulness of financial accounts, the targeting (or otherwise) of investments in science parks or technopoles, and the influence of investors on the entrepreneur's internal management of his high-technology firm. Second, it builds a model that explains the level of investment funds allocated (at the microeconomic level) by a set of factors measuring the investor's attitude to risk. The latter approach is econometrically based. It can be contrasted with two alternative approaches: the macroeconomic, and the stochastic. The macroeconomic, as illustrated by work like that of Salehizadeh (2005), would look at the role of macroeconomic variables like GDP per capita, long-term capital inflows and stock market listings to explain the level of venture capital investment. The stochastic approach, as represented by work like that of Mantell (2003), would model the investor's capital commitment to the entrepreneur by a stochastic process (e.g. a renewal process, deriving the probability that an entrepreneur's innovative project will be abandoned, due to failure to acquire adequate funding in a given time interval). By contrast, the approach of Chapter 10 is microeconomic, in focusing on the investor as an individual economic agent, investing in a specific high-technology firm. Further, it is behavioural, rather than anonymously stochastic, in focusing on individual investors' attitudes (e.g. to compulsory information provision, to adequacy of own due diligence, to extent of disclosure of information) as determinants of the level of investment.

Chapter 11 draws together the various threads from the earlier chapters. It emphasises the efficacy of the research method adopted for 'getting to the parts' about risk that alternative methodologies cannot reach. The primacy of the three risk classes identified in preliminary fieldwork (namely, agency, business and innovation) is established, based on qualitative and quantitative evidence. Investor and investee attitudes to risk are summarised. Models for explaining levels of funding are also summarised. It ends by drawing conclusions about areas in which practice may be improved.

The Appendices present four specimen instruments: a pre-letter, an administered questionnaire schedule (including the eight-point agenda), a basic data sheet, and a postal questionnaire. The second relates to the entrepreneur's interview schedule, but save for the investor/entrepreneur distinction, the instrumentation design is parallel for each type of interviewee.

Conclusion

The purpose of this chapter has been first, to establish the institutional setting of our research, and second, to indicate the basic form of our research methods.

We have indicated that significant changes have been taking place in the UK venture capital industry over the last decade. These have involved an increase in scale of funding, and a greater willingness to back high-technology businesses. However, there is evidence that the conservatism of approach by UK investors may be leading to under-investment in the high-technology area (compare Jaffe

(2000) for the US context). Finally, the policy context was briefly considered, focusing on the interests of both government and accounting bodies in fostering an improved environment for high-technology investing.

We then set out our research methods. These were described as being largely fieldwork based, involving face-to-face meetings with investors and entrepreneurs in high-technology areas. The tools of investigation were the administered questionnaire, and the postal questionnaire. Key concepts behind the development of the instrumentation were explored, involving the distinction between risk and uncertainty, and between qualitative and quantitative risk. Finally, a checklist of key areas of investigation (or agenda) was developed, covering matters like sensitivity analysis, certainty equivalence and financial modelling.

Having established the basic background of our research, we now turn to a further development of key concepts, and a detailed consideration of the fieldwork activity and the results it produced.

2   Risk and uncertainty

Introduction

Some key considerations of risk and uncertainty have been briefly laid out in Chapter 1. The purpose of this chapter is now to provide a more detailed treatment which focuses on our interest in high-technology firms, and on the venture capitalists and entrepreneurs that back and run them, respectively.

Our interest in risk and uncertainty focuses on decision making. This might involve a decision on the best launch of a product using light emitting polymers (this LEP technology is considered further in Case E, Chapter 8). Should it be a television screen, a mobile phone display, or a computer screen that is used to launch this technology? Part of the decision making involves making reference to similar events, or even identical events. Typically, in a high-technology context, the latter is ruled out. In our illustration, nobody, at the time of the field-work, had used LEP technology for such purposes. However, there were related technologies, indeed even different technologies, which had been put to similar purposes, from which we may learn. This illustration suggests that in practice the uncertainty attached to a product launch can be dealt with by a variety of methods (e.g. lessons learnt from related technologies). The methods may be qualitative, rather than quantitative, but provided they are used in a structured method, their adoption may well be better than ignoring uncertainty altogether, for want of quantitative methods.

This chapter will first develop this distinction between quantitative and qualitative uncertainty, and then will move on to consider our three main risk categories: *agency*, *innovation* and *business* risk. In elaborating agency risk, we shall give explicit attention to the principal–agent model on which it is based, and develop some relevant formal tools. The concepts of uncertainty and risk assessment are further elaborated, and then related to high-technology ventures. The last substantive section looks at intellectual property, an important asset of high-technology firms, and attendant risk considerations.

This chapter aims to provide tools for answering two questions, within an applied principal–agent framework (compare Reid, 1998; Sapienza *et al.*, 2000). As we know, the applied context is venture capital investing. Within this setting the venture capitalist is treated as principal, and the entrepreneur as an agent.

The questions are: How risky are investments? What affects risk most? As announced in Chapter 1, we aim to address these questions using interview evidence on attitudes to risk, obtained from a sample of UK venture capitalists and entrepreneurs in high-technology enterprises (compare Lefley, 1997). In Chapter 3, to follow, it is shown how this was done using two administered questionnaire schedules of parallel design. These allowed us to take respondents through a common agenda in face-to-face interviews. The detailed arguments will be left to Chapters 4 and beyond, but to motivate this conceptual chapter, and lay the basis for the tools of analysis we shall be deploying, we anticipate our findings as follows.

We report on two key findings. First, there is general agreement between venture capitalists and entrepreneurs concerning the relative riskiness of investment involvements, e.g. start-up, MBO. However, entrepreneurs rate individual investment types as more risky than venture capitalists across the whole spectrum of investment types. This finding suggests a common industry view on relative investment riskiness (compare Bhattacharyya and Leach, 1999), but a comparatively more risk averse attitude by entrepreneurs, in relation to venture capitalists (compare Beetsma and Schotman, 2001). This can be explained by the greater risk exposure of the entrepreneur, who is generally denied the risk-spreading opportunities that the venture capitalist enjoys through portfolio diversification. Second, a difference is found between venture capitalist and entrepreneur, concerning factors which affect risk the most. Venture capitalists are largely concerned with agency risk, focusing on the monitoring and control relationship with their entrepreneurs. By contrast, entrepreneurs are largely concerned with business risk and unconcerned with agency risk. This suggests successful shifting of agency risk from entrepreneur to venture capitalist. Venture capitalist and entrepreneur differ in their evaluation of the impact of innovation on risk. Thus the venture capitalist focuses on novelty in the market place and sales, whilst the entrepreneur focuses on getting to market and meeting innovation milestones. It is concluded that venture capitalists and entrepreneurs generally do view risk in the same light but, when their views differ, this is explicable either by function (producer or funder?) or by risk exposure. A formal language for discussing and developing such ideas is developed in 'Agency, innovation and business risk' on p. 22. As a preliminary to this, the concepts of risk and uncertainty are developed in the following section.

Qualitative and quantitative uncertainty

In classical decision-making contexts that involve uncertainty, a quantitative approach can be adopted. A famous example involves costing the breakages of bottles in a champagne cellar. There are hundreds of thousands of bottles, and every day several explode under the pressure of fermentation. It is not possible to say which specific champagne bottle will explode, or how many will explode. However, over the years a very precise average value has been determined for breakages, and the costs thereby incurred are known with a high degree of precision. Uncertainty dealt with in this fashion is usually referred to as 'risk', as intimated first in Chapter 1, in our brief discussion of Frank Knight (1921).

In our example of the breakages of bottles, 'hard' information is available, which depends on accurate evidence from past events, in an unchanged setting (the product, champagne, and its bottle, remain unchanged, as does the cellar). Therefore it is possible to attribute numerical probabilities to the event of a bottle breaking. Put more formally, this way of proceeding depends on what we have called elsewhere in this book (e.g. in 'Risk appraisal in high-technology ventures' on p. 5) 'the frequency limit principle'. A few symbols will help to elaborate what this means. Suppose an 'event' A (which may be something like the breaking of a champagne bottle) occurs N_A times in a set of N independent trials. Then its relative frequency is N_A/N. Further, suppose that as N becomes larger, this ratio settles down to a fixed value (as is known from hundreds of years of producing champagne, for example). Then we can call this value 'the probability of the event A'. It is usually denoted P(A). This is the basis on which the quality controller in the champagne cellar (or 'cave') proceeds. He has enough evidence to estimate very accurately the probability of a bottle breaking. This allows him to set 'bounds' within which variations in breakage should normally be confined. If these bounds are exceeded, investigation is warranted. (For example, to enquire into whether the bottles have been procured differently, or whether the temperature in the cellar has gone beyond usual limits.) Statistical quality control can be used to formalise this approach. Although mathematically complex, its essence should be reasonably familiar to those with accounting, finance and economics backgrounds. This is because quality control approaches can be related to the 'variance analysis' approach of management accounting (compare Arnold and Turley, 1996), or the principal–agent approach of economics and finance. In the example we have given, having determined whether the extent of variation is unusual, a kind of cost–benefit analysis must be undertaken by the quality controller, to determine whether taking any action (which may be costly) is justified in terms of the benefits it may offer.

This example, from a well-established traditional technology, with hundreds of years of experience and established standards, in terms of labour, materials and other associated costs behind it, cannot carry over readily to our high-technology contexts. In our new context, you do not have repeated trials under essentially unchanged conditions, with sufficiently large numbers of trials that a 'frequency limit' may be approached. Essentially a high-technology product is novel, and developers and users of it are breaking unfamiliar ground: there are no known frequency limits, as there is no history for the technology.

Fortunately, the economist John Maynard Keynes (1921), in his lifetime a very successful stock market advisor, and investment analyst, has provided us with another way of thinking about probability. It is useful in 'one-off' cases, like those relating to very new high-technology products. It involves the exercise of judgement (or the construction of a 'rational belief', as he called it), rather than the conducting of repeated trials. Such Keynesian probabilities may still be assigned numerical values. Thus we may ask, for example, venture capitalists who appraise the potential value of new technologies, what probability they attach to the successful commercialisation of the technology. Based on their rational belief, which may involve appeal to collateral evidence (like yardstick comparisons with related technologies) but no statistical evidence as such, they may assign a numerical probability to success.

Technically, Keynes's argument may be expressed as follows. If P certainly follows from Q, then we may say that Q 'gives' to P a probability of one. However, if P and Q are contradictory, and P does not follow from Q, then Q 'gives' to P (an impossibility) a probability of zero. But what happens in between these two extremes of 'the certain' and 'the impossible'? Keynes proposed a way of filling this gap, so we could talk of 'the probable' as lying between the certain and the impossible. For such cases, he said, we should associate a probability with P which is greater, the less its content goes beyond what is contained in Q. This provides a way of dealing with 'the probable' using numerical probabilities. These probabilities expressed what he called 'degree of rational belief'. They are numerical and obey all the same laws as the probabilities obtained from the classical frequency limit approach (e.g. they lie between zero and one). However, in using them we do not have to take on board the very unrealistic framework that lies behind the frequency limit approach (e.g. that repeated trials are conducted, under essentially unchanged conditions). In terms of our fieldwork investigation, this 'degree of rational belief' approach allowed us to have discussions about numerical probabilities with respondents without having to feel trapped in an unrealistic framework.

Of course, behind the judgements about such probabilities, and hence of risk appraisal, is the sifting and weighing of evidence. What if there is a paucity of evidence, or if evidence is complex and conflicting? This is not an improbable scenario in the high-technology area, where expert opinions, perforce constructed on just the limited evidence available, can often conflict widely. Remember the doomed prophecy of Thomas J Watson, Chairman of the Board at IBM, saying in 1943: 'I think there is a world market for about five computers'! Keynes (1921) too had a view on this, and argued that if the situation was one of considerable ignorance, it should still be possible at least to rank probabilities (as being greater or lesser), even though it may be rationally difficult to determine exact numerical probabilities.

This takes us into the realms of what we will describe as qualitative uncertainty. We have in mind a situation in which information on alternatives (e.g. engineering products for which no prototyping has been done) is so vague that it would not be rational to assign numerical probabilities. Such information may be called 'soft', being based on hunch, gut feeling, rumour, market sentiment, idle gossip, and so on. In the high-technology context, the use of such 'soft' information usually arises when scientific developments are essentially unique. They create situations which nobody has previously encountered. Even so, it is important to gather 'soft' information and to interpret it, when no 'hard' information is available. To that must be applied judgement, based on analogy, pattern recognition, and so on, in order to make a decision. As we observe below, just how far we may be willing to go in making judgements of this sort should depend on a kind of cost–benefit calculation.

To summarise this section, we have shown that a wide variety of uncertain situations are capable of calibration by thinking in terms of probabilities. These can be: precise estimates based on full information; statistical estimates based on accurate but incomplete information; 'degree of belief' estimates based on limited information'; or even ordinal (or rankings-based) estimates, based on a paucity of information. In effect, the latter ranking method amounts to determining risk classes (e.g. high/medium/low risk), rather than to assigning precise numerical probabilities. In designing our instrumentation (see Appendices to this book), we became aware that the full spectrum of approaches would be necessary in our investigation of high-technology investments.

Agency, innovation and business risk

Consider the three classes of risk which we have suggested may be relevant to our research landscape: agency, innovation and business risks. Of these three, specifically agency risk arises because information is not held in common (i.e. it is asymmetric) between economic agents (e.g. investor and entrepreneur), and such agents have different attitudes to risk. In our case, these agents are venture capitalists who provide equity finance and financial expertise, and entrepreneurs, who provide know-how about a new technology, and are knowledgeable about the prospects of its commercialisation. This agency approach rests on the foundations of what economists, including financial economists, call principal–agent analysis. When undertaking the empirical work we report upon in this book, we often had in mind, as an overarching model, the principal–agent approach, as applied to the venture capitalist (as principal) and the high-technology entrepreneur (as agent).

To start with, we shall develop ideas of agency in general terms, focusing on problems of incentives and information asymmetry following the lines of what Jensen and Meckling (1976) call the 'positive theory of agency' (see also Salter and Sharp, 2001). Then we shall move on to a more formal statement of the principal–agent model, illustrated by the venture capitalist–entrepreneur relationship. As we shall see, this will involve emphasising risk sharing, and the seeking of optimal contracting between principal and agent. The nature of the 'contract' will be explicitly considered below.

In general, agency theory (e.g. Reid, 1987) is based on the behavioural premise that economic actors seek to serve their own self interest. Given that they can hide some of their actions from others, they may rationally seek favourable ways of doing so, which will allow them to benefit personally from their unseen actions. We may think of the principal (e.g. the investor) and agent (e.g. entrepreneur) as seeking the best contractual terms possible, in the face of risk and asymmetric information. Thus, in a contractual arrangement, there is a danger of moral hazard, in that, post contract, agents may shirk (i.e. fail to work as hard as they could and/or personally may consume benefits which would otherwise accrue to others). In doing so, they obtain the benefits of perquisite consumption (i.e. perks), for which the principal bears a proportion of costs. The organisational answer to this danger is to assign a residual owner or claimant (in this case, the principal, or venture capitalist) who is entitled to any surplus created by the firm (in this case, the agent, or entrepreneur) after the disbursement of all remunerations. The theory therefore explains why venture capitalist–entrepreneur relations will be created, and the forms they may take. Given he or she is the recipient of any surplus created, the venture capitalist (as principal) should have no motive to tolerate shirking. He or she directs activities, and will seek, at the contract interface, to establish systems for monitoring and rewarding the entrepreneur (see Figure 2.1). This figure illustrates schematically the two parties to a principal–agent relationship (here, investor and entrepreneur, respectively). It shows the different roles of each party, and how each confronts the other over a 'contractual interface' – they are seeking to conclude a mutually agreeable deal. The figure shows how this 'deal' or 'contract' will be designed to encourage the entrepreneur (and his high technology firm) to act in ways which are aligned with the venture capitalist's aims. That is, the investor's goal will be to attenuate shirking and to elicit optimal effort. In such a fashion, the venture capitalist tries to reduce any informational advantage possessed by the entrepreneur (compare Healy and Palepu, 2001). This can arise from greater familiarity with high-technology products and better intelligence on the cap-abilities of rivals. This information asymmetry, coupled with moral hazard, pre-sents a circumstantial problem for the principal, for which (as the figure suggests) a monitoring and control system may provide an affective solution.

Economic applications of principal–agent analysis are well known (Ross, 1973; Mirrlees, 1976; Holmström, 1979; Radner, 1985). Extensions to cognate areas, like accounting, have been undertaken by the likes of Baiman (1982) and, in textbook form, by Kaplan (1982), Ezzamel and Hart (1987) and Scapens (1991). These extensions show how the firm itself creates a demand for informa-tion. Further, the need to monitor and control entrepreneurs' behaviour requires a flow of information from the firm to the venture capital investor. For example,

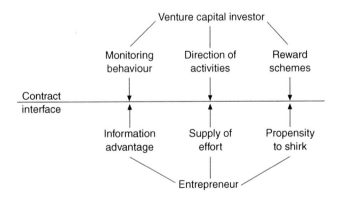

Figure 2.1 The principal–agent setting for investor and entrepreneur.

accounting measures of actual performance, financial analyses of decisions, budgets and financial plans may all contribute to the provision of a basis upon which the firm's performance can be assessed (Ouksel *et al.*, 1997).

The availability of appropriate financial controls and decision support can also be viewed as helping to direct the firm's behaviour in accordance with the venture capitalist's interests. In addition, if incentives such as entrepreneurial remuneration, or even entrepreneurial retention, are to be based on performance, there is an important role to be played by information on the financial dimension of that performance. To play these roles, such information has to be accepted by both venture capitalist and entrepreneur and should therefore possess sufficient 'hardness' and reliability to adequately reflect an entrepreneur's actions (Mutch, 1999).

Information provision may be influenced by a variety of factors relating to each specific principal–agent relationship. Obvious instances, relevant to our venture capitalist-entrepreneur setting, include:

- *Ownership and control* (Bricker and Chandar, 2000; Francis and Smith, 1995). The greater is the divorce of ownership and control (which, in turn, may mirror the size and complexity of the high-technology firm) the greater is the need for information about the firm to be made available to the venture capitalist.
- *Degree of incentivisation*. The extent to which incentive is induced by the entrepreneur's compensation package. For example, where the entrepreneur's rewards are heavily based on performance, which matches the venture capitalist's aims, the need for monitoring information (as a surveillance and control function) will be lesser (Nouri and Parker, 1996).
- *Sophistication of monitoring*. Per contra to the previous point, the more sophisticated is the monitoring system put in place, the less will be the need for the venture capitalist to base the entrepreneur's remuneration on the performance levels achieved.
- *Complexity and uncertainty*. The greater the complexity and uncertainty associated with the entrepreneur's role and work, the greater is the information asymmetry which exists, and the more the emphasis that will have to be put on monitoring inputs and outputs, as opposed to processes.

Following the above, more general discussion, the relevant principal–agent model may be expressed in more formal terms as follows. A new *contract* is designed by a *principal* (here, a venture capital investor), the success of which depends on the *effort* (α) of the *agent* (here, the entrepreneur, or owner-manager of a high-technology business), and random factors (like the probability of achieving a high-technology breakthrough) are captured by the term θ, the *state of the world*. In simple settings (see Figure 2.2), the latter may simply be dichotomised into 'good' and 'bad' states of the world. The outcome of contracting between principal and agent (namely, venture capitalist and high-technology entrepreneur) is a *payoff* (x) in dollars, pounds sterling, etc. This payoff increases with effort (at a decreasing rate), and with θ (e.g. higher values of θ could be used to denote better states of the world). Subject to these restrictions, we have a *payoff function* $x(.)$ which may be written $x=x\,(\alpha,\theta)$ which, in this context, relates to something like the value of the high-technology firm once the terms of the contract come to maturity in an agreed fashion by venture capitalist and entrepreneur (e.g. main market listing).

The principal (the venture capitalist) and the agent (the entrepreneur) are assumed to be rational economic agents, who wish to do the best they can for themselves, in terms of satisfaction, which here may be represented by the economist's conception of utility. Essentially, this tells you the psychic return you get from an activity, like consuming a good or making an effort on a task. The utilities of the venture capital investor (denoted v) and the high-technology entrepreneur (denoted E) are represented by the functions $U_V=U_V(x-y)$ and $U_E=F_E(y, \alpha)$, respectively, where y represents the 'cut' (or fee) that the entrepreneur gets from the venture capitalist. We assume that the U_E is increasing in y (at a decreasing rate) and decreasing in the entrepreneur's effort (α), at an increasing rate. We have seen above that the venture capital investor may be treated as the residual claimant. This has attractive incentive properties (e.g. attenuation of shirking by the agent). This *residual claim* may be represented as having the magnitude $(x-y)$. The *fee schedule* determines the relation between the contract payoff and the entrepreneur's remuneration according to the increasing function $y=y(x)$. The venture capital investor and the entrepreneur are assumed to be expected utility maximisers. This formal framework having been established, we can move now to consider optimal contracting.

The optimal agency relationship determines the fee schedule (y) and effort level (α) that maximises the venture capitalist's utility, subject to two constraints. First, α is chosen to maximise expected utility for the entrepreneur. Second, the entrepreneur's expected utility should not fall below its reservation utility level. The latter is determined by the best utility level achievable by the entrepreneur outside of the contract in question (e.g. by the entrepreneur seeking better terms with another venture capitalist). In a familiar way (e.g. Reid, 1987, Ch. 9) it can be shown that the optimal risk sharing involves setting equal the principal and agent's marginal rates of substitution between any two states of the world. To simplify, we will think of the 'state of the world' as just having two ('good' or 'bad') outcomes (e.g. the research milestone was, or was not met). If this is not completely observable, and if the effort of the entrepreneur is not fully known, then the simplest result (Reid, 1989, p. 290), which would see the venture capitalist bearing all the risk, and providing the entrepreneur with full insurance, would not apply (see Magee, 1998, for such problems in a cost allocation setting).

We are now in a position to consider more formally the contractual incentives for effort within the firm. This can be illustrated using the so-called box-diagram of Figure 2.2 (see Ricketts, 1986, for a general exposition of this technique). Therein, the letter I denotes indifference curves (i.e. curves of equal utility) for the venture capitalist (V) or the entrepreneur (E). The 45° line through the

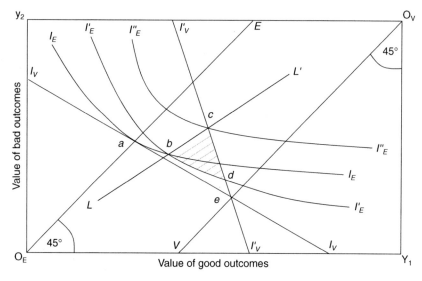

Figure 2.2 The implications of effort for efficient contracting.

entrepreneur's origin O_E is the 'certainty line' for the entrepreneur (in that values are equal along it, in good or bad states of the world). I_E denotes the indifference curve when the entrepreneur's effort is bad, and I'_E the indifference curve when the entrepreneur makes some effort. The entrepreneur is assumed risk averse, as reflected in the convexity of the I_E curve from below. The I_V curves denote the venture capitalist's indifference curves, which are linear, reflecting an assumption of risk neutrality. This assumption is made because the investor is considered to have a large, fully diversified portfolio of investment involvements. The application of entrepreneurial effort shifts the venture capitalist's indifference curve from I_V to I'_V. LL' represents the locus of indifference between effort and no effort. In Figure 2.2, the hatched area *bcd* represents the set of contracts which are Pareto superior to that at point *a*. Pareto superior points have the property that they make at least one party to the contract better off, without making the other worse off. At *a* itself, there is 'first-best' contracting, with all risk being borne by the risk neutral venture capital investor. Because the slopes of I_E'' and I_V' at *c* are not equal, Pareto superior-efficient contracts, if effort and states of the world are not fully observable, will not generally be first-best. Some risk will be borne by the entrepreneur. This involves the surrender of more efficient risk bearing, in order to increase the incentive for the entrepreneur to make effort that will raise the probability of the good outcome. In this context, it can be shown that a risk averse entrepreneur will never bear all the risk.

Finally, we need to consider how information systems can produce superior benefits (compare Fredrickson, 1992). It can be shown that monitoring allows risk sharing benefits to be attained, without diminishing effort, and that more reliable information encourages lazy entrepreneurs to offer more effort (Reid,

1998, Ch. 4). One way in which agency risk can be reduced is by superior information systems (e.g. a management accounting system, MAS). Within the high-technology venture, its form is driven by both internally and externally generated needs (see Mitchell *et al.*, 1995, 1999). We have given detailed and extensive attention to agency risk, partly because it is the most difficult to grasp conceptually, and partly because its effects are endemic. However, we must now turn (albeit briefly) to our other categories of risk, namely innovation and business risk.

Innovation risk arises because of the inability of forecasters, even technology-foresight specialists, to fully anticipate the development cost of a new technological product or service of a given quality or technical specification. For example, although a budget may be assigned for funding the development of a new technology which will lead to an 'innovative step', it may, in practice, prove to be inadequate. Typically, the problem of budget overrun (see Perez-Castrillo and Riedinger, 1999) is the main one of practical consequence, in terms of its impact on innovation risk. Alas, it is endemic. Not only are unexpected costs incurred for development towards the innovative step, which are much higher than initially projected, but also costs are incurred at considerably later dates than were originally envisaged. Such innovation risks generate irresistible needs for resource reallocation. These occur both across immediate needs within the firm, at a current point in time, and across diverse needs, at future points in time.

Business risk arises because of the inability of industrial economists, accountants and business forecasters to predict with any precision the prospective value of a new product in the competitive marketplace. Not only do innovation risks 'feed forward' into business risks (e.g. in the sense of timing of initial market entry of a product), but also business risks arise from action-reaction effects within the marketplace, as rivals attempt to accommodate to the marketplace implications of innovative steps, very often in a strategic fashion, for example by pre-emption, emulation, imitation, backward engineering, etc.

Whilst the above taxonomy of risk is not necessarily exhaustive, we would maintain that it captures the larger part of total risk in venture capital contracting. Further additional possible categories of risk (e.g. liquidity risk, Cumming *et al.*, 2005) can often be assimilated within our three proposed categories of risk.

Uncertainty and risk assessment

When it comes to uncertainty, ways of dealing with it in a new venture may require an awareness that risk appraisal may not go so far as making a probability judgement. An example of making a probability judgement would be that there is a 10 per cent chance that the market extent for a new high-technology product will exceed £100,000 sales per annum, and a 90 per cent chance that it will be £100,000 or less. There may be a desire by the decision maker to stop short of a probability judgement of this sort, because the vagueness of the evidence only permits the appraisal that a large market is much less probable than a small market. We have seen that economists like Knight (1921) and Keynes (1921) were both aware that not all uncertainties could be gauged against the yardstick of unique probability distributions. To Knight, uncertainty appraisal made an appeal to judgement or to pattern recognition, in essentially unique situations. Indeed, an intrinsic feature contributing to the uncertainty was that the situation had not been encountered before. This is, of course, the typical case of a new product launch from a high-technology venture.

By contrast, probability assignment made appeal to evidence on, or relative frequencies of, similar, independent past events. Keynes (1921) argued that the uncertainties attaching to events were essentially of three types. In the first, the information was so vague that events could not be compared; in the second they could at least be ranked according to higher or lower probability; and in the third, actual numerical probabilities could be assigned (as in our discussion of Keynes's 'degree of rational' belief in 'Qualitative and quantitative uncertainty' (p. 19)). Keynes's line of reasoning usefully extends the repertoire available for us to use for getting a grip on what we mean by uncertainty. His insight is philosophically persuasive; it also provides useful clues as to how one can enquire into an individual's evaluation of risk. Indeed, his insights have certainly influenced the design of our instruments.

Despite a trend in risk analysis to advocate the use of numerical risk estimation (Lefley, 1997), a concession often made is that an indication should be given of whether such estimates should be regarded as 'soft' or 'hard'. Economists naturally suggest a cost–benefit approach to vague information. The costs of using non-numerical risk assessments are that the cutting edge in decision making is lost, and advanced manipulation of probability statements (e.g. to compute compound or conditional probabilities, for example) is lost. The benefits are that the decision maker retains control by admitting that there are limits to the precision possible (e.g. by talking in terms of ranges, rather than points), and is thereby more open to the context of the decision. For example, the decision maker becomes more sensitive to features like the degree of dread of the downside, or the nature of risk which involves elements of the unknowable (e.g. because of lack of observation, time lags, etc.). Both these features are present in venture capital contexts. In fact, in experimental settings with human subjects, it is found that individual differences in understanding vague uncertainties are both reliable (in that they are persistent features of repeated judgements) and substantial (in that some understand vague uncertainty much better than others) (see Wallsten, 1990). Therefore, vague probabilistic forecasts may be preferred to precise ones, when it is felt that this is all the weight of judgement the data will bear.

With the exception of earlier work by Ruhnka and Young (1991), and more recent work by Liu and Chen (2006), little attention has been paid to the formal analysis of risk management in venture capital contexts. Our work aims to remedy this deficiency in the literature. Reid (1998) provided a base from which our further work was undertaken. There, a wide range of issues of risk management was addressed for both venture capitalist and entrepreneur. These included: chance outcomes and sure prospects; offsetting good outcomes against bad; effects of new projects on overall risk management; and risk-sharing. There, the design techniques applied to instrumentation (typically administered questionnaires and semi-structured interviews) provided hints on potentially fruitful new methods of measurement in risk analysis, which could be incorporated into the instruments which we developed for the current project.

Although, from the eighteenth century on, risk theorists like Bernoulli have argued that individuals faced with different prospects or gambles select the one that maximises expected utility or value, the behavioural analysis of decision makers subject to risk, in experimental situations, provides cautionary evidence. To illustrate, Kahneman and Tversky (1979) have discovered that experimental subjects display conduct which is anomalous, when viewed from a classical risk perspective. These anomalies are described as 'certainty and 'reflection' effects. In the former effect, subjects attach especial importance to certainty, and indeed certainty seems to be given a higher weighting than even something quite close to it, but still slightly uncertain. In the latter 'reflection' effect, it transpires that when losses are almost inevitably involved, subjects appear to weight rather highly a slim chance of avoiding any loss. Such evidence suggests looking at risk management in a fashion which goes beyond a narrow classical probabilistic approach, to a broader qualitative approach.

To illustrate, in Reid (1998, Chapter 8, Case J) attitude to risk is investigated in a high-technology firm producing *in vitro* diagnostic kits. When high levels of risk were involved in 'one-off' deals, prospective value was set at zero, because the frequency limit principle was abandoned. Further, for a sample of venture capitalists considering projects with limited downside risk, but an attractive upside, it was found that, even when probabilities were accurately assigned to upside and downside outcomes, the actuarial value was not used as a reference point (see also Reid *et al.*, 1997). Thus qualitative risk assessment appears to be very important in high-technology contexts. The argument that we should therefore go beyond narrow classical probabilistic approaches appears to have considerable force.

Risk and uncertainty in high-technology ventures

We have seen in Chapter 1 that new high-technology ventures make difficult business propositions. This is not just because the business and agency risks are high, but also because the innovation risk is high and cannot be handled by standard methods of risk appraisal. Lacking historical data on high-technology, we cannot compute risk in an actuarial sense. Faced with this dearth of evidence, risk must be assessed in a more subjective fashion. Although judgement is necessarily involved, a common way of trying to ground a subjective risk appraisal in reality is to seek advice from technology experts. This is one of the most frequently commissioned forms of third party due diligence. Those undertaking this work are familiar with development trajectories of related technologies, and with technology foresight techniques.

In high-technology ventures, when budgeting for the coming year, a major risk attaches to the allocation of R&D expenditures thought to be necessary for the next technological step (e.g. rather than 100 laboratory trials being necessary, it may be found that 500 are necessary). If R&D expenditure is proportionately a major outlay for such enterprises, any volatility in its component can have devastating effects for allocations to alternative uses (e.g. the training of personnel). It is enterprises of this sort, and their potential backers (typically formal venture capital funds), which are the focus of our research.

We have argued above that it is usually impossible to apply a 'frequency limit principle' to innovative events within a high-technology firm, because they are essentially 'one-off happenings', alternative ways of assigning probabilities have to be sought. We have therefore followed Fiet (1995a, 1995b), in moving our research forward, by thinking in terms of 'risk classes', rather than in terms of point estimates of probabilities. We find that simple classifications of risk (e.g. high, medium, low) are often adequate, if not perfect, substitutes for statistical estimates of probabilities. Our questionnaire design used Likert scales to determine (on a scale of 1 to 5) the perceived riskiness, by respondents (be they venture capitalists or entrepreneurs), of certain types of events (e.g. start-up, MBO, MBI). The principal risk classes we have used in this book are business risk, agency risk and innovation risk.

It should be noticed that another possible risk class, namely liquidity risk, may be partially subsumed under business risk. It refers (see Cumming *et al.*, 2005) to risks arising at exit (e.g. on initial public offering (IPO)) when matching up expectations of value to overt market conditions can be very difficult. Indeed it can explain a preference for late exit.

Consider further two of the classes of risk relevant to our book: agency and business risks. We have seen that agency risk arises because information is not held in common (i.e. it is asymmetric) between economic agents, and such agents have different attitudes to risk. In our case, these agents are venture capitalists and entrepreneurs. One way in which agency risk can be reduced is by superior information systems. Indeed, contemporary evidence seems to affirm this. Thus, in a comparative study of Indian and UK venture capitalists, Pruthi *et al.* (2003) found that the more seasoned investors focused more on strategy and on monthly management accounts, whilst the less seasoned focused on operational matters and specifics of accounting policy.

We have seen that business risk arises because it is hard to estimate the market clearing price for a new product. Business risk is itself affected by innovation risk. Further, business risk is affected by the strategic interactions of innovators, who are attempting to 'out-compete' one another in markets for new products.

Of the three classes of risk we have emphasised (agency, innovation and business) we would judge that agency risk is the one that has been most successfully confronted in the high-technology context. We now know that agency risk arises through incomplete alignment of the interests of venture capitalists and entrepreneurs (compare Reid, 1998). Such risks derive from inefficiencies, all of which ultimately revolve around problems of information and risk bearing. For example, the entrepreneur may be better informed than the venture capitalist about the product, and may also be more risk averse. If information were perfect, doubt and uncertainty would not attach to decision making and venture capitalists could choose best actions with complete confidence. However, information is *not* perfect, and venture capitalists have to proceed by using imperfect information as effectively as possible, at the same time as trying to remedy in some measure these imperfections. Thus the venture capitalist will be motivated to create an information gathering system which will help him to overcome his relative ignorance, and thus to decrease the risk of his decision-making environment. Indeed, if this does not happen, financial scandals may follow, as occurred in the Taiwanese IT sector from 2001 to 2003 (Sheu and Lin, 2006). There, it was found that information disclosure by entrepreneurs was significantly positively correlated with investment by venture capitalists. Concealing information limited the fund flow, which can lead to corruption. So it is evident that the investor should seek transparency from the entrepreneur. Proceeding in this way, the venture capitalist will be better equipped to avoid the tendency for the entrepreneur to pass all the risk on to him. The venture capitalist becomes a better judge of the performance of the entrepreneur, and refusing to accept all of the risk keeps the entrepreneur on his toes.

Although UK venture capitalists are becoming increasingly skilled at attenuating agency costs, they have not yet progressed so far as their US counterparts in using powerful, so-called 'boilerplate', contractual terms. Further, though they have relative success in managing agency risk, venture capitalists must increasingly turn their attention to business risk. This arises from the uncertain environment within which the quest for competitive advantage is pursued by the entrepreneur (e.g. in terms of innovation, new and existing rivals, substitutes, and shifts in customer tastes). This is a less controllable class of risk in that factors like the market attractiveness of a high-technology product sold by the entrepreneur are only partly (e.g. by advertising), but not entirely, amenable to manipulation. Along this dimension, therefore, contracting is frequently informal, but the relationship is relatively pro-active, which aims to compensate for the informality.

The relative ignorance of business risk on the part of the venture capitalist has partly arisen from a natural tendency to specialise in the controllable area of risk, namely agency risk. It would be inefficient for formal venture capitalists to attempt to proceed in the way that, say, 'business angels' (i.e. informal investors) might (compare Mason and Harrison, 1997, 2000). The latter might seek to address the problem of business risk by having such a close relationship (proactive, 'hands-on') with an entrepreneur that business risk is relatively effectively handled. From the formal investor's position of relative ignorance, information relevant to business risk is costly to acquire, and difficult to evaluate, and this proactive route is less attractive, and almost certainly not cost effective. Instead, the venture capitalist has to seek to 'incentivise' his relationship with the venture capitalist more effectively (see Kaplan and Stromberg, 2001).

This creates a demand by the venture capitalist for a more sophisticated management accounting system (MAS) within the innovating firm. Indeed the provision of outside equity (possibly in staged form) is typically contingent on the implementation of improved MAS. Thus the supply of superior accounting information naturally follows on from its demand (see Mitchell *et al.*, 1995). The way in which the supply of new information develops has been analysed in detail by Mitchell *et al.*, 1997. It is found that the variety and extent of procedures adopted will increase, as well as the frequency of provision of information. It was found that this stimulated internal accounting changes for monitoring and control purposes within the innovating firm, which in turn supported the use of such information for improved internal decision making.

Intellectual property

An important way of limiting innovation or technological risk exposure is to seek good protection of intellectual property (IP) rights over innovation (see Webster and Packer, 1996a), where IP refers to ideas over which the investor or author can assert proprietorial rights. Such rights (e.g. copyrights) can be bought, sold and licensed, just like physical property. Classically, IP protection is achieved through the patenting system. This is now worldwide in scope, in terms of patenting regimes (see Reid *et al.*, 1996), though the UK remains pivotal, to this day, as a place initially to file for a patent. The management accountant has an important role to play within both venture capitalist and entrepreneurial firms in estimating the prospective marketplace value of innovations. In doing so, they are subsuming part of what Cumming *et al.* (2005) call 'liquidity risk' into innovation risk. As we have seen earlier, part of liquidity risk may also be absorbed by the business risk class. Alongside lawyers, managers and technologists, management accountants often participate in the cost effectiveness calculation which surrounds the progression of the patenting process. Thus there is both an investment in technology per se to be considered (e.g. in lab space, personnel), as well as an investment in the institutions for protecting the marketplace value that the technology may command (e.g. defending the IP right in court).

Obtaining such protection may involve high-technology companies in major costs. Between the stage of filing for a patent and grant of a patent, there is an iterative process of presenting (and modifying) the case to patent officers. They have to be convinced that the company which is filing for a patent has indeed satisfied the criteria for an 'innovative step'. These are that the technology is novel, and that it can be industrially implemented. Having that case rebuffed, leading to requirements for further modifications of the technology on the part of the company, can have enormous resource implications. To satisfy such additional requirements, further prototype work may be necessary, extra testing undertaken, technical glitches smoothed out, etc. These all generate unanticipated costs, not the least of which are the opportunity costs created when company resources so diverted are prevented from being allocated to other potentially fruitful innovative activities. Further, protecting IP across other national (e.g. US, Germany, Japan) and transnational (e.g. European, World) regimes can be immensely resource-expensive, particularly when (as in some countries, like Spain) costly judicial procedures are almost inevitably involved.

Conclusion

We have seen that special problems arise in dealing with risk in high-technology ventures. First, the innovation risk is high. Second, there is no statistical track record to provide estimates of likely outcomes, in terms of timing, magnitude, and so on. Third, the complexity and novelty of the technological setting may make standard methods of risk appraisal irrelevant or ineffectual.

This presents a rather gloomy outlook for financiers, accountants and entrepreneurs seeking to manage risk in high-technology ventures. This gloom may be exacerbated by the tendency noted by Lerner (2002) for the level of venture capital activity to be cyclical, with lost opportunities in recessions, and over bought technologies in booms. However, there are numerous approaches which can be adapted to rising to this challenging situation, of which five have particular promise. First, one has to come to terms with adopting a subjective risk appraisal approach. True, evidence may be fragmentary, chaotic or contradictory; however, in the face of this, judgement must still be rational, and needs to be directed at calibrating risk. Second, even if the technological situation appears to be unique, there may be relevant yardstick comparisons that can be made. If precise comparisons are not possible, less precise comparisons must be sought. Less formal ways of making comparisons, like the use of analogy, must be contemplated. Third, expert evaluations can help to clarify complex risky situations in the high-technology area, where little history exists. Technology foresight is not just wild conjecture. There appear to be mathematical rules which govern progression in the speed of computer chips, and progression in their memory capacity, for example. This expertise can be tapped into by the buying of third party due diligence to do an independent appraisal.

This can be augmented by the so-called Delphic method. Like the oracle at Delphi, this seeks authoritative advice. It does so by appeal to a panel of third-party, independent evaluators. An example of the use of this technique, relating to decision making in a business context, is contained in Bacon and Fitzgerald (2001). In this case, the systemic framework of the authors was tested by surveying the views of 105 leading academics in 19 countries, using a structured questionnaire. The framework was revised in the light of feedback from this Delphic plumbing of opinion.

Fourth, if a rational basis for assigning a numerical probability does not seem to exist, this may not create an impasse. Logically, one should move from the more demanding informational context of cardinal numbers to the lesser one of ordinal numbers (namely, numbers used for ranking). The focus in this low-information, uncertain world is on distinguishing between higher and lower probabilities. This amounts to identifying risk classes. For example, if three high-technology project options can be ranked in order of probability of success, this amounts to identifying low, medium and high-risk classes.

Fifth, and finally, IP can, if properly assigned and protected, lower risk. In terms of risk classes like agency, business and innovation risk, for example, both business and innovation risk can be reduced by successfully being awarded a grant of patent in a high-technology product. This means that you guarantee a limited monopoly for the product, which greatly reduces business risk, and it also firmly establishes and protects achieving a research milestone, which reduces innovation risk.

We have now mapped out a wide range of possible strategies for handling different types of risks in high-technology ventures. We now turn to the task of examining how these risks are dealt with in practice, in our samples of UK (and some US) venture capitalists and entrepreneurs.

Part II
Sampling and evidence

3 Sampling, fieldwork and instrumentation

Introduction

This chapter is concerned with: how samples of venture capital (VC) investors and entrepreneurs were collected; how work was carried out 'in the field' (Glaser and Strauss, 1967); and how the 'instruments' (namely, administered questionnaire schedules) were designed for the interviews with venture capitalist and entrepreneurs (Miles and Huberman, 1984). Information on how the postal questionnaire (Appendix 4) was constructed will be deferred for Part V (Reporting and Investing).

The basic research philosophy we adopted in this study was that one best understands risk by direct examination of attitudes to risk, and how risk situations are managed, on the part of those economic agents (e.g. investors and investees) who actually bear risk. Our methodology is active, in that it requires direct fieldwork engagement, in terms of face-to-face discussion, between researchers, and VC investors and entrepreneurs (Burgess, 1984; Werner and Schoepfle, 1987; Shaffir and Stebbins, 1991). This is not to say that background reading, database analysis, and model building are neglected. These remain central research tasks. However, to these we add the commitment to developing a detailed, direct knowledge of the world of investors in high-technology companies, and the entrepreneurs whom they back (compare Moesel and Fiet, 2001; Moesel *et al.*, 2001). This provides a much richer, and more thought provoking flow of information into the 'research pool' in which one fishes for new insights and understanding, than does the conventional 'arm's length' method.

The principal stages which our research involved were:

*   Performing unstructured, preliminary, qualitative fieldwork (Woolcott, 2005).
*   Determining appropriate sampling frames for selecting our samples of venture capitalists and high-technology new ventures.
*   Designing two complementary administered questionnaire schedules (Oppenheim, 2000), suitable for face-to-face interviews with venture capitalists and entrepreneurs (compare Sudman and Bradburn, 1982; Neijens, 1987), based on the extant risk and VC literature.

- Interviewing venture capitalists and entrepreneurs in the field, using questionnaire schedules. In these face-to-face meetings, one researcher acted as interviewer, and the other as rapporteur (Willis, 2005).
- Constructing a quantitative and qualitative database (Reid, 1992), of the evidence gathered by interviews in the field (Burgess, 1984), suitable for both statistical and case study work (Yin, 1984, 1993).
- Analysing the database, along with additional evidence provided by venture capitalists and entrepreneurs (e.g. accounts, technology descriptions).

This chapter deals with each of these issues in turn.

Unstructured preliminary fieldwork

Our 'field' was the UK venture capital 'industry'. Our preliminary work within it was unstructured, because we were still seeking an appropriate framework for our enquiry. In terms of the methodology of our research, we aimed to let ourselves be open minded about the detailed structure of our enquiry until we had become familiar with key features of the field, and the principal players on it. A standard problem in fieldwork methods is how the researcher gets access to the field (Woolcott, 2005). We chose to gain access through the leading institutions of the venture capital industry. These were: first, the professional association of UK venture capital investors, the BVCA; second, the largest of the UK venture capital investors, Investor in Industry (3i). This turned out to be a very fruitful way of proceeding. The BVCA had 134 members, and they accounted for almost all the venture capital investment, by value, in the UK. Of these venture capitalists, 3i and Apax were the leaders in high-technology. In fact the top twenty or so venture capital 'houses' accounted for 90–95 per cent of high-technology investments in the UK.

Based on our success in this phase of the field research, we later went on to apply the same method as the above when we were investigating IP issues (compare 'Intellectual property' in Chapter 2 on p. 32). These issues are highly pertinent to high-technology firms which generate potentially valuable IP. This IP often needs to be protected by either copyright or patent methods. For this phase of the fieldwork, we sought contact with leading figures in the UK Patent Office. This institution deals with all principal forms of protection of intellectual property, from design and trademarks, through copyrighting, to patents. This part of the project was particularly relevant to entrepreneurial conduct, and the perceived value of entrepreneurial activity.

We turn, first, to how we dealt with venture capitalist issues. Partly because of previous success at making contacts within the industry, we were able to secure top-level contacts within our target institutions. This had the advantage of 'legitimising' our activity, once we had convinced opinion leaders within these institutions that our enquiry was sound, and of considerable potential value to the investment community. This value, we suggested, would arise from the insight it would offer into the functioning of the venture capital industry at the high risk end of the investment spectrum. Our argument was accepted, and, as a result, we obtained what fieldworkers call 'high communicators', 'key informants' or 'gatekeepers' to the field (compare Tremblay, 1982; Jankovicz, 2000).

We met our 'gatekeepers' at their places of work in London. In approaching these meetings, we had a fairly open mind about what we might investigate, and in how we would proceed. Certainly, we were willing to be guided, in terms of the best form our enquiry might take. A natural starting point was to compare UK experience with US experience. Although the UK has an age-old tradition in venturing, going back to the merchant adventurers (Lorenz, 1989), the modern form of venture capital is an American phenomenon (Wilson, 1985; Kortum and Lerner, 1999; Gompers and Lerner, 2001; Hsu and Kenney, 2005). Further, the US were quicker to recognise the importance of commercialising IP. They did this through NASDAQ, the first electronic stock market in the world. It has been a popular outlet for high-technology investments, and now accounts for a substantial proportion of trading on primary US markets. In making comparisons between the US and UK scenes over the period of the fieldwork, it should be pointed out that the 'boom and bust' nature of high-technology investing in the US (Lerner, 2002; J. Green, 2004; M.B. Green, 2004), including the 'dot.com meltdown', were not characteristic features of the UK venture capital scene at the time of our fieldwork. Indeed, it appears to be less prone to cyclical effects so characteristic of recent US experience. For comparative reasons, we therefore included two US case studies in Part IV.

The Director of 3i that we interviewed admitted 'we are relatively young in investing in high-technology'. However, he explained that, in recent years, there has been 'a thrust to invest in high-technology'. At the time of interview, in 2000, he estimated that about one billion pounds had been invested in high-technology in the UK. This was consistent with estimates provided by the BVCA (2001). In terms of the style of investing, he said that 3i's interest was 'in value growth, and in making sure that the company is structured to do that for us'. This involved 'the Board structure – we want the right people – and we want to know who is accountable for what'. When asked about issues of risk reporting, as discussed in the Turnbull Report (1999), he said 'we do not apply the full rigour of Turnbull and Cadbury etc., in terms of compliance and procedures, except in principle. That is, the company should be appropriately managed, and the Board should be independent' (compare Lin and Chou, 2005, for the Taiwanese context).

The Chairman of the BVCA whom that we interviewed (also in London) judged that the early purpose of the UK VC industry, when it emerged in the 1980s, was 'to revitalise British industry'. This was largely done through buyout activity. However, he pointed out that the emerging scene was very different. For the first time, high-technology started to figure strongly in the course of the 1990s. By the year 2000, the BVCA estimated that, of the eight billion being invested across all aspects of the UK VC market, one billion was high-technology. He felt that a large part of this was due to the digital revolution. When asked about risk reporting, he said, 'Turnbull is a great articulation of what we do anyway. You've got to work at it quite hard to assign categories of risk'. One aspect of the new attitude to investing in high-risk areas was to modify attitudes to downside risk or risk exposure. He claimed that 'things are changing – we're placing more emphasis on the fact that technology will generate sizeable value. If things go wrong, we wade in and change the people'. When asked whether this meant that venture capitalists had now become more inclined to assume control, he replied that 'we have shareholding control, and a seat on the Board. At the buyout end, we typically take control. At the technology end, we need portfolio spread – it is much more common to have several investors, but you always need a lead investor. Portfolio spread is very important'. Finally, when asked about categories of risk, without being prompted, he referred to what he called 'four degrees of risk'. These were, in his own words, 'market risk, technology risk, managerial risk, implementation risk'. These relate readily to our own categories of business risk, innovation risk and agency risk. In commenting upon these he said, 'we know market risk best, others know technology risk best'. His comments were influential in shaping the form our investigation assumed.

Our remaining unstructured fieldwork involved a visit to the Patent Office in Newport to speak to the Director of Copyright and other policy advisors. He was aware that our interest was in modern methods of protecting intellectual property in high-technology areas. His advice was valuable to our search for a suitable set of entrepreneurs to investigate, using an eight-point agenda (see 'Research methodology' (p. 9); Appendix 2 (second page); and Table 3.3 (p. 44)). In particular, he helped to sharpen our perception of appropriate forms of protection of intellectual property for digital products, especially those involving encrypting and enciphering (see case studies C and D in Chapter 7). The meeting also helped us to understand the increasingly blurred distinction between copyright and patenting regimes. For example, the Director of Copyright said 'the listing of a computer programme is automatically copyrighted. The person that creates it controls copying of it. For example, it can only be copied for personal use. The Patent Office would now encourage them to consider patenting'. He felt that the 1998 US *Digital Millennium Copyright Act* and the EU 2001 *Directive on Copyright in the Information Society* would both have far-reaching consequences for the operations of emerging high-technology companies.

We found the observations and suggestions made in our unstructured fieldwork to be of help in planning our sampling and instrumentation. In this way, we were put in touch with the most timely evidence, and were privy to high-level judgements about the most pressing areas for investigation.

Samples of investors and entrepreneurs

The second stage of the research involved: (a) determining sampling frames for both venture capitalists and high-technology companies; and (b) selecting samples, according to certain sampling criteria. The sampling frame for venture capitalists was obtained from the Venture Capital Report (VCR) CD-ROM. This listed most UK venture capital firms, under a number of headings. Our aim was to construct a random sample of twenty venture capital firms (venture capitalists), subject to their being actively involved in the high-technology area. The sampling frame for high-technology firms and their entrepreneurs was also obtained using the VCR CD-ROM. It was used to search for entrepreneurs who were developing, making or marketing high-technology products. In determining the 'technological intensity' of our sample of entrepreneurs, use was made of our contacts with the Patent Office at Newport. On-line facilities enabled us to select those entrepreneurs who were most patent-intensive in their innovative activities. We preferred this independent route of access to high-technology companies rather than the judgements of venture capitalists, which might be less objective. The number of venture capitalists interviewed was twenty, and the number of high-technology firms was five, in the first instance (see Chapter 7), subsequently augmented by a further five (see Chapter 8).

The venture capital backers of high-technology firms who agreed to be interviewed are listed in Table 3.1. A larger sample of UK investors was also approached using a postal questionnaire, as briefly described at the end of this chapter, and fully explained and analysed in Part V (Chapters 9 and 10).

The average fund size (in terms of funds managed) was £529m, the average number of venture capital executives was 32 and the average number of investments per year was 45. The biggest player by a magnitude was 3i. Schroder

Table 3.1 Venture capitalists participating in fieldwork

	Full-time VC executives	Investments per annum	Funds managed (£m)
3i (group plc)	285	320	2,000
Scottish Equity Partners	10	n.a.	150
Amadeus Capital Partners Limited	14	n.a.	88
Schroder Ventures	25	10	4,209
UK Steel Enterprise Limited	10	50	4
Wales International Fund Limited	n.a.	n.a.	n.a.
British Coal Enterprise	n.a.	n.a.	n.a.
Murray Johnstone Private Equity Ltd	23	25	373
Top Technology Limited	3	7	35
Thomson Clive Ventures	11	5	148
Catalyst	2	4	30
Wales Fund Managers Ltd	3	5	Not disclosed
Friends Ivory & Sime	10	68	110
Standard Life Investments	10	n.a.	Not disclosed
Penta Capital Partners Ltd	8	n.a.	142
WL Ventures Ltd	2	n.a.	2.3
Albany Ventures	4	n.a.	40
Bank of Scotland Structured Finance	120	n.a.	n.a.
Abingworth	6	5	79
3i (Scotland)	n.a.	n.a.	n.a.
Averages	32	45	529

Ventures appear to have a surprisingly large volume of funds, but this is misleading, and arises because the UK total is not 'cut out' of the global operations of the global financial body of which they are now a part (indeed it was not possible to do this).

These companies run the gamut from small specialist providers of venture capital backing for high-technology ventures to large structured finance providers who usually back funds rather than entrepreneurs. In the former case, the equity provision is direct and the degree of involvement with entrepreneurs can be close. In the latter case, the financial provision is usually directly to a fund, but the right to do 'direct' deals with promising entrepreneurs is retained, and occasionally exercised. Typically, the involvement with high technology entrepreneurs is more 'arm's length'.

From a portfolio balance perspective, the difference between these two forms of financing is considerable. It would be true to say that a portfolio of, say, 50 entrepreneurial firms, if chosen carefully, would be highly diversified. Indeed, the evidence is that the risk-spreading benefits of portfolio enlargement advance very rapidly, as the first dozen or so investees are drawn in (Statman, 1990; Cumming, 2006). If one is actually investing in funds (as in the structured finance case), rather than 'directs', it might be typical to have, say, 50 such funds in a portfolio. If each fund, in turn, invests in, perhaps, 50 entrepreneurs, the upstream provider of the ultimate source of finance capital is actually diversifying itself over $50 \times 50 = 2,500$ entrepreneurs. Its risk exposure on any one entrepreneur is therefore very slight. A beneficial consequence of this is that there has been a considerable willingness on the part of venture capitalists of this sort to see at least a small proportion of their total disbursement of finance capital put into very risky high-technology ventures. Generally, they will have no active interest in how this is done. However, if an entrepreneur within a fund to which they provide finance capital looks promising, the upstream provider of finance retains the right to get directly involved. This can be highly advantageous, once a technology has been technically and commercially proven.

The bulk of the investors were located in, or close to, London. Edinburgh, were London not so globally dominant, would also be regarded as a major financial centre. It too is important to the flow of venture capital to high-technology companies, and we conducted several interviews there. Finally, for regional diversity within the sample, we interviewed several venture capitalists in Cardiff and Glasgow.

The first set of investees numbered five in all, and were chosen according to three criteria: (1) that they appeared under a high-technology heading in the *Venture Capital Report Guide to Venture Capital in the UK and Europe*; (2) that they were highly active in patenting to protect their intellectual property in the high-technology area, as evidenced by searches on the Patent Office database *esp@ce.net*; and (3) that they were in, or close to, technology parks attached to London, Oxford or Cambridge. These are actually quite stringent criteria and, once willingness to be involved was determined, produced a clearly defined short-list. The final selection was made, according to the dictates of 'theoretical sampling',

Table 3.2 Entrepreneurs participating in fieldwork

Case A – Drug development
Case B – Thermal imaging
Case C – Copy protection
Case D – E-commerce acceleration
Case E – Light emitting polymer displays
Case F – Laser and infrared detectors
Case G – Animal robotics
Case H – Electronic micro-displays
Case I – Automated baggage security inspection
Case J – E-commerce retailing

by appeal to the principle that, to be included, an entrepreneur should be especially informative about the diversity of entrepreneur types. Table 3.2 (under A to E) lists the entrepreneurs' firms which initially participated in our research.

The technologies represented are diverse, and run across several disciplinary areas, including computer science, electrical engineering, biochemistry, mathematics, electronics, physics, and telecommunications. In practice, the companies were all close to, or within reasonable distance of, the so-called M4 high-technology corridor in England. These entrepreneurs are considered in some detail, by miniature case studies or vignettes, in Chapter 7.

A further tranche of funding subsequently allowed us to augment these five case studies by another five, after a further period of fieldwork, including site visits in Edinburgh (Scotland) and Boston (USA). These further interviews of entrepreneurs (denoted F to J in Table 3.2) were all undertaken using the same instrumentation (QA) as in interviews for entrepreneurs A to E. The technologies of F to J complement and extend the compass of the initial investee sample. There is complementarity, for example, between Cases D and J, which deal with aspects of e-commerce; and between E and H, which deal with large format and micro-format LEP displays, respectively. Another dimension that the cases F to J introduce is triangulation, defined by Fielding and Fielding (1986, p. 24) as 'a situation in which a hypothesis can survive the confrontation of a series of complementary methods of testing'. Not only are case studies themselves (as expounded in Chapters 7 and 8) a form of alternative to statistical methods of testing (as in Chapters 5 and 6), but also the different sites (Scotland and USA) for cases F to H and I to J respectively, provide a different perspective from the sites for cases A to E, which were all in England, hence achieving the desired triangulation.

Instrumentation design

The interview schedules, or 'instruments', were used as the basis of measurement in our fieldwork. As such, their design is of crucial significance to the success of the fieldwork, and the analysis which follows it. Based on our findings in the unstructured fieldwork, we decided that an administered questionnaire (AQ) form of instrumentation was appropriate for interviewing both the

Table 3.3 Eight-point agenda for administered questionnaire (AQ)

Risk Premia
Investment Time Horizon
Sensitivity Analysis
Expected Values
Predicting Cash Flow
Financial Modelling
Decision Making
Qualitative Appraisal

---

investors and the entrepreneurs. This approach guides the interviewee through a set of agenda items (e.g. financial modelling), in the course of which further detailed enquiry is made (which can be quite structured) under each agenda item (see Appendix 2 for the full AQ schedule, the second page of which sets the agenda). There were identical agenda items in the administered questionnaire interviews for both venture capitalists and entrepreneurs (see Table 3.3). All respondents were given notice of these agenda items in a so-called pre-letter (see Appendix 1) which was sent out when we were confirming our agreed interview time.

In covering this agenda, we frequently dealt with relatively sophisticated respondents (the investors and entrepreneurs) in our interviews, many of whom were trained in economics, commerce, business administration, finance, accountancy and cognate areas, so the depth of inquiry was often considerable. Both concrete data on risk handling were gathered, as well as attitudinal data. For example, we were interested in both concrete facts like 'which variables are used in sensitivity analysis?', and also in attitudinal variables like 'how important is staff morale to risk appraisal?'.

Also of relevance to instrument design was the distinction between 'hard' and 'soft' analysis. Both types were relevant to our work. To illustrate, we asked the investors what variables were used in any sensitivity analysis they applied to their business model. This is a type of 'hard' analysis, as it allows reference to be made to specific parameters (e.g. time scale, discount rate) and quantitative features (e.g. 10 per cent parameter variation). We also asked the venture capitalists how they went about determining a 'reference point' or 'base case' of what they expect to happen. This is a type of 'soft' analysis, requiring qualitative judgements on what would be a suitable reference point (e.g. another business or technology). As in previous work by the authors on risk in the UK venture capital industry, we aimed to combine such 'hard' and 'soft' analysis (see Reid *et al.*, 1997) in our book.

Exploring the interview agenda

Each heading of the eight point agenda in Table 3.3 was explored as follows.

Risk premia

The first thing of interest to us was whether or not risk premia (Atrill, 2006, Ch. 5; Damodaran, 2006, Ch. 4) were attached to the discount rates used in investment decisions (compare Thompson, 1997; Bhattacharyya and Leach, 1999). If so, how was the size of the risk premium calculated? For example, was the cost of capital taken as a reference point in adjusting the discount rate by a premium? Were risk classes of investment opportunities recognised, and if so, did they provide reference points for setting risk premia? Was a risk return locus of a certain 'shape' (e.g. slope) borne in mind when setting risk premia, and if so, what factors influenced its shape?

Investment time horizon

Was a payback period (Atrill, 2006, Ch. 4; Damodaran, 2006, Ch. 5) method of investment appraisal used (compare Arnold and Turley, 1996)? If so, how forward looking was it, and what determined the time horizon on the payback? Was it that, beyond a certain point, outcomes were too risky, or was it that they were too complex? Were payback decision rules modified by cash flow considerations? If so, were discounted cash flow methods used, and how were discount rates assigned? Did the firm have a target discounted cash flow (DCF) rate of return? If so, how was it set? Would payback periods be reduced for highly risky situations? More generally, were target rates of return and payback periods interdependent?

Sensitivity analysis

Was sensitivity analysis applied to investment decisions? Was this applied in NPV contexts (Atrill, 2006, Ch. 4; Damodaran, 2006, Ch. 5)? What determined the range of parameters (e.g. of costs) utilised in the sensitivity analysis (Quiry *et al.*, 2005, Ch. 20)? Was breakeven a relevant reference point in sensitivity analysis? Were different values assigned to costs and revenues independently, or was there recognition of their inter-dependence? If the latter, what forms of inter-dependence were considered, and could they be quantified? Were probabilities attached to costs and revenues in sensitivity calculations? If so, how were they assigned? Was a reference point used of what was expected to happen, around which a sensitivity exercise was constructed? If so, what factors were taken into account in determining what was expected to happen?

Expected values

Were 'certainty equivalents' used? If so, were values and probabilities separately estimated, and then certainty equivalents calculated, or were certainty equivalents estimated directly (Damodaran, 2006, Ch. 8)? If the latter, what factors had a bearing on the setting of these estimates? For example, was consideration given to risk variation, year by year, over the prospective lifetime of an investment involvement? Was there inter-dependence in the assigning of certainty equivalents (e.g. across years, with higher risk attached to later years)? To extend the latter, could different methods of assigning certainty equivalence be applied in any given year, depending on whether a cost or a revenue was being considered?

Predicting cash flow

Were quantitative probability estimates made of cash flows (Atrill, 2006, Ch. 2) (i.e. in effect, could the probability distribution of prospective cash flows be estimated?) (Damodaran, 2006, Ch. 5)? If so, were they used to compute the actuarial or expected value (EV) of the NPV of a project? In such a procedure, would a positive EV of the NPV lead to the project being adopted, or would this be moderated by a further qualitative risk assessment? Were calculations made of the probability that the total PV of cash inflows might be less than the project cost (i.e. the probability that the project would run at a loss)? If so, what level did this probability have to reach for the risk to be considered unacceptably high?

Financial modelling

Was a model constructed of the firm's financial objectives? If so, was it an optimising model? If the latter, what were the objective(s), and what were the constraints? What variables might appear in the financial model? Were inter-relationships between these variables considered explicitly? Was the model used to plan ahead? Could the future profitability of the firm be estimated, and were predictions like these used to modify the long-run strategy of the firm? Were simulation methods (e.g. Monte Carlo techniques (Quiry *et al.*, 2005, Ch. 20)) used to examine possible performance paths of the business over time (compare Brigham, 1992; Dupire, 1999)? If so, what was the time frame of interest, and what parameters and decision rules were varied across simulation runs?

Decision making

Were explicit decision trees (Quiry *et al.*, 2005, Ch. 20) constructed to evaluate different project scenarios? If they were, was a distinction made between decision points and outcomes? Were probabilities attached to outcomes? If so, on what basis were these probabilities assigned? Was the best action decided upon the basis of the highest expected returns? Could the best actions involve delay or waiting, or was the best action sometimes contingent on something (e.g. information acquired over a waiting period)?

Qualitative appraisal

Was qualitative risk assessment important to these investors? Were arguments constructed for and against an event occurring (e.g. successful high-technology product launch)? What were the requirements set on valid arguments? Was a hunch or an intuitive feel regarded as an acceptable form of argument? Was the context of an argument allowed to colour its salience? Was a 'more than even chance' of an event occurring a particular focus of qualitative risk assessment? Were arguments for and against an event occurring weighted in some formal way? Was a score-carding technique used in assessing risk qualitatively (compare Kaplan and Norton, 1992)? If so, how were scores assigned and aggregated? Was an expert system used in decision support for qualitative risk assessment? (see Hardman and Ayton, 1997).

Interviewing in the field

The respondents who were willing to be interviewed for the project have been described in 'Samples of investors and entrepreneurs' (p. 40). Once those venture capital houses with an interest in technology investments had been identified from the VCR database, additional research was conducted before an approach was made. Typically, the VCR gives brief biographies of directors working in their organisation. In additional, most venture capital houses have fairly comprehensive web sites which hold additional information about the particular roles played by individuals. Therefore, the researchers were often able to focus on a specific person within the company when making the initial contact. Given the fast-moving nature of the venture capital world, occasionally the chosen individual had moved position, or even company. However, just having a name to mention made it easier for the secretariat to find an alternative respondent in the relevant area.

When someone agreed, in principal, to a meeting, then they were sent an initial pre-letter (see Appendix 1) explaining the project, and a copy of the interview agenda. Confidentiality was assured, in the sense that no individuals would be identified, nor would anything be attributed to a specific organisation. This was usually enough to guarantee co-operation, and an interview time was therefore arranged, usually through correspondence with secretarial staff or a personal assistant. Confirmation of the agreed schedule was sent by the researchers previous to the meetings and, without exception, the practicalities ran smoothly.

The interviews with venture capital investors were conducted using the administered questionnaire schedule (Appendix 2) and were undertaken at their places of work over the period September 2000 to March 2001. Both researchers were present at each meeting with venture capitalists; one to act as interviewer, and the other to act as rapporteur. In this way, the interviews could be conducted in a free-flowing fashion, and the respondent was helped to feel at ease by being 'engaged' in a conversation, rather than simply feeling quizzed on sensitive data about his organisation. The meetings were not tape-recorded, which was again an attempt to make the venture capitalist feel more relaxed and willing to speak. Instead, the detailed notes which were taken of the conversations were later transcribed, while the meetings were still fresh in the researchers' minds. In this manner, only the most salient points were recorded. This is a useful technique, and one which limits the need for later data reduction. This avoids problems of data overload so frequently encountered by fieldworkers who record extended meetings during the course of their research, and then have all conversation transcribed. It is our observation that much of this evidence is never used, hence our own method, which emphasises data reduction and salience.

The meetings could take anything from one to three hours to complete, in following the given agenda. Very often, the professional background of the investor was in accounting or in finance, though many were also scientists by training, with additional MBA qualifications, either from Ivy League universities in the United States, from Oxford or Cambridge in the UK, or from the top European business schools, like the LBS and INSEAD. They were all extremely bright, fast-thinking individuals, and happy to talk in detail about some fairly technical approaches to risk management.

Following the interviews, we were often given additional company literature, and encouraged to access the company web site, or to get back in touch with any further queries. Respondents were then sent thank you letters, and promised a copy of the summary responses obtained. This was subsequently mailed out in the form of an accessible university working paper.

In terms of the entrepreneurs interviewed, the methodology adopted was essentially the same. The way in which respondents were chosen is again described in the 'Sample of investors and entrepreneurs' (p. 40). Thus, after an initial search of the relevant databases, individuals were identified, contacted, sent a pre-letter and agenda, and a meeting was arranged. A basic data sheet (see Appendix 3) was also mailed out for completion prior to the interview. This covered basic features of the firm like line of business, size, and financial structure. Again, both researchers attended each of these meetings, which took place early in 2001. And again, following the meeting, additional company literature was obtained, where possible, and respondents were thanked by letter. This documentation later proved helpful in drafting the case studies of Chapters 7 and 8.

Database construction

The data gathered by interviews with venture capitalists lent itself to statistical analysis (see Chapter 5), and so there was a requirement for formalising and coding the data obtained. A Microsoft Excel spreadsheet was found to be sufficient for our needs. This allowed us to codify all the data, in a form suitable for subsequent manipulation, both for descriptive and inferential purposes.

The variables identified in the administered questionnaire fell into one of the following types: binary; categorical; numerical; and string. Some of the variables acted as filters; thus a respondent's answer to the question, 'Do you attach a risk premium to capital investments?' was coded as a binary '1' for 'yes', or

'0' for 'no'. If the database contained a '1' for the relevant variable, then the question, 'What size is this risk discount?' would have a response; otherwise, it would not. This enables the researcher to filter the data, when it comes to analysis, and to ignore missing data, where a response would not be expected anyway.

In many cases the variable responses were attitudinal. For example, they might contain information about the respondent's opinion as to the importance of various factors. In such cases, a Likert scale was used (Oppenheim, 2000), so that attitudes (e.g. to risk) were easily translated into categorical variables, on a six-point scale.

Some of the responses from the questionnaire were numerical, and could be entered (with some care) directly into the database. For example, the payback time horizon on investments could be given in months or years. Usually, one thinks of payback in terms of annual figures. However, there were occasions where a respondent expected payback in, perhaps, 18 months. Thus on the database this variable contains the number of months, which allows greater accuracy and increased variation in the responses.

Finally, some of the responses given by respondents were string variables, or textual responses. In these cases, when analysing the data, the researchers would refer back to the original transcript of the meetings. The size of the sample meant that there were not enough responses to make it worthwhile attempting to code these text responses, and so the most efficient way to deal with this information was to look up the printed transcript of the meetings. The additional comments given by venture capitalists were, however, useful, and add a flavour of authenticity to the findings garnered from our statistical analysis (see Chapters 5 and 6).

Analysis of database

The data, once coded in the manner described above, can be manipulated and analysed in a number of different ways. Summary statistics were computed to give us a feel for what the data were able to tell us. This successfully prompted further investigation into specific areas. Graphing functions were also used for exploratory data analysis. The way this was conducted is discussed below in Chapter 4, where we compare venture capitalist's and entrepreneur's conduct with respect to risk analysis.

A more sophisticated analysis of the data is also possible, using the SPSS software package. The Excel calculations allowed us to compare descriptive statistics, and to present some interesting graphs. However, the work done using SPSS allowed us to make some useful statistical inferences, and to discover which variables had the most impact upon the dependent variables in which we were most interested. Chapters 5 and 6 report on the analysis thus performed, and provides a more technical analysis and interpretation of the data than does Chapter 4.

Finally, a further word should be said about the investees' data which were also gathered from entrepreneurs. While evidence from the initial sample of five investees (subsequently extended to ten) did not always lend itself to statistical analysis, except by specialised techniques like concordance analysis (see, especially, Chapters 5 and 6), it was ideal for case study analysis, particularly if enriched with company specific evidence like product description, price list, financial PR. These companies were deliberately chosen to be illustrative of the types of firms that we were looking for, namely patent-intensive, high-technology, and in receipt of venture capital funding. So, while entrepreneurs did indeed provide numerical data, which can be used in narrative analysis, as in Chapter 4, and in specialised statistical analysis in Chapters 5 and 6, they also enlivened the depth and range of information that we obtained. This gives us an additional and revealing perspective on how entrepreneurs handled risk on a day-to-day basis. We report on this case study analysis in Part IV (Chapters 7 and 8).

Conclusion

This chapter has introduced the methods by which both investors and entrepreneurs were sampled and interviewed. Then the ways in which the data were coded, stored and analysed were explained. Our key concerns, when starting the fieldwork, were:

- How do we find our venture capitalists?
- How do we find our entrepreneurs?
- What should the administered questionnaires cover?
- How do we analyse the data?

We started our research by approaching key experts in the areas of concern. These included the chairman of the BVCA, and a leading investment manager at 3i. These key fieldwork contacts were able to bring us up-to-date with happenings in the venture capital world. Further, the Director of Copyright at the Patent Office was able to give us a clear view of contemporary practice in the protection of intellectual property. Thus the work started off on a sound footing, and we commenced the fieldwork with confidence.

The venture capitalists were selected to be representative of those having an interest in high-technology investments. They were also chosen to give a good coverage of the UK, covering key areas like the city of London, the financial centre of Edinburgh, and additional sites in Glasgow and Cardiff. Careful due diligence, using published sources like the VCR guide, as well as companies' web sites, meant that we were well informed when it came to selecting our respondents for interview.

We were as careful when we sought out our entrepreneurial respondents. We made sure, by using both patent and venture capital databases, that our respondents fulfilled all the criteria laid out in the research agenda. That is, they had to have been patent-active in recent years, located in a high-technology sector, and in receipt of venture capital funding to back their company. These criteria were applied to entrepreneurs in England, Scotland and the USA.

When designing the administered questionnaires, our aim was to ensure comparability between venture capitalist and entrepreneur attitudes. Therefore, the agenda were the same for each administered questionnaire. We were interested first of all in 'hard' information, and the use of accounting or financial techniques to analyse this type of data. But we were also interested in 'softer', more qualitative evidence, and how widespread this was as a means of assessing risk in venture capital investments. Thus our questionnaires developed from ideas prompted by our initial meetings with the key figures, and from our reading of a wide body of economics-, accounting- and finance-based literature.

The data from the fieldwork were analysed in three ways. First, comparative statistics were presented to highlight areas of conflict or difference between venture capitalist's and entrepreneur's preferences. Second, detailed statistical analysis was conducted of the larger body of evidence, the venture capitalist's data. And finally, a series of case studies was constructed to illustrate, in an accessible format, the methods used by entrepreneurs for managing risk in the running of their businesses. Chapters 4 to 8 report upon this analysis, within the frame of analysis described above.

Finally, the last body of evidence to be referred to in this book relates to a postal questionnaire (see Appendix 4) sent to 114 VC investors in the UK, with the focus of enquiry being on risk and financial reporting, intangible assets, and the level of VC fund provision. The sampling frame was again created from BVCA and VCR sources. Details of instrumentation and sampling are given in Chapter 9, and the full analysis of this additional body of evidence is given in Part V Reporting and Investment (Chapters 9 and 10). For the moment, this chapter (Chapter 3) concludes the background institutional, empirical and conceptual analysis necessary to an understanding of the rest of this book. Therefore, we now turn to our substantive analysis of risk appraisal and VC in new high-technology firms.

4　Venture capitalists' and entrepreneurs' conduct

Introduction

In this chapter, our aim is to investigate how UK venture capitalists and entrepreneurs went about handling risk, when high-technology was involved (compare studies of this sort elsewhere e.g. by Liu and Chen, 2006, for Taiwan). Our evidence was gathered using the instruments discussed in Chapter 3. There, we explained how we interviewed both venture capitalists and entrepreneurs using two AQs of parallel design (Mitra, 2000; Liu and Chen, 2006). These allowed us to take respondents through a common agenda in face-to-face interviews (compare Fried and Hisrich, 1995, who used a less structured approach, but recorded the proceedings). In these interviews we covered: risk premia; investment time horizon; sensitivity analysis; expected values; predicting cash flows; financial modelling; decision making; and qualitative appraisal. During these interviews, which could take several hours, we gathered considerable bodies of evidence on how venture capitalists and entrepreneurs handled risk. For each interview, we gathered over 80 numerical responses, and over 40 qualitative (text) responses. These were coded, and then stored in a database for future analysis.

This chapter reports on this analysis in a narrative fashion. Initially, there were twenty VC investors and five entrepreneurial case studies. The venture capitalists accounted for the bulk of the funds invested in the UK. The entrepreneurs were fewer in number, but illustrated the diversity of entrepreneurial types. This body of data was subsequently increased by a further five entrepreneurial case studies (see Chapter 8). Chapters 5 and 6 take the analysis of this chapter further, by applying inferential techniques on the quantitative evidence about venture capitalists. Chapters 7 and 8 look at fuller evidence on entrepreneurs, much of it qualitative, in a case study framework. Finally, Chapters 9 and 10 examine risk reporting, and the level of funds allocated. Wherever possible, we have made reference to our general taxonomy of risk types (namely, agency risk, business risk and innovation risk).

Assessing risk

In our interviews we defined a risk premium as the additional return which induces venture capitalists to accept additional risk (see Appendix 2). The great bulk of venture capitalists did attach risk premia to their discount rates, usually without reference to the cost of capital. It was usually claimed that there was so much 'head-room' in risk management plans that the cost of capital became an insignificant factor. In detail, methods of fixing risk premia varied, but, in general, similar principles applied. A representative investor's comment was: 'We do it on the basis of IRR calculations. Early-stage technology companies require a higher rate of return ... you're looking at about 60 per cent per annum. We double the IRR because we're in a high risk sector'. The investor who said this made two things clear: first, it is useful to think in terms of risk classes; and second, stage of investment is one of the most obvious of such classes. Entrepreneurs were less sure than venture capitalists that they thought in terms of risk premia. On reflection, most thought that they did. For example, one said

> we might look at adding another 5 to 10 per cent as a risk premium on the discount rate. One method I would use is adjusting the discount rate for an amount, as a way of accounting for perceived risk.

Attitudes to risk

In our interviews (compare Mitra, 2000, for such techniques in an Indian context), we thought of risk classes as categories of similar degrees or types of risk (Q.2, AQ, Appendix 2, compare Cumming *et al.*, 2005; Smolarski *et al.*, 2005; Liu and Chen, 2006). Grouping risk in this way can aid effective risk management. Most venture capitalists (95 per cent) thought of their investments as belonging to appropriate risk classes. One investor, typical of many, said that, when risk classes needed defining, 'we would do it by stage of investment'. Another investor, again quite typical, said 'we'd look at risks in specific areas – for example, technology, market and manager (people) risk'. The latter comment is notable for its reference to our chosen risk categories of 'innovation risk', 'business risk' and 'agency risk'.

Both venture capitalists and entrepreneurs were able to rate investment opportunities by risk class. This might be done by stage of investment (see results in Figure 4.1 and 4.2, compare Rosenberg, 2003). Both venture capitalists and entrepreneurs were asked to say how risky they rated different types of investment, using a six-point Likert scale (Oppenheim, 2000, Ch. 11). Options were listed in the following order: seed, start-up, other early-stage, expansion, MBO, MBI, turnaround, replacement, follow-on. Figures 4.1 and 4.2 represent the perceived risk of investment types, according to the views of venture capitalists and entrepreneurs, respectively. The length of the bars in Figure 4.1 and 4.2 represent average perceived degree of risk, for venture capitalists and entrepreneurs, respectively (see also Reid and Smith, 2000).

Riskiness of investment types

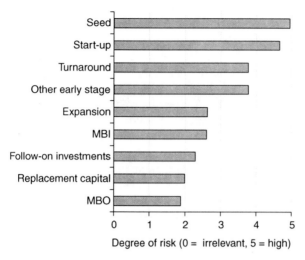

Figure 4.1 Venture capitalists' attitudes to risk.

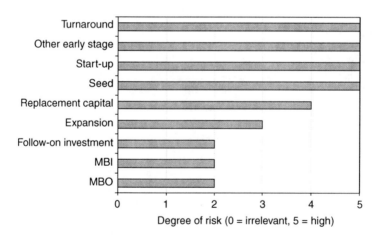

Figure 4.2 Entrepreneurs' attitudes to risk.

The entrepreneurs rated seed-corn, start-up, turnaround, and other early-stage investments as being the four most risky. Entrepreneurs actually rated the same four investment stages as having equal highest risk. Thus both venture capitalists and entrepreneurs seem to follow what is suggested by theories of venture capital (e.g. Chan, 1983; Chan *et al.*, 1990) and small firms (e.g. Jovanovic, 1982; Frank, 1988). That is to say, they both emphasise the importance of market experience. The entrepreneur has to 'learn by doing', when it comes to small business management. The learning curve has to be steep, as competition is usually strong. At start-up, learning has scarcely begun. Arguably, the entrepreneur is not well prepared for dealing with surprise events that impinge on the firm. Also, the investor is usually quite unsure of how to appraise the ability of the entrepreneur. It takes time and skill to put incentives and checks in place that will ensure the entrepreneur is 'singing from the same song sheet' as the investor. In short, agency risk is high. Seed-corn and start-up are therefore judged to be especially risky, by investor and entrepreneur alike. We also observe from Figures 4.1 and 4.2 that venture capitalists and entrepreneurs both view turnaround as highly risky. This is because turnaround often follows on from a period of bad performance, certainly of the entrepreneur, but possibly also the initial investor(s). Turnaround is often associated with major restructuring within the firm, as well as re-contracting of the investor/entrepreneur relationship. This all increases risk. Finally we observe, from comparing Figures 4.1 and 4.2, that entrepreneurs generally perceive all types of investments to be more risky than do venture capitalists. The only exception to this are MBI and follow-on investments, where entrepreneurs are intrinsically better informed than venture capitalists, thereby reducing their risk perception. The result that entrepreneurs are more risk averse than venture capitalists is consistent with our view on agency risk, in that the investor creates a fund of investments (i.e. firms) over which risk can be diversified, whereas the entrepreneur is entirely exposed to the risk of his or her own firm alone (compare Reid, 1998).

Agreement between investor and entrepreneur is apparent for the MBO (but see another side of the evidence in Chapter 5). It is natural to think of this as the least risky type of investment as the company, and the team who run it, are very much a known quantity. Indeed, the management team will be even more incentivised by the buy-in. By contrast, the MBI is more of a 'shot in the dark', from the investor's standpoint, as it involves a new team which has to be 'experience rated'. Entrepreneurs are more sanguine about this class of investment, probably because they could conceive themselves being bought-in to a new company. However, it is important not to be facile in reaching such judgement. For example, it may be that entrepreneurs, who know more about MBO teams than do investors, may be, correspondingly, relatively cautious about this investment form (see Chapter 5).

Follow-on investments were judged by venture capitalists and entrepreneurs as being relatively low risk. However, the low average perceived risk does mask some diversity of opinion. To illustrate, several venture capitalists observed that 'it all depends on the follow-on'. This suggests that follow-on per se may not be less risky than other forms of investment. It could be that 'sample selection' is occurring, with the more risky follow-on opportunities being screened out by venture capitalists. The same could be said of replacement capital. It may be quite low risk (on average) from an investor standpoint, but they were aware that some forms of replacement (e.g. following the death of a dynamic founder) could be fraught, and highly risky. This may be why entrepreneurs scored follow-on investments as being more risky than did venture capitalists. They are more likely to be aware of the potential this has to disrupt established firm operations. Done skilfully, the firm may benefit; done poorly, the firm may suffer. This is why entrepreneurs perceive capital replacement as involving significant risk (Wright and Robbie, 1996a, 1996b). When responses are looked at in the more disaggregated fashion of this paragraph, we see nuances of interpretation arise that are masked by the use of mean scores responses. Chapter 5 explores such issues further, using mean ranks, rather than mean scores.

Factors in risk appraisal

Venture capitalists and entrepreneurs were presented with a list of fifteen factors which could have a bearing on their risk appraisal of an investment (see Q.5, Sheet 5, AQ, Appendix 2). The factors which respondents had to consider in this way included: market opportunities, the global environment, the local environment, the quality of the proposal, the management model (Goodman, 2003), the business model (Frigo and Sweeney, 2005), the sales model, the scale of the business (Keuschnigg, 2004), and so on.

As Figure 4.3 indicates, venture capitalists thought that (on average) the management team was the most important factor in the risk appraisal of an investment. This factor is an aspect of agency risk. Other factors relevant to agency risk were: the extent of motivation and empowerment within the potential entre-

Figure 4.3 Most important factors in risk appraisal (venture capitalists).

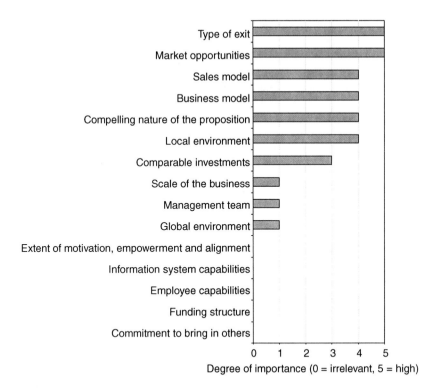

Figure 4.4 Most important factors in risk appraisal (entrepreneurs).

preneur's company (third ranked); and employees' capabilities (fourth ranked). Overall, these high rankings of organisational factors suggest that agency risk is very important to risk appraisal (compare Hyytinen and Toivanen, 2003; Pruthi *et al.*, 2003). Put simply, agency risk has its source in the uncertain and incomplete contractual relations between investor and entrepreneur. Entrepreneurs drive the firm forward, but the success with which they do so depends not just on their skills, but on how they, and the venture capitalists, handle incomplete information and uncertainty.

This agency relationship between the investor and entrepreneur (owner-manager) has been examined in detail by Reid (1996, 1998, 1999); Wright and Robbie (1996b); Pruthi *et al.* (2003) and was given due attention in Chapter 2 (especially in 'Agency, innovation and business risk' (p. 22)). From a theoretical standpoint, if the entrepreneurial firm has under-performing management the investor is entitled to intervene and to take control (Chan *et al.*, 1990). After investment has occurred there is said to be a problem of moral hazard, typical of agency situations. That is, there is an incentive for risk to be shifted towards the investor (as principal) by the entrepreneur (as agent) (see Ricketts, 2002, Ch. 5). This effect is caused by the natural inclination of the entrepreneur to avoid the disutility of risk by letting more of the risk be borne by the investor, once the deal is done. The investor can avoid this undesirable outcome by extending the frequency and range of information required from the entrepreneur (see Mitchell *et al.*, 1995, 1997, 1999).

From our interviews, we concluded that venture capitalists used information systems heavily to manage 'agency risk'. When we asked them about predicting cash flow, we found that three-quarters of venture capitalists explicitly modelled inter-relationships between variables in cash flow projections. Almost all venture capitalists used such techniques for planning. One investor explained his method as follows: 'We do a lot of investment monitoring – especially where the funds are investing. We're always working with the managers very closely. We measure profit against initial financial projections.' We found that most venture capitalists were committed to modelling the future profitability of their firms. This exercise was important to the formulation of long-run strategy for the firm (compare Frigo and Sweeney, 2005; Reid and Smith, 2006; Waites and Dies, 2006). When engaged in formal modelling, the investor often drew upon entrepreneurial opinion. One investor explained this symbiotic relationship as follows: 'The assumptions you input to produce the model are assumptions about how the business will run. It's an interactive process.' Though a desire on the part of investor and entrepreneur to manage risk is evident in all principal–agent relations in practice, it is particularly strong in the high-technology setting. Here, risk is unusually high, and information asymmetry is unusually acute (compare Liu and Chen, 2006; Sheu and Lin, 2006; and also Randjelovic *et al.*, 2003, in an eco-entrepreneurial setting).

Consider now the venture capitalists' assessment of the most important factors in risk appraisal compared to those of entrepreneurs (see Figures 4.3 and 4.4). It is interesting to note that the three factors ranked as very important by venture capitalists (namely, management team; extent of motivation; empowerment and alignment; and employee capabilities, all agency effects), were among those ranked as *least* important, or not even relevant (=0), by entrepreneurs. This highlights the different impact that agency problems have on investor and entrepreneur. The investor (as principal) is worried about how the entrepreneur (as agent) is running the firm in which he has invested. Due to a lack of information, he may not be able to make an accurate assessment of the entrepreneur's capabilities. The evidence of these tables is that the investor's concern about the entrepreneur's ability is not misplaced. Thus, factors like employee capabilities, motivation and empowerment were regarded as irrelevant to risk assessment by entrepreneurs (see Figure 4.4). These are, of course, a prime source of risk (i.e. agency risk) to venture capitalists. As if to emphasise this divergence in point of view, entrepreneurs ranked information systems as being irrelevant to risk assessments. However, as previous research (Mitchell *et al.*, 1995, 1997, 1999) has found, an improvement in the MAS is one of the first things that venture capitalists require of their entrepreneur. These data illustrate very clearly the nature of agency risk. For example, the problem of moral hazard, so much the headache of the investor, is clearly displayed by the evidence in Figures 4.3 and 4.4.

Also notable in these tables are the importance to both venture capitalists and entrepreneurs of factors like: market opportunities; the business model; the quality of the proposal; and the sales model. These factors all relate to 'business risk'. The main source of this is uncertainty about the future value of the entrepreneur's business. This arises primarily because market opportunities are hard to judge. Even if they do prove to be promising, it is not known whether the entrepreneur's untried ability will be up to exploiting such new market opportunities, especially when faced with competitive pressure. The business model, market opportunities, the sales model, and the quality of the proposal, are all regarded as important to risk appraisal, by both venture capitalists and entrepreneurs. Thus they display a common interest in dealing with business risk. Indeed, to the extent that the investor 'solves' the agency problem, or to put it another way, efficiently 'manages' agency risk, investor's and entrepreneur's interests are well-aligned, and they can then focus jointly on dealing with business risk. A final point to be made in comparing Figures 4.3 and 4.4 is that type of exit is only a moderate factor in risk appraisal for venture capitalists, but it is the most important factor to the entrepreneur. This key difference is again illuminated by the agency approach. The investor typically has many investment involvements. For each one, he may have several exit strategies (e.g. trade sale, market listing). Compared to this, the entrepreneur is relatively risk exposed. His or her exit is the sole source of payoff, and needs to be good. A flop on exit (e.g. a collapse of share price on flotation) is more damaging to the risk exposed entrepreneur than to the diversified investor.

Turning again to 'business risk', this was further illuminated as a concept when we asked venture capitalists and entrepreneurs about their use of sensitivity analysis. One entrepreneur said, 'From market assessment you can work out what a reasonable revenue and cost line would be. Management as a whole does the market analysis and we take a top down approach. We tend to be quite rigorous in doing a careful analysis of the market.' This suggests that 'business risk' is best managed by allowing an interaction between entrepreneur and investor. We have already seen that this is true in the handling of 'agency risk'.

Features of innovation risk

Finally, we turn our attention to innovation risk. To illustrate this, we asked venture capitalists and entrepreneurs how they rated certain features of innovation (see Q. 45 and sheet 45 of AQ, Appendix 2). As before, we used a six-point Likert scale, with zero denoting 'irrelevant'. There were six features of innovation to rank. In the case of venture capitalists (see Figure 4.5), these were rated (on average), in decreasing order of importance, as

- new product introduction compared to rivals
- the time that the entrepreneur's company planned to take to develop its next generation of products
- the expected percentage of sales to be gained from new products

- the actual extent of new product introduction compared to the company's business plan
- the number of key items in which the company was first or second to market
- the expected breakeven time (namely, payback period) for new products, or the company as a whole.

Thus venture capitalists emphasised novelty, timeliness and sales. Their concept of novelty was in relation to the market place (e.g. novelty as against the latest efforts of rivals). Venture capitalists want to know that entrepreneur's products are sufficiently new to beat rivals' new products in the marketplace, and that this can be repeated with further new products in the future. Entrepreneurs (see Figure 4.6), compared to venture capitalists, were more interested in technology per se, or in winning technological races. On average, entrepreneurs' ratings were (from highest to lowest): the number of key items in which the company might be first or second to market; the extent of new product introduction versus competitors; closely followed by the necessary time expected to develop the next generation of products. Venture capitalists generally rated all innovation features more highly than did entrepreneurs. Thus

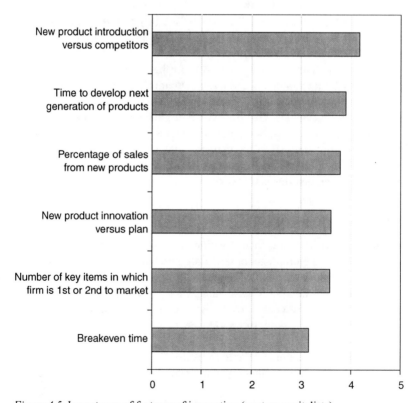

Figure 4.5 Importance of features of innovation (venture capitalists).

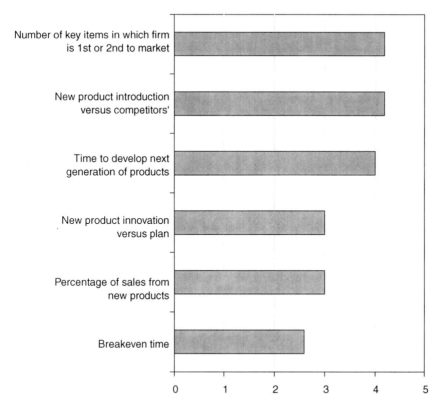

Figure 4.6 Importance of features of innovation (entrepreneurs).

venture capitalists seemed aware that innovation had to be the basis of the entrepreneurial firm's competitive advantage (compare Freel, 1999). They also said that capitalising on such advantage meant gaining a market presence.

Entrepreneurs, by contrast, seemed more concerned with hitting technological goals. 'First to market' only has value if, once you get the product to market, it will be enthusiastically bought. It is conspicuous, and very telling, that venture capitalists rated 'first to market' second bottom, whilst entrepreneurs rated it first. Further, entrepreneurs rated percentage of sales from new products as second bottom, whereas venture capitalists rated it third from top. So, even though entrepreneurs (as we have seen) worry more about business risk than do venture capitalists, they show less awareness than venture capitalists of the importance of markets.

Non-financial factors

So far, numerous facets of risk have been considered, in a framework which is largely concerned with accounting, economics and finance. In this final section, we extend the discussion to factors which are, broadly speaking, outside the financial world. We considered it important to look at factors which were outside the scope of the usual accounting discourse, for example, because observation suggests that matters like public image can overwhelm the numerical side of accountancy if public confidence is lost in a company. We therefore determined upon a list of factors which could be crucial to risk appraisal, but which might nevertheless be neglected if too blinkered an approach were adopted. Our final list of those non-financial factors which might be important to the risk appraisal of investment was: entrepreneur's public image; customer services; quality of product; legal considerations; and staff morale (see Figures 4.7 and 4.8).

Admittedly, several, or possibly all, of these factors can be reduced to an economic or financial measure, and thereby 'absorbed' into an accounting framework. For example, staff morale might be raised by better pay, customer service could be improved by heavier staffing, and legal problems can be bought off. However, at a certain level, these strategies will not work. Once the public image of a company, or its products, is damaged, it is very difficult to turn it around. If staff morale is low, money alone will not change this – good staff are likely to leave, and company performance will suffer. This is why is it important to investigate factors that do not necessarily fit into neat accounting categories, but can have disastrous effects on risk, the consequences of which are very rapidly observed in accounting performance indicators (e.g. in cash flow, or in profit).

Again, we used a six-point scale to measure how important venture capitalists and entrepreneurs perceived the five non-financial indicators to be. The results are displayed in Figures 4.7 and 4.8. Three important points can be made about them. The first point to observe is that both venture capitalists and entrepreneurs judged these factors to be of some importance – none was judged irrelevant. Indeed, most factors were judged to be of considerable importance.

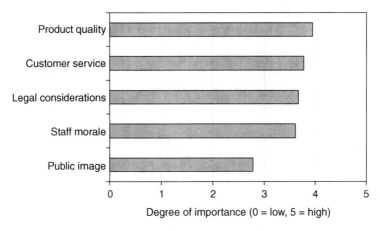

Figure 4.7 Importance of non-financial factors (venture capitalists).

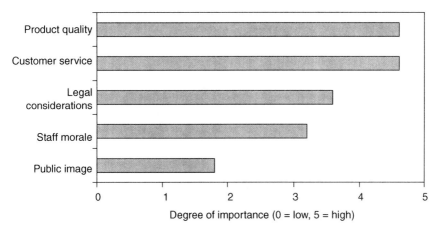

Figure 4.8 Importance of non-financial factors (entrepreneurs).

Second, it is generally the case that the venture capitalists were less worried about these factors than the entrepreneur. This reflects, as discussed earlier in this chapter (compare 'Attitudes to risk' (p. 53)), the relatively higher risk aversion of the entrepreneur, compared to the investor. There are two minor exceptions to this. (a) Staff morale is thought to be of greater importance by venture capitalists than entrepreneurs. The difference is slight, and possibly not significant, but may reflect the investor's greater concern with agency risk, which certainly embraces issues like staff morale. (b) Venture capitalists think that the public image of entrepreneurs is more important than do the entrepreneurs themselves! This is probably *not* paradoxical. Venture capitalists might well value the reputation of being ethical or prudential venture capitalists. To go outside this province would take them into an area of avoidable risk. By contrast, entrepreneurs are already committed to their firm, with their given range of products and services, and will have had to accept the risk inherent in their public image, along with the desire to continue running their firms.

Third, and most conspicuously, venture capitalists and entrepreneurs rated the relative riskiness of these five factors in the same way. This is important, because it suggests a good alignment of venture capitalists' and entrepreneurs' interests on non-financial issues. This may be part of what is meant by the common phrase used by venture capitalists and entrepreneurs, having concluded a deal, that 'we get on with one another' or 'we see things in the same way'. Mutual assumptions of common interest can then be made on this level, and the pursuit of goals in the financial direction can then be the focus of their energy.

Conclusion

This overview of investor and entrepreneur behaviour in the face of risk has focused on four questions:

- How risky are investments?
- What affects risk most?
- What aspects of innovation affect risk?
- What non-financial factors affect risk?

We found that there was general agreement between venture capitalists and entrepreneurs about which investments were relatively more or less risky. However, entrepreneurs were shown to rate individual investment types as more risky than were venture capitalists, right across the spectrum of entrepreneur types (e.g. seed, expansion, MBO). Likert scales were used to calibrate these differences. This suggests entrepreneurs were more risk averse than venture capitalists, as implied by agency theory (see also Reid and Smith, 2004).

When it came to factors affecting risk most, there was a clear difference between venture capitalists and entrepreneurs. Agency risk was largely the concern of the investor. The entrepreneur's first priority was dealing with business risk, and agency risk did not figure large in the entrepreneur's mind. This suggests that this component of risk had successfully been shifted on to the investor. Business risk was also a clear concern of venture capitalists, who placed as much (if not more) emphasis on matters like market opportunities and sales as entrepreneurs. The only area of considerable divergence was on type of exit. This loomed large in the entrepreneur's mind, presumably because of higher risk aversion, but was of only middling importance to the investor.

On matters of innovation, investors' and entrepreneurs' attitudes to risk differed considerably. The investor focus was on novelty in the marketplace, and on sales. Entrepreneurs were more concerned with getting to market, and with meeting innovation plans. This emphasises the importance of the symbiotic relation between investor and entrepreneur, so far as risk management in the innovation area is concerned. Each brings a different focus to the investor–entrepreneur relationship, and these complement each other.

Finally, we looked at non-financial factors, and found venture capitalists and entrepreneurs to be in accord, so far as their relative importance was concerned. However, the more risk averse nature of the entrepreneur's attitude to risk, compared to the investor, was also apparent.

We conclude that venture capitalists and entrepreneurs generally see risk in the same light, but, that when views differ, this is explicable either by function (e.g. are you a producer or funder?) or by attitude to risk (which itself may reflect risk exposure).

Part III
Statistical analysis

5   Investor and entrepreneur

Statistical analysis

Introduction

This chapter is the first component of Part III of this book, on statistical analysis. It builds on the work of Chapter 4, which has essentially been 'exploratory data analysis'. In developing that material, no formal statistical analysis, using inferential tools, was used. Rather, the emphasis was on the 'shape' of the data, and what this implied for a variety of analytical frameworks, including principal–agent analysis of investor-investee relations.

This chapter takes that treatment a step further, by utilisation of a range of inferential techniques, including tools that are well suited to the statistical analysis of data in rankings form (e.g. the ranking by riskiness of investment vehicles). In reconsidering the treatment of Chapter 4, it will shift from that chapter's simple representation of responses on a five-point scale (as in Figures 4.1 and 4.2 on investors' and investees' attitudes to risk), to a more sophisticated approach that emphasises mean ranks, rather than average scores. These 'mean ranks' data will be re-interpreted, and used in an explicitly inferential framework. We shall then relate our statistical concordance to a new, and revealing, geometrical analysis of concordance that will further link the treatments of Chapters 4 and 5 to that of Chapter 6.

Attitudes to risk

It has been argued that an effective risk management strategy, faced with complex uncertain classes, is to reduce complexity and thus to aid decision support (e.g. in the allocation of investible funds). Quite natural risk classes, in the VC context, are stage of investment (e.g. start-up, MBO), and area of business activity (e.g. innovation, business strategy). For example, Cumming (2006), in looking at the determinants of VC portfolio size, using Canadian data, has identified important factors as being stage of development, deal staging and technology.

It became evident in the previous chapter (Chapter 4) that the VC investor looks at risks in particular areas, and can rate such risks on a subjective scale (which we have calibrated using a Likert scale). For example, investors looked at different investment stages (e.g. MBO, MBI, start-up, follow-on), and were able to rate them by riskiness, giving rise to Figure 4.1, where risk was rated on a six-point scale. An alternative representation is now given in Figures 5.1 and 5.2, where *mean rankings* are used, rather than the *mean scores* of Chapter 4. In the mean rankings case, illustrated in Figures 5.1 and 5.2, the length of each bar is the average rank assigned to any investment stage, where averaging is over investors' opinions for each investment stage, and a low average rank means low risk (e.g. as for the MBO) whereas a high average rank means high risk (e.g. as for seed-corn and start-up capital). As there are nine investment stages to be ranked, rankings can never be zero, and cannot exceed nine (the number of stages considered in all) in magnitude.

There can be subtle differences in interpretation arising from the use of mean ranks data (as here) compared to mean scores data (as in the previous Chapter 4). In comparing Figure 4.1 to Figure 5.1, we see that there is little difference in perceived risk evident from the two methods. Most risky is seed, least risky is MBO, and the only reversal of attitude is over the MBI and expansion. However, when it comes to the entrepreneurs' views on risk, the calibration adopted does make a clear difference, as a comparison of Figure 4.2 and Figure 5.2 indicates. By mean rank, seed and start-up are viewed by entrepreneurs as more risky than turnaround and early-stage using a ranking measure, whereas turnaround and early-stage are viewed as more risky than seed and start-up using an attitude measure (i.e. a mean score, as in Figure 4.2). That does not detract from the analysis of Chapter 4, but is a reminder that the calibration of views on risk is a subtle matter.

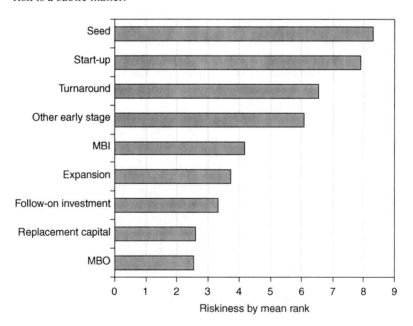

Figure 5.1 Venture capitalists' rankings of risk of investment stage, by mean rank.

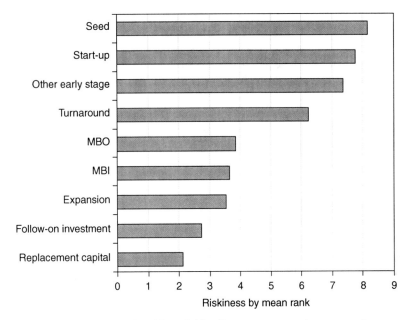

Figure 5.2 Entrepreneurs' ranking of risk of investment stage, by mean rank.

An advantage of using the ranking method of this chapter is that, despite taking the analysis one step away from raw data on attitudes to risk, it does present more promising possibilities for utilising inferential tools. The initial setting out of that framework will be undertaken here, and a brief application of it will be used in 'Concordance of investors' and entrepreneurs' Opinions: an alternative approach' (p. 71) on concordance of the views (or otherwise) of venture capital investors and entrepreneurs on risk. It is left to Chapter 6 (and especially 'Detailed statistical analysis' (p. 87)) to deploy more fully the techniques now to be set out next.

Statistical analysis

The general problem we are considering is that of ranking k objects by n judges. In our case, these 'judges' will be entrepreneurs or venture capitalists. The elaboration of this framework for statistical inference is given below. It is somewhat technical, and may be skipped by readers who do not have training in this area. The narrative re-commences in the last paragraph of this section. To resume, the 'objects' could be the nine investment stages of Figures 5.1 and 5.2. The choices of the judges define a ranking matrix, $R = R_{ij}$ $i = 1....k$; $j = 1....n$. The typical element R_{ij} defines the rank of the ith object by the jth judge. In our case, it might be the rank of an investment involvement (e.g. MBO, MBI) in terms of risk, by a venture capitalist. Here, our technical treatment follows Gibbons

(1985, Ch. 13). Formally speaking, $R_{i1}.......R_{in}$ is a permutation of the first n natural numbers. The jth column is the collections of ranks assigned to the jth object by the n judges. The ranks in the columns of R indicate how much agreement there is between judges. If there were complete agreement in the ranking of the jth object, for example, every element of the jth column would be identical. If this were true of every column, it could be said that the judges were in complete agreement. The column totals, called, say, $R_1.......R_n$ will be some permutation of the numbers $1k...........nk$. The average column total is k $(n+1)/2$. For perfect agreement between rankings, the sum of squares of deviations of column totals from this average will be:

$$\sum [jk - k(n+1)/2]^2 = k^2 n(n^2 - 1)/12 \tag{5.1}$$

The actual observed sum of squares of deviations will be:

$$S = \sum [Rj - k(n+1)/2]^2 \tag{5.2}$$

Expression (5.1) can be shown to be equal to ks_t where s_t is the total sum of squares of deviations of all ranks from the average rank. Now ks_t is the sum of squares of the columns total deviations when the judges are in perfect agreement i.e. there is complete concordance. Its value for any set of k rankings must lie between 0 and $k^2 n(n^2 - 1)/12$. The maximum value occurs when there is complete agreement, and the minimum value occurs when each judge assigns ranks randomly, indicating complete lack of agreement. If we think of the judges' judgements as simply samples, lack of agreement between judges is equivalent to statistical independence of the k samples.

A measure of the agreement between judges (or 'concordance', or 'dependence between samples') may therefore be defined by the ratio of S to its maximum value, that is:

$$W = S/ks_t = 12S/k^2 n(n^2 - 1) \tag{5.3}$$

The W in (5.3) is known as Kendall's *coefficient of concordance*. When there is complete concordance, W is equal to equal to unity, and when there is complete disagreement, W is equal to zero.

Tests of significance of W arise from interpreting $R_{1j}...............R_{kj}$ as ranks of a random sample of size n from a population of k variates. The null hypothesis is that these variates are independent. If they are independent, there is no association between the ranks of the k variates (i.e. of the k sets of ranks of n objects). In this case W is zero. If they are completely dependent (i.e. in complete concordance) there is complete agreement and W is unity. Thus the appropriate rejection region against the null hypothesis occurs for large values of W.

Under the null hypothesis, the ranks which judges assign are completely random for the k variates, which is to say that the $(n!)^k$ assignments of ranks in the rankings matrix R are equally likely. The sampling distribution of W can be approximated in various ways, for example using the beta distribution. A common approximation is that:

$k(n-1)$ W is chi square (χ^2) with $n-1$ degrees of freedom.

We shall now illustrate how these new tools can be used to treat our evidence on risk in a more formal way than hitherto. Norusis (1993) has written the user's guide for the use of this under SPSS – the software package we used to under-take computation of the W test. Wherever possible, we include a 'probability value' when a statistical test of investors' responses has been performed. This will be indicated by the use of notation like prob. $=0.004$, where 'prob.' refers to 'probability value' (compare Wonnacott and Wonnacott, 1977, Ch. 9). To recap, it means there are only four chances in a thousand that the responses made could occur purely by chance. Thus, one can have considerable confidence that such responses closely reflect the reality of the investors' world. For busy readers, only dipping into this chapter, we record that, by convention, results are said to be 'significant' if the probability value (prob.) is less than one-tenth (0.1), 'very significant' if the prob. is less than a twentieth (0.05), and 'exceptionally significant' if the prob. is less than one thousandth (0.001). Otherwise, results are thought to be insignificant (i.e. for a prob. less than 0.1). In reporting the prob., this allows the reader to put his or her own interpretation on the signific-ance of a result. This form of reporting will be used throughout the rest of this book, whenever statistical or econometric analysis is used.

In terms of statistical inference, both sets of rankings displayed in Figures 5.1 and 5.2 are highly significantly different in statistical terms from a random assignation of ranks, using the above Kendall W test of concordance [$\chi^2(8)=97.90$, prob. $=0.000$; $\chi^2(8)=31.487$, prob. $=0.000$, respectively]. Further, a comparison of the mean rankings of investors and entrepreneurs suggests that their rankings are *not* statistically significantly different, at the 7 per cent level [$\chi^2(8)=14.533$, prob. $=0.069$]. Additionally, if we use Likert scores data, as in Chapter 4, rather than mean ranks data, to compare investor and investee appraisals of risk, we do not find significant differences between investor and investee attitudes to risk [$\chi^2(8)=0.869$, prob. $=0.410$]. Thus the conclusion of Chapter 4, namely that there was general agreement between venture capitalists and entrepreneurs about which investments were relatively more or less risky, is sustained by the findings of the more rigorous statistical procedures used here. Further, the finding is robust with respect to the way in which views on risk are calibrated, be they mean scores or mean ranks.

Concordance of investors' and entrepreneurs' opinion: an alternative approach

An illuminating alternative way of examining concordance, which does not seem to have been used in the literature, is now illustrated in Figure 5.3. Here, the raw data are mean ranks of investors (vertical axis) and entrepreneurs (horizontal axis), as given in Tables 5.1 and 5.2. Thus, each 'observation' in Figure 5.3 itself embodies further observations (on investors and entrepreneurs) about their subjective rankings of risk for the various investment types illustrated: A, B, ... to I, for seed, start-up, ... to follow-on. Complete concordance would imply all observations would lie on the 45° line going through the points (2,2) and (9,9). As we see, 'eye-balling' the data suggests that there is very little divergence of opinion. This confirms earlier evidence, in Chapter 4, and above in this chapter. The main divergence is on point E, which relates to the MBO, which entrepreneurs rank as being much more risky than investors (hence E lying well below the 45° line on which investors' and entrepreneurs' views agree). This could be because entrepreneurs, as actual or potential participants in an MBO may be far more aware of possible (maybe even hidden) risks than are investors. A similar argument may apply to point C (other early-stage), which entrepreneurs consider considerably more risky (in a mean rank sense) then do VC investors. A regression line (fitted by least squares) through the paired mean ranks of Figure 5.3 gives the equation

$$y=0.516+0.901x \quad \bar{R}^2=0.084 \tag{5.4}$$

$$(t=0.827)\,(t=7.862)$$

prob.: (0.436) (0.000)   F=61.811, prob.=0.000

where y refers to investors' rank and x refers to entrepreneurs' rank. In brackets, under the coefficients, are t-values and, under them, probability values. The intercept is not statistically significantly from zero (prob.=0.436), and the slope coefficient (0.901) is highly statistically significant (prob.=0.000), and somewhat less than unity. Thus the fitted regression line lies close to the 45° line, reflecting considerable agreement between investors and entrepreneurs about the risks of each investment stage. This alternative display of evidence, which uses mean ranks and regression, rather than concordance estimates, gives very similar results to those of 'Statistical analysis' (p. 69) above. Further, the graphical display of the extent of concordance provides a useful summary device for readily communicating similarities of views between investors and entrepreneurs, when it comes to their perceptions of the riskiness of various investment stages.

Factors in risk appraisal

In Chapter 4, a wide variety of factors of relevance to risk appraisal were considered (see Figures 4.3 and 4.4 of 'Factors in risk appraisal' (p. 72)) from the standpoint of both the VC investor and the entrepreneur. There the focus was on how each economic agent *scored* (as opposed to ranked) riskiness, for a wide range of factors, from the management team to the local environment. Here, in this chapter, the focus shifts from mean scores, in this sense, to mean ranks of

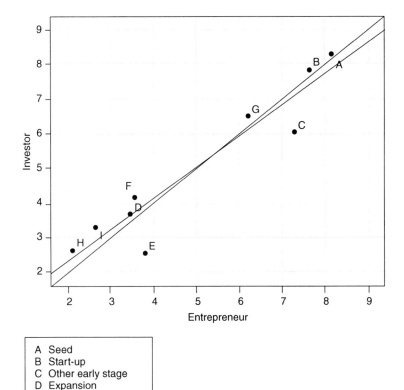

Figure 5.3 Investors' and entrepreneurs' mean rank scores of riskiness, by investment types.

Notes
a 45° line for *x* = *y* (if there is complete concordance between investors' and entrepreneurs' opinions on risk)
b Fitted regression line *y* = 0.516 + 0.901*x* for least squares fit to actural investors' and entrepreneurs' mean ranks of riskiness

those factors for riskiness. Figures 5.4 and 5.5 express the evidence in this alternative way.

There is an immediate and obvious difference between these tables and those of the corresponding Figures 4.3 and 4.4 of the previous chapter. It is that the possible scores are much higher in Figures 5.4 and 5.5, as the respondent is undertaking rankings over fourteen alternatives, whereas in Figures 4.3 and 4.4 the respondent is ranking each factor of potential importance on a six-point

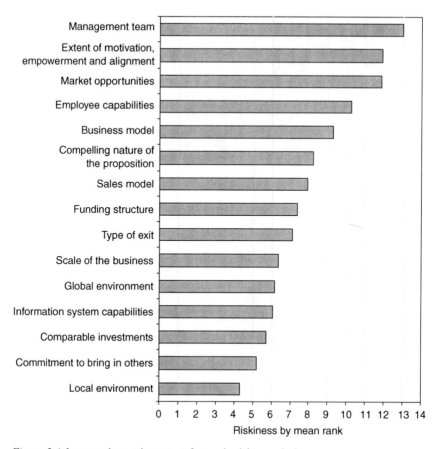

Figure 5.4 Investors' most important factors in risk appraisal.

Likert scale. As a consequence, all factors receive a score in the entrepreneurs' appraisals reflected in Figure 5.5, whereas five factors were ranked as unimportant to entrepreneurs in Figure 4.4. Arguably, Figure 5.5 is therefore more informative than Figure 4.4.

Turning to Figures 5.4 and 5.5 themselves, a key difference is that certain factors are ranked much higher in importance for risk appraisal by VC investors, compared to entrepreneurs. Of especial note in this respect is the factor O, of 'extent of motivation, empowerment and alignment' which has a mean rank score of 11.8 for VC investors, but a mean rank of only 6.15 for entrepreneurs. This is exactly the difference one would expect from a principal–agent perspective (compare Chapter 2, 'Agency, innovation and business risk' (p. 22)). The VC investor (as principal) focuses on incentive issues, like alignment of interests, which the entrepreneur downplays. *Per contra*, factor C, 'the local environment' is perceived to be much more important to entrepreneurs (mean rank = 0.10) compared to VC investors (mean rank = 4.2). The entrepreneur is preoccu-

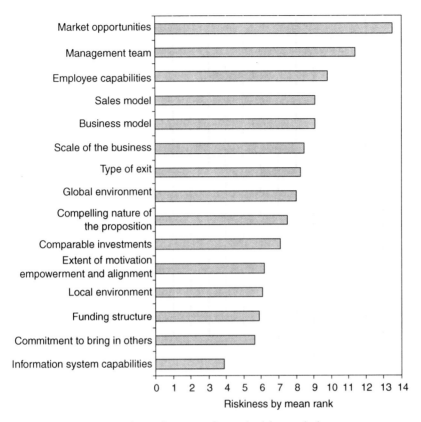

Figure 5.5 Entrepreneurs' most important factors in risk appraisal.

pied with local 'time and place' information, which is largely uncharted territory to the VC investor. Not unrelated to this point is that factor N, 'information system capability', has a low mean rank (of 3.95) for entrepreneurs, but a high mean rank (of 6.05) for VC investors. This is again consistent with agency theory, in which one sees the principal (here, the VC investor) being more concerned with using information systems to monitor and control than is the agent (here, the entrepreneur).

Figures 5.4 and 5.5 also offer the opportunity to extend the narrative discussion of Chapter 4 to the inferential. In terms of statistical inference, both sets of rankings (by mean rank) displayed in Figures 5.4 and 5.5 are highly significantly different from a random assignation of ranks. Again, using the Kendall W test of concordance introduced in 'Statistical analysis' (p. 69), we find the diagnostics: $\chi^2(14)=98.952$, prob.$=0.000$; $\chi^2(14)=24.519$, prob.$=0.000$, for investor and investee, respectively. Further, in this case, as contrasted with the evidence that relates to rankings on investment stages above, a comparison of the mean rankings of factors important in risk appraisal, suggests investors and entrepreneurs

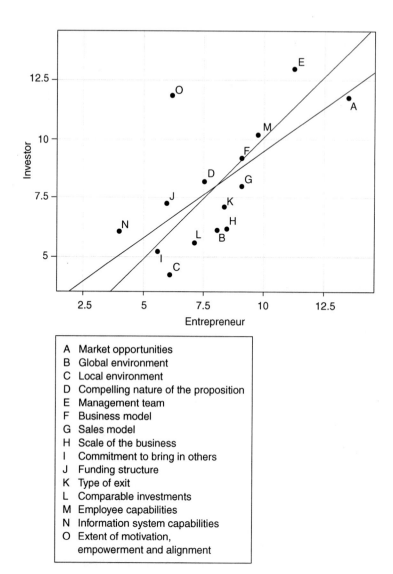

Figure 5.6 Investors' and entrepreneurs' mean ranks of importance of factors for risk appraisal.

Notes
a 45° line for $x = y$ (if there is complete concordance between investors' and entrepreneurs' opinions on importance).
b Fitted regression line $y = 2.144 + 0.731x$ for least squares fit to actural investors' and entrepreneurs' mean ranks on importance of factors for risk.

themselves have views that *are* statistically significantly different, at the 5 per cent level [$\chi^2(14)=23.408$, prob.$=0.05$]. As we have seen above, these differences can be explained within a principal–agent framework. In brief, views expressed on factors important to risk appraisal are themselves statistically significant, for both investors and entrepreneurs, and the views significantly differ between these two parties to the principal–agent relationship.

Finally, in Figure 5.6, we follow the logic of Figure 5.3, in terms of inferential techniques. Here, the raw data are again mean ranks of VC investors (vertical axis) and entrepreneurs (horizontal axis), this time relating to the importance of factors to risk appraisal (as in Figures 5.4 and 5.5), rather than to investment stage (as in Figures 5.1 and 5.2). Again, complete concordance in the views of VC investors and entrepreneurs would imply all observations would lie on the 45° line, which goes through points (5,5) and (10,10). By contrast with Figure 5.3, we see that there is sometimes a considerable divergence of opinion between VC investor and entrepreneur. These divergences included O (extent of motivation, empowerment and alignment), E (management team), and N (information system capabilities). These factors were all scored as being relatively more important to the VC investor compared to the entrepreneur. On the other hand, factors which were important to risk appraisal from the entrepreneur's standpoint included C (local environment), A (market opportunities) and H (scale of business); all more operational issues, of more significance to the entrepreneur (as agent) than to the VC investor (as principal). Overall, we find that whilst both investor and entrepreneur rank factors similarly, the weight they attach to rankings can be quite different. In particular, the investor, who very much 'calls the shots' in determining the contractual relationship between investor and entrepreneur, is putting much more emphasis, as one would expect, on agency factors (e.g. motivation, alignment, employee capabilities, information systems, etc.) relating to monitoring and control, whilst the entrepreneur is more focused on operational issues of running a successful high-tech business (e.g. markets, local environment, scale of operations).

A regression line (fitted by least squares) through the mean rank scores of Figure 5.6 gives the equation

$$y=2.144 +0.731x \quad \bar{R}^2=0.395 \tag{5.5}$$

$(t=1.122)$ $(t=3.182)$

prob.: (0.282) (0.007) $F=10.125$, prob.$=0.007$

where y refers to investor mean rank and x refers to entrepreneurial mean rank. In brackets, under the coefficients, are t-values and, below that, the probability values. In this case, the intercept is not statistically significantly different from zero (prob.$=0.282$), and the slope coefficient is indeed statistically significant (prob.$=0.007$), and considerably less than unity. The magnitude of this slope coefficient (0.731, compared to 0.901 for Equation 5.4) suggests far less agreement (or concordance) between investor and entrepreneur, as compared to the evidence displayed in Figure 5.3. This judgement is reinforced by the fitted regression line, which now considerably deviates from the 45° line of complete concordance, as do most observations. What we have unearthed here is that views expressed in mean ranks can be particularly illuminating about agency-type effects.

Conclusion

This chapter has aimed to extend the narrative work of Chapter 4 into the domain of statistical inference. In doing so, the treatment has been more detailed and more technical in nature, but slightly narrower in scope, focusing only on investment stages, and factors influencing risk appraisal.

Two statistical tools have been expounded and utilised, both focusing on ways of comparing investors' and entrepreneurs' views about risk. The first was a concordance technique, which leads to the useful tool, in this context, of Kendall's coefficient of concordance (W). This was able to show that investors and entrepreneurs largely agreed on the risk of investment stages, but agreed far less on the key factors impacting on risk appraisal. The second, a regression technique, displayed on a grid chart, is based on familiar devices, but in combination appears to be a new way of representing the extent of concordance. It provides both a statistical measure (from which precise inferences can be drawn) and a graphical representation, which supports well the intuition one seeks from the statistical analysis.

Both techniques were shown to support further the agency view of investor-investee relations. For example, VC investors focused more on incentives and information systems, whilst entrepreneurs focused more on markets, growth and the local environment. Chapter 6 will now drive forward the more extensive use of concordance techniques.

6   Risk appraisal by investors

Introduction

We have seen above that the forms of evidence we gathered are of both the quantitative (e.g. what is your IRR?) and qualitative (e.g. what are the objectives of your financial modelling?) variety. This chapter focuses on the quantitative evidence. By contrast with Chapter 4, which is largely narrative in its approach to statistical evidence, here we focus on *inferences*. That is to say, we ask what may be inferred from the data, with a reasonable degree of certainty. In doing so, we continue the work of Chapter 5, which was also inferential in character. In that chapter, we focused on the relative judgements made by entrepreneurs and venture capital (VC) investors about risk classes (e.g. categorised by stage of investment). By contrast, here we focus on the investor evidence (compare Proimos and Wright, 2005, for an Australian example).

Our sample of 20 investors, which we will exploit over many dimensions of risk appraisal, offers ample inferential opportunities. Subsequently (in Chapters 7 and 8) we will turn our attention to the very different form of evidence, case study based, which is available for investee firms and their entrepreneurs. These offer opportunities for theory construction (based on 'thick' evidence) and validation, in the sense of 'filling' theoretical categories (e.g. agency risk). The creation and analysis of illustrative case studies will be the task of the next part of the book, namely, Part IV.

The present chapter itself has two principal parts. In the first ('General statistical analysis'), general quantitative evidence from the investor's administered questionnaire schedule (see Appendix 2) is subjected to statistical analysis. Our treatment proceeds steadily through each section of the interview schedule. Statistical tests are applied to all questions which investors could answer in a quantitative fashion. Interestingly, this includes questions which some might regard as qualitative in nature. To illustrate, they might involve judgements that can be calibrated (e.g. how important is the use of sensitivity analysis to investment decisions?). As we shall show, questions of this sort actually can be treated in a statistical fashion, using methods that 'map' from attitudes to real numbers.

In the second substantive part of this chapter ('Detailed statistical analysis'), we focus largely on two specific investor issues that have been explored earlier in other ways (see Chapters 4 and 5): (a) the perceived riskiness of investment types (e.g. MBO, MBI); (b) the perceived importance of general factors in risk appraisal (e.g. those which are relevant to business and agency forms of risk). We also look at, in less detail, the perceived importance of specific non-financial indicators in risk appraisal (e.g. public image, staff morale), and the perceived importance of innovation to investment decisions (e.g. percentage of sales from new products). The new issues addressed in this second part of the chapter now relate to novel issues of interpreting rankings data (e.g. judgements by investors of what factors are most important), involving the decomposition of average rankings, hence exploring what lies behind the concordance statistics of investors.

General statistical analysis

This first substantive section looks at the eight categories of the investors' interview schedule in turn (see Appendix 2). The 20 investors in the sample were aware of our general framework through a pre-letter sent to them by us (see Appendix 1) and usually several personal telephone calls from us. They knew we were investigating the way in which UK investors appraised risk in backing high-technology firms. Further, they were aware that our enquiry would look at: risk premia, the investment time horizon, sensitivity analysis, expected values, cash flow prediction, financial modelling, decision making and qualitative risk appraisal, in this order. In that sense, they were forewarned, and investors' responses are likely to be well-considered, rather than 'shots in the dark'. We consider their responses below.

Risk premia

This area of enquiry was the first in our administered questionnaire (Q.1–Q.5, Appendix 2). We found that it was standard practice (84 per cent did this) to attach risk premia, (Atrill, 2006, Ch. 5), to discount rates in making an investment decision (Damodaran, 2006, Ch. 4), (prob. = 0.004). Because this result is so significant, it may be said to represent received practice among VC investors. However, evidence is less clear-cut in investors' use of the cost of capital (Quiry *et al.*, 2005, Ch. 20). They were asked whether they used the cost of capital as a reference point in setting risk premia (ibid., Ch. 5). Only a third said 'yes', and this result is not statistically significant.

When it came to risk classes, the evidence was very clear-cut. The great majority of VC investors (95 per cent) recognised investment opportunities as lying in risk classes (prob. = 0.000). Further, most (89 per cent) also used such classes as reference points in setting risk premia (prob. = 0.001). Both these results are highly statistically significant. Again, they represent received practice among VC investors.

As the UK VC market may now be considered 'mature', many of its investors being what Terry (1994) has described as 'seasoned', they are often familiar with advanced investment concepts (see, for example, Rahl (2000)). One of these is the risk–return locus of portfolio selection theory (Ezzamel and Hart, 1987, Ch. 6; Brigham, 1992, Ch. 4; Quiry, 2005, Ch. 21). This is sometimes loosely called the 'risk–return trade-off' (see also 'Conclusion' of Chapter 7). The great majority of investors (89 per cent) said that they had in mind a particular form for the risk–return locus (often called the 'risk–return trade-off') when they were assessing the risk of an investment opportunity. This result is highly statistically significant (prob. = 0.001).

Thus, as regards risk premia and risk–returns, investors appear to be sophisticated, and to share advanced practice. They utilise heavily risk premia and risk classes, and assess risk in a way which can be interpreted within the framework of modern portfolio selection theory. However, this need not always involve explicit computing of correlations (far less the solving of quadratic programmes), but rather the using of the mental construct of portfolio selection to assist in making judgements about additions to a portfolio. The extent of formality in procedures varies widely, yet within a common portfolio selection framework.

Investment time horizon

As a general issue, we were interested in how far-sighted our investors were, and whether they used formal techniques to cope with patterns of investment over time (Q.6–12, Appendix 2).

The use of the quite crude device of a payback period was quite common (53 per cent) but not statistically significant. It may well be that it is only used as a secondary instrument decision rule, as a constraint in decision making, or as a tie-breaking device, see Damodaran (2006, pp. 199–200). When it was used, there was rather little dispersion in how far investees looked ahead (months to payback). 'Far-sighted' investors wanted payback in no more than six years (the average was four years) and 'short-sighted' investors wanted payback in as little as a year and a half ahead (here, the average was two and a half years). Payback periods naturally varied, depending on the technology in which the VC investor was putting his or her money. Overall, this evidence does seem to point to short-termism in investment practice in the UK, by at least some groups of VC investors (namely, those using simple 'rules of thumb' methods of investment appraisal like 'payback').

However, practice was generally sophisticated. The great majority of VC investors (84 per cent) recognised that there was a certain point beyond which an investment had outcomes that were either too risky (or too complex) to be worth pursuing further. This finding is highly statistically significant (prob. = 0.004). Thus most investors (88 per cent) set a target rate of return (prob. = 0.002), and most (87 per cent) were sophisticated enough to know that target rate of return and payback period were intrinsically linked (prob. = 0.007). These results are highly statistically significant, and indicate that VC investors inhabit a sophisticated investment environment.

Sensitivity analysis

Sensitivity analysis, Damodaran (2006, Ch. 9), was an area in which our evidence (Q.13–20, Appendix 2) suggested investor practice could be improved. The sensitivity analysis of investment decisions was thought by investors to be of only average importance. Practice generally was not uniform, and few of the results reported in this section of the interview were statistically significant.

Thus, for many investors, important commercial insights may be being lost. The purpose of sensitivity analysis is to show how a project's expected outcome (e.g. in terms of IRR) changes in response to shifts in key parameters like price and advertising. It seeks to show investors how they can have the best impact on outcomes. This must surely be an important tool.

Indeed, there was a sophisticated 'sensitivity attuned' element amongst investors. Thus there were those who did subtle things like attaching probabilities to costs and revenues, and who did recognise that costs and revenues were intrinsically linked. Further, when sensitivity analysis was used, it was constructed around a reference point, in most cases (89 per cent); and this result is highly statistically significant (prob. = 0.001). Parameter variation in sensitivity analysis tended to be at what might be called the 'timid' end of the spectrum. The average parameter variation about the reference point which investors used was just 33 per cent, and the maximum variation was 50 per cent. It is certainly quite easy to imagine scenarios in which key parameters (e.g. advertising) should be subjected to much greater variation than this in sensitivity analysis.

As it seems likely that sensitivity analysis will improve investment decisions, its relative neglect needs to be explained. This is not an area of direct enquiry in our study, but we have received illuminating hints from 'asides' made during interviews with investors. From these, two main explanations emerge. One is that due diligence is expensive, and sensitivity analysis consumes time and resources. Further, it can impede decision making. Thus it increases complexity, and moves against the grain of 'yes/no' decision-making, by generating scenarios which can be difficult to evaluate. If one is screening scores of investment prospects, a less 'woolly' tool, while cruder, may be more efficacious. Another explanation of the neglect of sensitivity analysis is that sufficiently user-friendly software tools are not yet available. Certainly, traditional spreadsheet methods with programmed cells will work, but they are inflexible, time-consuming, and difficult to 'cast an eye over' rapidly. New software tools are required which are cheap and flexible, and are capable of rapidly conveying only the salient features of a sensitivity analysis (e.g. by using eye-catching graphics). As such tools are developed – and currently this is emerging as an active software market – so might sensitivity analysis become a more integral part of investment practice.

Expected values

In our interviews with investors (Q.21–24, Appendix 2) we treated expected values as representing the investor's estimate of the long-run average value of the investment, assuming no unforeseen changes in circumstances. We found that most investors (74 per cent) did indeed use expected values in making investment decisions (prob. = 0.004). Further, an interesting result is that these expected values were determined directly (e.g. by what we have called 'rational belief' in Chapter 2), rather than indirectly (e.g. by some statistical or actuarial calculations) by the great bulk (85 per cent) of investors (prob. = 0.023). Both these findings are statistically significant.

However, there was generally not much refinement in the use of expected values (compare Ezzamel and Hart, 1987, Ch. 8). For example, we did not get statistically significant responses to questions about risk variation over a project's lifetime, or the assigning of expected values differently for costs and revenues. This does not mean that all investors lack finesse in this respect, but rather that practice is patchy in this area. Our finding on sensitivity analysis is not unrelated to this point. More complex handling of expected values would be facilitated by having better software tools for sensitivity analysis, as more (or less) likely scenarios can be readily generated and analysed in this way.

Predicting cash flow

The efficient management of cash flow is crucial to many aspects of business operations (Quiry, 2006, Ch. 40). This is especially true of high-technology project management, where it is often hard to construct accurate forecasts of costs and revenues. Parts of the 'jigsaw' of operations are often constructed by different groups: sales, by marketing staff; capital outlays, by technologists and product development staff; and operating costs, by accounting, personnel and other staff. Forecast errors can be large, especially in areas like product design costs, where radically new technologies are being brought on-stream. As Brigham (1992, p. 377) says, 'it is almost impossible to overstate the difficulties one can encounter in cash-flow forecasts'.

With these thoughts in mind, we approached investors in high-technology companies with some caution when enquiring into how they predicted cash flow (Q.25–27, Appendix 2). However, the evidence proved to be surprisingly clear-cut. First, uncertainty was intrinsic to appraisal in this area; and second, there was little enthusiasm for basing decisions on purely technical evidence, like the sign and magnitude of the NPV of a project (Brigham, 1992, Ch. 8; Quiry *et al.*, 20056, Ch. 16).

Investors were asked whether they made explicit estimates of how probable cash flows were. In effect, we had in mind a kind of approach that amounted to estimating the distribution of probabilities of prospective cash flows – though we did not expect investors necessarily to explain themselves in this way. We found that the great bulk (89 per cent) of investors did estimate expected cash flows (Q.25, Appendix 2). This result is highly statistically significant (prob. = 0.001). Though about one third (65 per cent) said they would use these estimates in calculating project NPVs, this result is not statistically significant (prob. = 0.332).

Further, there was great resistance to using NPVs mechanically. When asked whether a positive expected NPV alone would lead investors to adopt a risky project, the results were surprisingly negative. The great majority (87 per cent) of investors would moderate the investment decision by further qualitative risk assessment. This response is highly statistically significant (prob. = 0.004). The general picture that emerged was one of investors who do use formal techniques, like probability weighted NPV analysis, but who heavily support this by other forms of evidence, including the non-quantitative. This may be due to an intuitive sense that a drawback of simple NPV rules is that they ignore managerial flexibility, and specifically the real options that can be exploited post-investment (Quiry *et al.*, 20056, Ch. 20).

One slightly worrying feature of investment conduct was a reluctance to contemplate the downside implications of projects. In interviews, attitudes could be quite cavalier, and it was clear that many investors would look bravely into the eye of a storm in which an investment was a total loss. Only just over a half (59 per cent) of investors would estimate the chances that the present value of cash inflows might be less than the project cost (in effect, the probability that the project would be loss-making) (Q.27, Appendix 2). Many investors were intrigued by the question (Q.27.1, Appendix 2) which asked how poor their chances of success on a project had to be before they regarded the risk as unacceptably high. Opinions differed widely, and no consensus was apparent. Neither of the above responses was statistically significant.

The latter results are rather surprising. This is especially so in the light of a climate established in risk reporting, since the Turnbull Report (1999). To illustrate, one approach might be to adopt the VaR approach to downside risk (Quiry *et al.*, 2005, Ch. 48; Jorion, 2000; KPMG, 1997). VaR is a measure of the maximum expected loss, over a given time period, for a given confidence level. It is defined against a background of normal market conditions. To illustrate, it might be said that the annual VaR of a high-technology project might be £10 million at the 99 per cent confidence level. This means that there is only one chance in 100, under normal market conditions, of this project leading to a loss of over £10 million. This is both a more conservative and (arguably) more realistic view of the project's risk exposure than saying, bravely, 'we'll take it on the chin if we lose the lot'. It is also a more readily communicable measure of risk to other (actual and potential) stakeholders in the company. As ever better software for producing VaR estimates becomes available, following the lead of JP Morgan with their RiskMetric™ proprietary software, this tool is likely to become more widely used in the context of high-technology investing. As well as being a valuable decision-making tool, VaR can also be used both for resource allocation and for performance evaluation (Jorion, 2000, Ch. 14), so it is likely to become ubiquitous, even though it may never supplant qualitative risk assessment.

Financial modelling

In the informal encounters we have had with a variety of investors (e.g. in meetings, committees, conferences, receptions, etc.), it has been common to contrast

US and UK investment styles. One way of summarising this is the phrase 'in the UK you run the numbers, in the US we back the man' (compare Goodman, 2003). We did not go out to test this sort of view, but our results do indeed suggest that financial modelling is particularly important to the UK high-technology investing culture. There was considerable consensus across investors in replies to all of our questions on financial modelling (Q.28–36, Appendix 2), and all results were statistically significant.

We found that most (89 per cent) investors did construct an explicit financial model of the investee firms (Q.28.1, Appendix 2). This result is highly statistically significant (prob.=0.001). However, most investors (72 per cent) did not construct an optimising model (i.e. a model which would automatically identify the best form of financial model for the firm which the investor was backing) (Q.28.1, Appendix 2). Even so, financial modelling was quite sophisticated. For example, almost three quarters (72 per cent) of investors explicitly considered inter-relationships between variables in their financial modelling. This is statistically significant (prob.=0.096). However, while using NPV analysis for decision support, investors were reluctant to let techniques alone dominate the investment decision. There was also some conservatism amongst investors in the use of techniques.

We asked (Q.36, Appendix 2) whether simulation methods, like Monte Carlo techniques (compare Dupire, 1999; Quiry *et al.*, 2006, Ch. 20), were used by investors to examine possible performance paths of the entrepreneur's firm over time. These methods can be used to subject entrepreneurs' plans to random 'shocks' generated in computer simulations. These can point out the potential vulnerability of business planning to unforeseen circumstances. Though some had heard of these techniques, the answers were unanimously negative. In fact, this reluctance to use simulations was not shared by all entrepreneurs (see Chapter 7), some of whom had perceived their potential benefits. For example, simulations, because they involve random 'shocks' to different parts of the financial model, can expose weaknesses which arise from unexpected, but possible, coincidences of events. Sometimes their consequences can be very damaging. By exposing these possibilities, simulations can allow investors to insert what are often quite inexpensive 'circuit breakers' or 'firewalls' which will prevent or eliminate these vulnerabilities caused by merely unusual coincidences.

Other questions (Q.33–35, Appendix 2) we asked of investors, about financial modelling, all concerned their projections, plans and forecasts. It seems investors in high-technology companies are very active on all these fronts. We found that almost all investors (95 per cent) used financial modelling to plan ahead (Q.33). Most (83 per cent) were able to estimate the future profitability of the entrepreneur's firm (Q.34), and all investors (100 per cent) used predictions about the entrepreneur's firms to influence its long-run strategy (Q.35). All these results are highly statistically significant (prob.=0.000; prob.=0.008; prob.= 0.000, respectively). Though they do not enable us to compare US and UK investing styles, they certainly do strongly support the view, that UK investors are very strong in their use of financial modelling.

Decision making

Although all investors were likely to use a range of decision-making tools, several of which have already been discussed above, in this part of our investigation we were particularly interested in decision trees (Q.37, Appendix 2). These are 'logic maps' of how a sequence of decisions may be taken (Quiry *et al.*, 2005, p. 381). Each decision point has several alternatives, and the number of possible routes through a decision tree (the mapping out of all possible routes in a tree-like diagram) is considerable. The best route is the one that maximises the ultimate payoff.

We found that most investors (79 per cent) did indeed think in terms of decision trees when evaluating different project scenarios. This result is highly statistically significant (prob.=0.019). Further, most investors (88 per cent) could distinguish between decision points (or 'nodes') and outcomes – a kind of test of competence in handling decision trees (Q.37.1, Appendix 2). This result is also highly statistically significant (prob.=0.004). In our interview settings, it became obvious that explicit decision trees were often constructed in quite different ways, by the various investors who used them. In fact, there is no standard way of constructing them, and different approaches may be the result of tailoring the method to appropriate investment contexts.

When it came to dealing with risk in decision tree contexts, some interesting differences emerged. It was not universal to attach probabilities to outcomes (Q.38, Appendix 2), with less than two thirds (63 per cent) of investors doing so. Indeed, this result was not statistically significant (prob.=0.359). Further, and more surprisingly, investors were not highly 'payoff sensitive' in their conduct. Only about a quarter (26 per cent) of investors decided on their best action on the basis of highest expected value (Q.39, Appendix 2). This result is statistically significant. These two findings are at least consistent, but suggest something about decision analysis which the standard approach (namely, payoff maximisation) does not embrace.

The reason why direct payoff maximisation seems to be rejected by investors is that they often appear willing to suspend, or delay, their investment evaluations. This hints at their adoption of 'real options' reasoning (Quiry *et al.*, 2005, Ch. 20). We used the phrase 'suspend, or delay' advisedly, at the start of this paragraph, because 'time shift' would not be such a fitting term. This latter term would still allow payoffs to be reduced to a comparable basis, by adjusting them with discount factors. However, investors seem to have something else in mind: something which is more like the suspending of judgement, or an allowance made for events to unfold before finally committing to an investment.

When asked whether a best action might involve delay or waiting, most investors (95 per cent) replied in the affirmative (Q.40, Appendix 2). This result is highly statistically significant (prob.=0.000). When asked whether a best action might be dependent on something (Q.41, Appendix 2), like information acquired over a 'waiting period', most investors (89 per cent) again replied in the affirmative. This too is highly statistically significant (prob.=0.001). The first action involves temporal delay, the second, contingent delay. For example, in the first case, a process of a certain expected length (e.g. an experimental laboratory process) must work itself out; and in the second case, a contingent condition (e.g. the grant of a licence) must be met. While these conditions are being met, the decision tree is not so much being put 'on hold', according to the investor opinion we have sampled, but rather being used to go through a series of 'exit' branches, of a set of nodes in the decision tree which involve 'wait/ continue' alternatives. In real options reasoning, this is called the option to defer progressions, or the 'option to delay' (Damodaran, 2006, p. 258).

Qualitative appraisal

The last topic dealt with in the investors' interview agenda was under the agenda heading of 'qualitative appraisal'. Its particular focus was on the score-card (Kaplan and Norton, 1996), as a framework for translating a company's strategic objective into a set of performance measures (for illustration see Mendoza *et al.*, 2002, for three company case studies on this technique). We asked our investors whether they used any type of score-carding method in their investment appraisals (Q.42, Appendix 2). Opinion was evenly split on this, and the result is not statistically significant.

Rather in the fashion of earlier questions about risk classes, we asked investors whether they used 'scenario analysis' to create 'best', 'middle' (most likely) and 'worst' case scenarios for investments (Q.44, Appendix 2). About three-quarters of investors (72 per cent) agreed that this was how they proceeded. This result is statistically significant (prob.=0.098). Further, it was asked whether such scenario analysis relied more on 'soft' or on 'hard' information (Q.44.1, Appendix 2). Most investors (79 per cent) agreed that it relied most on 'soft' information. This result is also statistically significant (prob.=0.057). Again, we get this finding that formal techniques will be heavily used by investors, deploying 'hard' data, but a considerable admixture of 'soft' information will be employed before an investment decision is actually made.

Detailed statistical analysis

A number of areas of enquiry were subject to more detailed statistical analysis than the simple testing upon which we have reported above. They all concerned cases in which investors had to make judgements, or express opinions, about the riskiness of alternatives, the relevance of certain factors to risk appraisal, and so on. Chapters 4 and 5 have already reported on some of this evidence. In Chapter 4, this was done in a narrative fashion, supported by a number of charts. In Chapter 5, it was analysed more rigorously, using concordance and regression techniques. The latter chapter gave a detailed account of ranking methods, as applied to data obtained from our AQ. This approach will be further developed in the present chapter.

Here, we will extend the inferential analysis, and support it by having a more detailed look at the rankings evidence. There are two issues which will be treated thoroughly in this way: (a) the riskiness of investments, as perceived by investors, by type of high-technology investment (e.g. start-up, MBO etc.) (Sheet 3 of AQ in Appendix 2); and (b) the commercial factors influencing risk appraisal by investors in high-technology firms (embracing factors relevant to agency and business risk) (Sheet 5 in AQ, Appendix 2). Briefer treatments will be accorded to: (c) the non-commercial factors influencing risk appraisal by investors in high-technology ventures (Sheet 43 in AQ, Appendix 2); and (d) the impact of innovation features on high-technology investment (e.g. impact of time to new product or first to market on appraisals made by investors of high-technology investment opportunities) (Sheet 45 in AQ, Appendix 2).

Riskiness of investment

In Chapter 4, we have already seen how, on average, investors rated the riskiness of various types of investment involvements. Recall (compare Chapter 4, 'Attitudes to risk' (p. 53)) that nine types of investment were to be ranked in order of riskiness. The underlying rating of riskiness on which ranks were computed was done using a six-point scale. These ratings of riskiness enabled us to compute a ranking of investment opportunities. Going from highest to lowest risk, the average rankings were: seed; start-up; turnaround; other early-stage; expansion; MBI; follow-on investment; replacement capital; MBO. Various narrative and statistical accounts of this ranking have been reported and discussed above (see Chapters 4 and 5), and from this a coherent account of this average ranking emerged (see also Reid and Smith, 2002).

However, average rankings mask variations in opinion by investors. We therefore give detailed consideration to the full set of rankings for investment risks, labelled A to I in Table 6.1. Only 18 of the 20 investors are labelled, because of incomplete data (Investors 2 and 20 are missing). Rankings were obtained from the ratings of riskiness on the six-point Likert scale (of Chapter 4), to create a rank order of riskiness, as displayed in the table. There is no unique way of undertaking this conversion. The technique shown in Table 6.1 is intuitively appealing in that the sum of ranks (for the nine alternatives) is 45 (namely, $1+2+\ldots 9=45$) under the tied rank method we used, even if 'fractional' ranks are used. Along the top of Table 6.1 are the investment types (A=seed, B=Start-up, etc.) which are ranked, and on the left-hand side column are the investors who did the rankings. To illustrate the method, Investor 1 ranked D (expansion), E (MBO), H (replacement) and I (follow-on) as least risky. Here, the calibration adopted is that the least risky will be given the lowest rank. As four items are ranked as least risky (D, E, H, I), they will have a shared mean rank of $(1+2+3+4)/4=2.5$. Note again, that, in this method, fractional ranks are permitted. As four items have now been ranked, the next in the order is 5 (which here is unique) and this refers to F (the MBI). All the rest, namely seed (A), start-up (B), other early-stage (C) and turnaround (G) were given equal (maximal) risk ratings by Investor 1. They therefore share the mean of the remaining ranks, namely $(6+7+8+9)/4=7.5$. Again, note a fractional rank is

Table 6.1 Individual investors' rankings of risk of investment types

	RiskA	RiskB	RiskC	RiskD	RiskE	RiskF	RiskG	RiskH	RiskI
Investor 1	7.5	7.5	7.5	2.5	2.5	5	7.5	2.5	2.5
Investor 3	9	8	6.5	6.5	2.5	2.5	2.5	2.5	5
Investor 4	7.5	7.5	5	2.5	1	2.5	5	5	–
Investor 5	8.5	6	6	3	1	3	8.5	6	3
Investor 6	8.5	8.5	6	3.5	1.5	6	6	1.5	3.5
Investor 7	8	8	6	5	3.5	3.5	8	1	2
Investor 8	8.5	8.5	6.5	2.5	4.5	2.5	6.5	1	4.5
Investor 9	8	8	6	4.5	2.5	2.5	4.5	8	1
Investor 10	9	8	6	2.5	2.5	2.5	6	2.5	6
Investor 11	8.5	8.5	5.5	5.5	1.5	5.5	5.5	1.5	3
Investor 12	8.5	8.5	6.5	5	2.5	4	6.5	1	2.5
Investor 13	7.5	7.5	7.5	3	3	5	7.5	3	1
Investor 14	8	8	5	5	2	5	8	2	2
Investor 15	8	8	5.5	3	3	5.5	8	3	1
Investor 16	8.5	6	3	1	3	6	8.5	3	6
Investor 17	8	8	6	3	3	5	8	1	3
Investor 18	8.5	8.5	6.5	2	2	4.5	6.5	2	4.5
Investor 19	8.5	8.5	7	5.5	2.5	2.5	2.5	2.5	5.5
Average	8.24	7.82	5.94	3.53	2.44	4.15	6.65	2.74	3.16

Notes
RiskA Seed; *RiskB* Start-up; *RiskC* Other early-stage; *RiskD* Expansion; *RiskE* MBO; *RiskF* MBI; *RiskG* Turnaround; *RiskH* Replacement capital; *RiskI* Follow-on investments; Ranks were computed by imputing mean ranks to tied ranks.

possible. Proceeding in this fashion for all investors, the complete set of rankings is as in Table 6.1. Note that the row sum, in every case, for each VC investor, is forty five, even with fractional ranks.

We can now learn much from an analysis of the fine detail of agreement and disagreement amongst VC investors. Up to now, we have simply focused on mean ranks. As the last row of data of Table 6.1 indicates, these mean ranks would give a ranking of riskiness from high to low as follows: seed (A), start-up (B), turnaround (G), other early-stage (C), MBI (F), expansion (D), replacement capital (C), MBO (E). This agrees with much of our earlier analysis and discussion (subject to slight variations due to method adopted, or number of VC investors who reported). What we now also see is that there are some areas in which VC investors agree quite a lot, and other areas in which there is considerable variation of opinion. Certainly, there is greatest agreement that seed-corn (A) investment is the riskiest (see column under RiskA in Table 6.1). Similarly, the VC investors, as a group, are in considerable agreement that start-up (B) and early-stage (C) are fairly risky. Next, there is what might be called 'close agreement' that an MBO (E) carries a medium level of risk. However, there is quite a dispersion of opinion about expansion capital (D), with some (like Investor 16 and Investor 18) thinking it is of little risk, and others (like Investors 3, 11 and 19) thinking that it is of great risk. The diversity of forms that expansion capital can take may explain this variety of opinions. For example, it might be used just to expand existing plant (low risk), to move to a different location (medium risk), or to create an overseas marketing network (high risk).

We may now return to asking, as we did in Chapter 5, whether investors are, overall, in agreement about the rankings. This may be tested using the Friedman statistic, but we have preferred a second method, using the Kendall statistic (for both approaches, see Gibbons, 1985, Ch. 13; Norusis, 1993, Ch. 20). In fact, the two are logically related, but the Kendall test (usually called, we have seen, Kendall's W) is more naturally interpreted as a coefficient of concordance, as expounded in Chapter 5. It measures the extent to which investors are in agreement. Kendall's W ranges from the value zero, which indicates no agreement among VC investors; to unity, which indicates complete agreement among VC investors. Technically, as demonstrated in Chapter 5, Kendall's W has a chi-squared (χ^2) distribution, which allows you to test whether the extent of agreement among investors is statistically significant. Now let us refer to our application of Kendall's W test. Its value was computed (using SPSS software) as 0.720. Being nearly three quarters of the way to unity, this suggests that investors strongly agreed in their rankings of investments, by degree of risk. This intuition is confirmed by the chi-squared test: the result is highly statistically significant (prob. = 0.000).

The extra information we have gleaned from this form of analysis is that, whilst there may be diversity of opinion amongst investors, particularly as regards specific investment types (e.g. expansion capital), it remains true, overall, that there is considerable consensus in the UK investment community on the riskiness of investment types. It is not just that, on average, the rankings look right (in relation to the theory of finance, for example), but that individual investors are themselves close to average opinion on this matter. On this matter, by reference to a number of investors (e.g. Investors 1, 7, 13, 14, 18) one sees a considerable resemblance to the average investor's opinion of riskiness, as represented by the last row at the bottom of Table 6.1. Finally, the inference is clear, under rigorous testing with Kendall's W, that the concordance amongst investors on riskiness is considerable, and highly statistically significant.

Commercial factors influencing risk appraisal

In Chapter 4 and 5 we saw how investors rated a wide variety of factors that were important in risk appraisal. Again, a six-point Likert scale was used, this time to measure importance for risk appraisal, rather than riskiness itself. It was found that, for investors, factors relating to agency and business risk were ranked highly in importance, such as management team (A), motivation and empowerment (O), and employee capabilities (M), these all being features relevant to agency risk. This kind of result is confirmed by the evidence in Table 6.2. There, the average rankings, by VC investors, of factors most important for risk appraisal are: management team (E); extent of motivation and empowerment (O); market opportunities (A); and employee capabilities (M) (in descend-

Table 6.2 Individual investors' rankings of importance of factors for risk appraisal

	AppraiseA	AppraiseB	AppraiseC	AppraiseD	AppraiseE	AppraiseF	AppraiseG	AppraiseH	AppraiseI	AppraiseJ	AppraiseK	AppraiseL	AppraiseM	AppraiseN	AppraiseO
Investor 1	13	7.5	2.5	13	7.5	13	13	13	7.5	7.5	7.5	7.5	2.5	2.5	2.5
Investor 3	10	7.5	4.5	13.5	13.5	7.5	4.5	10	13.5	4.5	1.5	1.5	13.5	4.5	10
Investor 4	13.5	5.5	5.5	5.5	13.5	9.5	9.5	3	5.5	1.5	9.5	1.5	13.5	9.5	13.5
Investor 5	7	1	7	7	13.5	13.5	7	7	7	13.5	2	7	7	7	13.5
Investor 6	7.5	7.5	1.5	12.5	12.5	12.5	4	1.5	7.5	7.5	12.5	4	12.5	4	12.5
Investor 7	14	10	1.5	4.5	14	4.5	4.5	4.5	10	10	1.5	7	14	10	10
Investor 8	14.5	8	3.5	3.5	11.5	11.5	8	14.5	3.5	3.5	3.5	3.5	11.5	8	11.5
Investor 9	13.5	13.5	7	1	13.5	7	10	10	3	3	3	5	10	7	13.5
Investor 10	14	6	3	10	10	10	10	3	1	14	6	3	10	6	14
Investor 11	13	4	4	13	13	13	8.5	8.5	4	8.5	4	1	8.5	4	13
Investor 12	9	4	4	9	13.5	6	13.5	1	4	9	9	2	13.5	9	13.5
Investor 13	13.5	5	2.5	9	13.5	9	9	9	1	5	13.5	2.5	5	9	13.5
Investor 14	10	4	10	4	14.5	4	10	1	4	10	10	10	14.5	4	10
Investor 15	9	1.5	4	9	14	9	9	4	1.5	9	9	14	9	4	14
Investor 16	14.5	7.5	1	7.5	14.5	11.5	11.5	3.5	3.5	3.5	3.5	7.5	11.5	7.5	11.5
Investor 17	12	8	2.5	12	12	5.5	5.5	1	5.5	2.5	12	12	12	5.5	12
Investor 18	10.5	1	10.5	5	15	10.5	2.5	10.5	2.5	10.5	10.5	5	10.5	5	10.5
Investor 19	14	8.5	2	8.5	14	8.5	2	8.5	8.5	8.5	8.5	8.5	4	2	14
Average	11.81	6.11	4.25	8.19	12.97	9.22	7.89	6.31	5.17	7.31	7.06	5.69	10.17	6.03	11.83

Notes

Appraise A Market opportunities; Appraise B Global environment; Appraise C Local environment; Appraise D Compelling nature of the proposition; Appraise E Management team; Appraise F Business model; Appraise G Sales model; Appraise H Scale of the business; Appraise I Commitment to bring in others; Appraise J Funding structure; Appraise K Type of exit; Appraise L Comparable investments; Appraise M Employee capabilities; Appraise N Information system capabilities; Appraise O Extent of motivation, empowerment & alignment. Ranks were computed by imputing mean ranks to tied ranks.

ing order of importance), and so on. This agrees with our earlier results on the importance of the factors to an agency view of investor behaviour. We have already discussed (in Chapters 4 and 5) why investors may have viewed the importance of factors in this way, both by reference to the broad risk classes of agency risk and business risk, and by reference to the personal testimonies of investors.

Here, we want to explore the diversity, or otherwise, of VC investor opinion on specific factors. The form of Table 6.2 allows us to do this. It gives all the rankings of VC investor opinions over the eighteen investors who provided replies (just two of our sample did not, for this question). The factors ranked were 15 in number from market opportunities (A) to extent of motivation empowerment and alignment (O). Again, the calibration adopted means the greater the importance of the factor, the higher the ranked value. It can be seen that there was very little disagreement that management (E) was the most important factor. Notice this is very much more important, on average, than funding structure (J). This shows that UK investor behaviour is not, in some sense, so distant from the presumed US patterns. In the US, it is said that 'the man is more important than the model'. For 'the man' (or woman) we can substitute the owner-manager or entrepreneur. This view is reflected in the rankings data, where funding structure (J), the sales model (G), or even the business model (F) are ranked well below the management team (E), which is the most important, and the extent of motivation, empowerment and alignment (O), which is the next most important, based on the evidence of Table 6.2.

We also want to confirm, as in earlier analysis (see Chapter 5) that there is an 'industry view' on the matter, in the sense of significant overall agreement, or concordance, amongst VC investors (compare Reid and Smith, 2003). There is certainly widespread agreement that the management team was the most important factor in risk appraisal (as indicated initially by the risk ratings displayed in Figures 4.3 and 4.4). It was the only factor which was at the top levels of importance for all investors. Market opportunities, the extent of motivation, empowerment and alignment, and employee capabilities were also high in consensuality, with few investors ranking these below the top three in importance. Some lower ranked options, nevertheless, were subject to considerable agreement. Thus information system (IS) capability, ranked twelfth out of 15, was viewed in a variety of ways. Investors 4, 7, 12 and 13 regarded IS capability as very important, whilst Investors 1, 3, 6, 11, 14, 15 and 19 viewed this as being quite unimportant. Most variation in opinion seems to have occurred for several middle-ranked factors. Of these, 'type of exit' was the factor that attracted most disagreement from investors, in the sense of its importance to risk appraisal. It is variously ranked as most and least important by VC investors. This, in turn, may reflect the diversity of exit types (e.g. IPO, trade sale, etc.) all with rather different risk implications.

Other important middle-ranked factors which were the subject of some disagreement included 'scale of the business' (H) and 'funding structure' (J). That is to say, they were not middle-ranked just because all investors thought they should be. Instead, some investors thought they were very important, and others that they were of little importance, with some in between. There may be good reasons for this. To illustrate, consider the 'scalability' of a high-technology business. Some are well suited to being scaled up (e.g. if they involve mass production of a high-technology product like a simple diagnostic test). Some are not suited to being scaled up (e.g. if a firm specialised in design or research capabilities). For cases such as this, the sense of it could be captured by saying that it was only for a few factors that there was relatively little consensus on their importance to risk appraisal.

Looking at the overall picture, for these rankings on factors important to risk appraisal, the Kendall W has a magnitude of 0.393. This is considerably lower than the value of W computed for the rankings of riskiness of investment types (as in the previous section). In that case, there was clearly high investor concordance. However, this value of W is well away from its value under complete lack of concordance (W=0). In fact, one is very unlikely to get, by chance, such a level of agreement indicated by the data, concerning which factors were important to risk appraisal. The result, unsurprisingly, is highly statistically significant (prob.=0.000). We conclude again that there does seem to be an industry 'view' or consensus amongst investors in this case, on which factors are important to risk appraisal. This evidence further buttresses the view that agency and business risk are crucial to overall risk appraisal.

Non-commercial factors influencing risk appraisal

In the previous section we have focused on the importance of commercial factors (namely, economics and financial factors) for risk appraisal. However, we need to recognise that careful risk appraisal needs to look beyond strictly commercial factors. Sometimes this is purely a matter of the moral, legal and ethical framework within which high-technology businesses function. Then the law, which largely reflects moral and ethical values, proscribes or discourages certain types of action, e.g. in relation to the environment. In other cases, certain non-commercial factors, like public opinion, do convert readily into economic and financial implications. VC investors were asked to rate five such non-commercial factors, by order of importance on a six-point scale (Sheet 43, Appendix 2).

Our VC investors ranked the non-commercial factors in the following order of importance for the risk appraisal of new investment opportunities (from high to low): quality of product; customer service; legal considerations; staff morale and investee's public image. As compared with the rankings discussed in the two previous sections, investors displayed considerably more disagreement. The highest ranked choice (on average), quality of product, was rated right across the scale from two to five by different investors. Public image, the lowest ranked on average, was never ranked as most important by any investor, but given all the other ranks by some investors.

Despite this relative diversity of opinion, investors' views of the importance of non-commercial factors to risk appraisal were quite coherent. Kendall's W came out yet lower, in this case, at a value of 0.229. Though lower, this value of W is well above zero, and is in fact highly statistically significant. Again, we do seem to have an 'industry view', this time emphasising the importance of non-commercial factors to risk appraisal.

The impact of innovation features on high-technology investment

We conclude this chapter, by looking again, briefly, at investor judgements and attitudes, with reference to innovation features. VC investors were asked how important were certain features of innovation to their willingness to invest in high-technology companies (Sheet 45, Appendix 2). We saw in Chapter 4 (Figure 4.5) that there were six such features, and they were ranked by VC investors (on average) as follows (from most important to least): time to develop next generation of products; percentage of sales from new products; new product introduction versus plan; number of key items in which the company was first or second to market; and breakeven time.

In fact, although the time to develop the next generation of products was ranked first, there was considerable diversity of opinion about its importance. The only ranks which investors did not nominate were the bottom two. Greatest consensus was actually held on the following feature of innovation: the import-ance of introducing new products to challenge competitors' products. At the other extreme, payoff, which on average was ranked least important, was given each of all the ranks by some investor or another: a great diversity of opinion. Kendall's W is just 0.117 in this case, suggesting some, but not great, concor-dance. In fact, this value of W is of only marginal statistical significance (prob.= 0.061). Under usual conventions (e.g. 1 per cent, 5 per cent significance), we would not regard this result as statistically significant. The results for innovation features are not chaotic, but they are probably sufficiently diverse that it is not possible to say that there is an 'industry view' (or consensus) on the key features of innovation to look at, when contemplating investing in a high-technology company.

Conclusion

This chapter was divided into two parts: general, and detailed, statistical analysis of risk handling and attitudes to risk. The first looked at the very wide range of risk issues which we addressed in our fieldwork interviews with VC investors. From this, a coherent (and generally statistically significant) picture of VC investor conduct towards high-technology companies emerged. We found that investors:

- assign risk premia and expected values, and use risk classes
- adopt relatively short time horizons
- follow quite sophisticated procedures in investment appraisal.

To illustrate the last point, they used sensitivity analysis, cash flow prediction, financial modelling, and decision trees. However, they often missed out on using some advanced techniques of analysis, including VAR (Quiry *et al.*, 2005, Ch. 48); simulation methods (e.g. Monte Carlo methods) (Atrill, 2006, Ch. 5) and real options (Quiry *et al.*, 2005, Ch. 20); Ghemawat, 1991).

The second part of the chapter looked in a detailed statistical way at how investors went about investing in a risky high-technology environment. We focused mainly on attitudes to risk, and factors influencing it. In a less detailed way, we also considered non-commercial factors and innovation. Our aim was to discover if there was a kind of 'industry standard' or consensus by VC investors concerning what was most important, in terms of level of risk, and factors determining it. Largely, that turned out to be the case. We found that the industry:

- is agreed on what are high-risk and low-risk investments
- is agreed on what are the key commercial factors affecting risk
- however, when it comes to the influence of non-commercial factors on risk this consensus starts to crumble
- so far as features of innovation in risky environments are concerned, consensus starts to break apart
- thus there do remain areas in which practice in the face of risk is uncertain. Further research and practitioner guidance would seem to be indicated, and would, indeed, be welcomed.

Part IV
Case study analysis

7   Case study analysis of risk appraisal by entrepreneurs

Introduction

This part of the book (Part IV, Case Study Analysis) is concerned with enriching the empirical content of the book, by providing detailed illustration of numerous actual investment processes, using the common framework adopted earlier (e.g. in Chapters 4–6). The approach is different, but the evidence base is the same. Here, in Chapter 7, we introduce the data gathered by interviews with the directors, sometimes chief financial officers, of five high-technology companies. It is these directors we are identifying as entrepreneurs. In writing the cases, we have aimed to provide illustrative case studies of risk handling in practice (compare Yin, 1993).

Five of the cases were selected because they met a number of criteria relevant to our research mission. First, a selection of investee companies was chosen from the *Venture Capital Report Guide to Venture Capital in the UK*, under the various technology headings available. Second, the Patent Office database, *esp@ce.net*, was searched to establish which of the companies that had received VC funding were also actively patenting. From this, a judgement sample of five of the most promising high-technology businesses was made by appeal to the quality of their intellectual property. The final sample included companies in technology parks close to London, Oxford and Cambridge. A further sample of three UK firms was added, using the same criteria, then finally another two from the USA were added. The latter two were obtained by a similar method of 'sieving' options, and they were utilised because they improved the 'triangulation' properties of the full ten case study examples. This chapter is firmly based on both reflective research and practical fieldwork. To help make Chapter 7 self-contained, a connection with the relevant instrumentation and technical literature is made in the early part of the case discussion.

Case A – Drug development

Company A was a drug development business, aiming to create products primarily for the treatment of cancer. For example, thanks to university colleagues, the company was able to claim expertise in a particular enzyme that could 'extend the life span of a cell, and which in cancer patients plays a role in allowing the cells to repeatedly divide and grow'. The company had recently merged with an important biotechnology company, and was listed on both the London Stock Exchange and Nasdaq. They anticipated that the additional expertise in vaccines, immunotherapy and gene delivery, brought about by this merger, would create 'a group which has a broadened and enhanced product portfolio with a key area of focus on cancer'.

This company's director perceived the riskiest investments in high-technology companies, by stage of investment, to be in seed, start-up, and other early-stage projects, as well as, perhaps surprisingly, in management buyouts (compare Chapter 4, 'Assessing risk' (p. 53)). In terms of the factors that impinged most upon his own investment decisions, market opportunities (business risk) were the most important, along with the management team and employee capabilities (agency risk), and the funding structure. This provides some support for the agency approach expounded in Chapter 2 ('Qualitative and quantitative uncertainty) (see also the case study evidence of Smith, 2005). Concerning technological breakthroughs, being first to market and speedily developing the next generation products were the most important aspects when evaluating potential investments (compare Chapter 2, Section 2.3).

Director A would indeed attach a risk premium (Atrill, 2006, Ch. 5; Damodaran, 2006, Ch. 4) to the discount rates used in high-technology investment appraisals. This was done relatively flexibly, perhaps by adding 5 to 10 per cent to the discount rate used. The company's cost of capital was a relevant reference point, in this regard. In addition, they also used risk classes to categorise potential investments, and would use these classes to determine the discount rate to be applied to the decision. In line with his relatively technical interpretation of the risk inherent in the allocation of business resources, this director had in mind a particular risk–return trade-off. He explained that 'within a range, there's probably a fairly linear relationship but, at certain points, there's a "super-return", and that relationship breaks down either above or below that line.'

The nature of this company, drug development, meant that payback periods were very long (Atrill, 2006, Ch. 4; Damodaran, 2006, Ch. 5), and could date either from as far back as initial laboratory research, or to as far ahead as the clinical trial period, or beyond, to market (compare Uher and Toakley, 1999). Thus, while payback period was considered, it could be difficult to define. During the initial research period, and up to as far as two years along the line, if progress were unsatisfactory, the company would cease operation of a particular product line.

This company used DCF techniques and determined the discount rate by applying a range of probabilities, based on industry averages, to potential outcomes of clinical trials, with increasing probability of success as the product moved through from Phase 1 to being close to approval. The probabilities thereby derived were applied to the expected cash flows for the products at the relevant stages of development. NPV calculations were also used in Company A's sensitivity analysis. This was carried out for each product on variables like potential market share, market penetration, sales revenues, and therapeutic indications. In conducting this analysis, the variables could range from plus to minus one hundred per cent. To a degree, some costs and revenues could be said to be inter-dependent. However, as Director A explained, 'drugs are price inelastic and the margins are very high. The cost of goods for a drug and the likely sales revenue have no direct relationship'.

Expected values were used to help the company make decisions (compare Damodaran, 2006, Ch. 8). Given the nature of pre-clinical trials, each phase had to be completed before the next. As every step of the way was a binary decision – either they did, or they did not, proceed to the next stage – the company was able to avoid the cost of expensive clinical trials if the product failed a particular stage. Company A was, in this way, better able to manage its technology risk.

This company made explicit predictions of cash flows (Atrill, 2006, Ch. 2), but would not expect to adopt a risky project based purely on a positive NPV (Damodaran, 2006, Ch. 5). This is where their sensitivity analysis came into play, along with additional qualitative assessment. They would not invest in projects with a very low probability of success; not because they were particularly risk averse, but rather because of a lack of resources: 'we have a lot of opportunities and not a lot of cash'.

As we might expect from his earlier responses, this director modelled explicitly his company's financial objectives (compare Quiry *et al.*, 2005, Ch. 20). Rather than having a single model, with an optimal outcome for the company as a whole, separate models were constructed for individual projects, and each had its own objective. Then, the decision as to which project to adopt was subjective. The company was constrained in its modelling by cash considerations, and by human resources. Therefore the phasing of costs was of prime importance. It was quite possible for the company to 'maintain a number of projects by juggling the time scales', so one might be put on hold, while another was progressed (compare Gifford, 1995). Thus a main function of this company's financial modelling was to help in the decision as to whether or not to pursue a project. But it also had the role of helping management to estimate the company's share price.

As well as the highly sophisticated quantitative analysis that this company undertook – it had even used simulation methods in the past – they also performed detailed qualitative appraisals. For example, SWOT analysis was used to examine the pros and cons of following particular strategies, for example, assessing the level of customer service was a key feature when considering new investments. Used in conjunction with decision-trees and scenario analysis (Quiry *et al.*, 2005, Ch. 20), this was considered to be a 'very useful decision tool with a product with such a long gestation period'.

Case B – Thermal imaging

Company B produced infra-red microprocessors, using thermal imaging technology, and placed a strong emphasis on affordability. The applications of a typical product would include security and surveillance, process control, non-destructive testing and healthcare. Rather than being a university spin-out company, as are many UK high-technology businesses, this had instead been funded by the Ministry of Defence.

The director of Company B seemed unable to use risk premia in his analysis of new product developments, and worked to no overall target rate of return. His explanation for this was that the nature of each product line, and the innovative nature of the company, made it very hard to gauge how successful a product might be. So, although the demand for his products existed, and an equivalent product did not, the only way to judge market reaction would be to 'go on gut feeling', based on such thin evidence as there was.

Director B thought that the riskiest stages of investment were seed and start-up (compare Chapter 4, 'Attitudes to risk' on p. 53). He identified many factors as being highly important when making risk appraisals within his company. Under the categories defined for our research purposes, he considered the most important business risks to arise from: the global environment; the sales model; and scale of the business. He attached importance to agency risks, such as: the nature of the management team; employee capabilities; and a commitment to bring in others. He thought that technology risk was related to the percentage of sales from new products; and the extent of his own new product introduction, compared to that of competitors.

Whereas risk premia were difficult, if not impossible, to calculate, he thought that the time horizon for investments could more easily be judged. Therefore, differing lengths of payback periods were used (Atrill, 2006, Ch. 4). Some products had a payback period of seven to eight years, while more recent products had a 36-month time horizon. As the director explained, 'we have to balance it, otherwise we'd run out of money very quickly'. To a degree, he felt under pressure from investors to set target times for payback, as 'investors want to see some returns'. However, they would not carry on regardless if one sector were not delivering for them, choosing to withdraw rather than to pursue it any further.

For this company, sensitivity analysis (Atrill, 2006, Ch. 4), was extremely important, especially when contemplating moving into unknown or completely new markets. The company had previously employed professionals to produce for them a sensitivity model, which they now used to analyse each market segment in which they operated. This included details on volume, material prices, labour content and selling prices. They would let the sensitivities range widely in conducting their analysis, and would attach probabilities to relevant figures based on expected market demand.

While it was difficult for Company B to predict sales levels, they did try to calculate expected values, conducting a probability analysis on the sales. These calculations incorporated sales budgets and probabilities for individual market segments, which were based on their knowledge of the macroeconomy and reports from 'world class' consultants.

Company B produced an explicit model of the firm's objectives. This was not an optimising model, such as the sort that might show the best possible outcome, given various inputs. Instead, until recently, the objective of the firm's financial modelling had been to predict when the company would run out of money. The director explained that the objectives of financial modelling changed with time, and that, with breakeven in sight, he now intended to looking in much more detail at the sensitivity analyses and salesman's predictions of achieving predicted sales levels than he had done in the past. Given that the company had spent several years on product development, the product costs were now fairly well defined, and so modelling was now going to have to focus on sales figures. The director anticipated additional complications in future financial modelling. As he explained, 'what becomes more difficult is when you're both selling and developing next generation products'.

Decision trees were clearly important to this company's choice of strategy. They would develop flowcharts through eight stages from product concept to manufacture, getting feedback on things like marketing. The engineering process followed standard industry questions and answers, which helped the company to reduce the consequential technology risk. Probabilities were assigned on the basis that risk was reduced if the company knew more about the potential outcomes. So for each business segment in which this company operated, the business outcomes were continually monitored, as the company moved through its decision tree.

Case C – Copy protection

Company C worked primarily in the TV and digital field and claimed to copy protect 'anything'. Their company literature states that they 'develop and market digital rights management, electronic license management and copy protection technologies for the consumer interactive software, enterprise software, home video and music markets'. The company's headquarters were in California, with additional bases in London and Tokyo. The business was marketed in terms of: the flexibility it offered; the compatibility of its products with a wide range of hardware and software configurations; the level of security provided (which could involve issues of encrypting and enciphering); and the facility for consumers to use their products as creative marketing tools.

Director C said that, because they were investing in 'untested' technology, his company did not use discount rates. Therefore risk premia were not favoured when making investment decisions. Instead, they were more interested in maintaining a profit margin of 40 per cent. Their cost of capital was taken to be the three per cent interest rate earned on their substantial bank balance, and again, was not considered in discount decisions, because 'it's not important'. The company had started with a core competence in its technological area. It had then extended its function by buying out other companies working in similar areas. This growth by acquisition was used as an alternative to internal growth, as best explained in the director's own words: 'we typically invest $1 million in a company, and get 10 to 20 per cent of the share capital of the company. Then we aim to buy the company outright, if it will not dilute our profit and loss account. We demand a seat on the Board, and so on. We invest in technology that is untested.' This investee company is therefore an interesting variant, in which some investor functions are absorbed.

Again, risk classes were not used to separate potential investment opportunities, as they were all considered to be risky. Indeed, the very nature of this company meant that it was concerned with managing investments at the riskiest end of the spectrum, considered by this director to be seed, start-up, other early-stage and turnaround investments. The most important factors considered by Company C, when making risk appraisals, were the potential market opportunities, and the expected type of exit. On the technology side, it was important to be first to market with new products, and the extent to which they could achieve this, compared to rivals, was crucial.

Payback, as a method of capital investment appraisal, was not used within this business, although the director did admit that 'we typically give it a year – for example, we'd put someone on the Board and see how it goes. We will stop spending time on it if it isn't working'. This business was in the fortunate position of being 'cash rich', and so payback and DCF methods were not necessary to them. They focused more closely on profit margins, and the effect that any new investment would have on their share price: 'it mustn't dilute what we've got'.

Company C did not specifically perform sensitivity analyses as, according to the director, it would 'suggest financial modelling, which we don't do'. Likewise, breakeven was unimportant, as the nature of the products in which they invested meant they would either make a loss, or a huge profit: 'they either bomb or go berserk'.

While neither sensitivity analysis nor breakeven analysis was used by Company C, what *was* important to them was the calculation of expected values. In every situation where the company wanted to assess the expected value of a project, they would employ a consultant to get a specialist opinion on the possible outcome. Generally, they were investing in projects with a time horizon of anything up to five years, which they considered to be long-term. The first year of any particular project was the most important, during which Director C thought that his company added valued, for example, though improved management. Beyond the first year, risk was considered to become much higher.

We have seen above that breakeven analysis and DCF methods were not used in this company. The director explained that 'we don't use cash at all [and] can't estimate revenues'. They did, however, estimate the chances that a project might run at a loss, knowing from experience that only one third would work out. If there were perceived to be at least a 50–50 chance of success for any particular, Company C would undertake that project.

All investments made by this business were signed off by the Board of Directors who, in turn, were accountable to the shareholders. For this reason Company C felt the need to produce a model (albeit small) of a particular investment, in a one-page spreadsheet format. This conformed to a defined house style and contained an analysis of the following main variables: the software engineers' time and buildings costs, which accounted for 85 per cent of costs; and revenue. Such models were not used to help the firm plan ahead, although its future profitability could be estimated, and its long-run strategy influenced by the people they put on the Board of Directors of investee companies.

Company C used 'serious' due diligence and decision trees to evaluate different project scenarios within the firm. For example, the first decision might be to choose between a digital and an analogue technology. The decision as to which strategy to follow would be made following advice from lawyers, technology specialists and marketing experts. It was interesting to note that Director C thought 'accountants are almost never involved' in creating project scenarios.

The lack of DCF analysis and limited financial modelling suggests that Company C was more likely to use qualitative rather than quantitative methods to make appraisals of investments. This was, in fact, the case. Director C explained how this worked: 'Every six months or every quarter our guy in the States provides a list of possible investments. This list of 50 investments goes to a team of 12, who consider it and use score-carding to whittle it down from 50 to six, asking things like "is it a core business?", and so on.' In addition, the company used 'scenario analysis' to evaluate potential outcomes from different investments. This would rely more on 'soft' information like, for example, 'is a digital TV going to be used in the TV in the home in 5 years, rather than analogue? If so, we must move our technology over to digital.'

Case D – E-commerce acceleration

This company had been founded, and was still based, in Cambridge. It developed both hardware and software products that enhanced the security of internet transactions. The company was skilled in techniques of encrypting and enciphering. Through its public relations literature, it claimed to 'help global e-businesses maximise information security, system saleability and transaction processing speed in electronic commerce and public key infrastructure applications'. This business, which was founded in 1996, had managed to achieve main market listing on the London Stock Exchange by the year 2000. It had offices across the world, including on both coasts of America, and in key European locations. Though this company was in the same generic area (namely, e-commerce) as Case J of Chapter 8 (to follow), its business activity was different. It was highly knowledge intensive, whereas Case J may be described as highly market intensive. Cases D and J agreed on only five out of eight practices (see Table 8.1 of the next chapter).

Director D said that he would attach a risk premium to discount rates, and referred back to venture capitalists when asked how this premium might be calculated. Whereas previously venture capitalists might have been looking for a rate of return of around 20 per cent, now, he thought that could be as high as 30 or even 40 per cent. More likely, though, was that they would be looking for a multiple, or 'five times return on their investment, in a three to five year time horizon'. This Director thought that it was difficult to determine a cost of capital for his company, and preferred to think in terms of being able to 'cover' whatever projections had been made, for example, by adding 10 per cent.

By far the riskiest investments, according to Director D, were in seed investments, although start-up and other early-stage, along with turnaround projects, were also relatively risky. In terms of the factors that this director classified as important, market opportunities (business risk) and the market team (agency risk) came out on top. Technologically, the speed at which his company could develop and introduce to the market new products, compared to the speed of his rivals, was the most important factor, and one way of protecting intellectual property. Risk classes were important to this company; any project which fell into a high-risk category would be expected to yield a higher return. However, to quantify this would be difficult, so the extent of risk inherent in such projects would be made on judgement. The risk–return curve for this company was said to 'get steeper', the riskier the project, until the point at which one might be trying to lead a market, where it would 'go through the ceiling'.

Payback was one of several criteria used to analyse potential investments. The company would be looking for a return within two years for a medium risk investment, and would wait a while longer for a higher return. They thought in terms of milestones, and would stop work on a project if it failed to achieve any of these. Director D thought that, with high-technology, the highest risk lay in long-term investments. He would therefore expect, for example, a 50 per cent return for a project that might last five years.

Sensitivity analysis was fairly important to Company D, and NPV calculations were used in such analysis. For example, this director might change the sales forecast by, perhaps, 20 per cent, in order to see what effect this had on the project's NPV. When performing sensitivity analysis, the director would be most interested in the effect on the company's two or three 'core competencies', and would try to identify any bottlenecks, whilst evaluating the impact on the company's existing business. In addition, he would be looking to identify the opportunity costs of making an investment. While the company was limited by the amount of its technical resources, the director did note that 'once you're looking at the revenue side, the cost side becomes much less important'.

Director D thought of costs and revenues as being linked, and had them modelled as such on a spreadsheet. He also recognised that, as projects developed and moved from phase to phase, so costs (for example, sales expenses) might change from being fixed to being variable: '18 months down the road they would become linear'. Probabilities would effectively be assigned to expected costs and revenues. This director was fairly sceptical about what people might tell him, and so would weight estimates accordingly.

This company did think in terms of expected values, though the evaluation tended to be more qualitative, and based on what the product might be worth on the market. Recalling the milestones used to monitor projects, the director said that 'we have a road map for scenarios of our development probabilities'. The reasons given for thinking things through in such as clear and logical manner were: '(a) cost estimates are done by people who over-analyse; and (b) sales people sell it on why it's such a great idea'. Thus Company D's analysis enabled it to take a measured view that fell somewhere between the wildly pessimistic and optimistic views available to them from elsewhere.

While this company was quite happy to use methods like DCF and NPV, a positive NPV alone would not be enough to induce them to accept a project, because they needed 'an assessment of projects for other things than just cash'. They were willing to accept projects that had a very low chance of success, although the director admitted that, in doing so, 'you would normally look at how you can "switch the tap off" after six months', should it prove to be a failure. With their portfolio now much bigger than it had been, they felt able to support a high level of risk for the odd project or two.

Financial modelling, as mentioned previously, was used in this company. Its objectives were to examine the effect of new projects on the company's existing portfolio, in terms of breakeven, margins, and various other ratios. The modelling was 'highly flexible', given its use mainly for scenario analysis. It would include such things as 'take-up rates', i.e. the adoption of a particular technology by customers. The most important variable was labour. The models were continuously being rebuilt with an aim to proving that the company had made profits out of particular technologies; that is, that they were creating, rather than stealing, trade.

Director D did not use qualitative methods like score-carding to appraise potential new projects. However, the company would perform a project review, scoring it on how well it had achieved various milestones; in other words, carrying out a post-investment performance appraisal. We have seen that scenario analysis was used, and that this would tend to group projects into low, medium and high-risk categories. For individual projects, this would consist more of 'soft' information, such as the customers' perception of the company's service provision.

Case E – Light emitting polymer (LEP) displays

Company E was involved in the exciting new technology of Light Emitting Polymers (LEPs) for flat panel displays and lighting. An extension and improvement on liquid crystal displays (LCDs), which have problems of poor visibility and high power consumption, LEPs are claimed to offer virtually unlimited possibilities. The company literature sold the product in terms of what it might offer in the future: 'a TV screen you can roll up, a full colour video display as thin as a CD and light enough to hang anywhere, a TV wristwatch'. Company E was backed by 'strong financial investment, unmatched core-technology intellectual property, engineering expertise, strategic licenses and partnerships, and management know-how'. Although this company was heavily involved in LEP technology, as in Case H, of the next chapter, its purpose is different. The applications areas of Case E are large ('macro'), like 'moving' posters; whereas the applications of Case H are small ('micro'), like mobile phones. This seemed to make a difference to business practice too, as Cases H and E agreed on only five out of eight practices (see Table 8.1 of the next chapter).

Director E thought that seed, start-up and other early-stage investments in high-technology were the riskiest, by stage of investment. When thinking about the risk–return trade-off, he considered it to be 'more of a hockey stick than a straight line', explaining that there was a point at which no return could compensate for the level of risk exposure. Director E explained that his company was in the business of developing intellectual property, based, as they were, on a university campus. As they had not yet launched any new products, a discount rate was not something that was considered relevant; nor, indeed, were risk classes used. Market opportunities and the global environment (both business risk) were considered to be the most important considerations when thinking about a new investment.

Company E would, informally, set a payback time horizon of three years on new projects. This period was chosen to please investors, and to ensure that future financing would be forthcoming: 'funding would get more difficult if you looked at a four or five year time horizon'. In addition to the payback period, the investors also determined the required company IRR of 30 per cent, and the management team were incentivised by stock options. Pressure from these external funders had increased in recent months since, as Director E noted, 'all funds are currently sitting on bad investments, so the risk premium is now higher, because all the dot.coms crashed'.

For this company, there were points at which the development and launch of a new high-technology product was considered to be too risky, or too complex, to make it worth pursuing any further. For example, they would always want to ensure that they had absolute rights to the intellectual property before moving into a new niche market. Sensitivity analysis was moderately important to Company E, who used NPV calculations in their analyses. Since global markets were the target for this firm's technology, exchange rates were an important variable. In addition, they would perform sensitivities on professional fees, for example, for patents, and on local markets and environments. So, to illustrate, aspects of employment law were an important consideration in California, whereas cultural differences were an issue in Japan. The variables were permitted to range widely in the sensitivity analysis, because the company was 'taking big bets'.

Breakeven was a fairly important reference point for Company E, possibly in part because of its psychological impact, but also because of its signal to investors: 'it signifies you've got out of the loss-making development side, and can look forward to profitability'. Again considering the future, Company E did use expected values, and made an attempt to use probabilities and to predict revenues. As the company was still in its development stage, an important factor when trying to determine expected values was the rate at which they could develop their technology: 'we can't expect someone to take a license until this bit works'.

While the company attempted some sort of revenue prediction, this, in itself, was not enough to enable them to make a decision whether or not to go ahead with a new project. Therefore, further qualitative analysis would be performed on the management team (consideration of the agency risk); the extent of intellectual property backing (technology risk); how well established the market was, and what competition the company was up against (both business risk). Any project considered to have a below average probability of success would not be pursued.

The financial modelling undertaken by this company was done with the main objective of predicting cash flow, and thus determining funding requirements. In addition, it was used to try to predict resource requirements, in terms of both physical plant and machinery, and employees. As many of the company's employees were scientists, they could not be recruited quickly, so it was important to plan for their requirement up to six months in advance. The key variables in the financial modelling therefore included costs of personnel, and revenue.

The company used decision trees in their planning and in research, but not in terms of deciding upon overall company strategy. They did assign probabilities to possible outcomes, however the chief financial officer interviewed was unsure as to the basis on which this might be done. The highest expected value would not necessarily determine the action to be taken. For example, another strategic option might be to be defensive, in terms of protecting the company's product and market (Reid, 1993, Ch. 7). And the best action would not generally involve delay, or waiting for something to happen, because 'it moves so fast you can't do anything'. However, the best action *could* be contingent on something, such as the grant of a patent.

Company E chose not to undertake any form of score-carding (Kaplan and Norton, 1992), in evaluating alternatives. They did, however, use scenario analysis to help them plan, and this would rely upon both hard, factual information, and softer, more qualitative evidence. For this, they would use 'whatever we can get hold of'. This might include feedback from the university, who were happy to comment on ideas and proposals put forward by the company. In addition, they would also actively seek expert advice and or evaluation of proposals.

Conclusion

The five cases above all exhibit a clear awareness of the three types of risk that we have identified as being important. In terms of business risk, the companies examined generally thought that it was very important to pay close attention to matters like sales opportunities, and the local environment in which they functioned. Agency concerns, such as the capabilities of the management team, and a commitment to bring in or to devolve responsibility to others, were highlighted as major issues. And so far as the risk inherent in high-technology was concerned, it was crucial to get products to market before rivals were able to react.

The directors interviewed were all agreed that the riskiest investments, by stage, in high-technology companies, had to be those which were seed-corn or other early-stage investments, where the track record had yet to be established, and where returns were uncertain. They appeared to concur over the shape of the risk–return locus (Quiry *et al.*, 2005, Ch. 21; Damodaran, 2006, Ch. 3), which can be graphed as in Figure 7.1. In this figure, points to the left of A represent the lowest degrees of risk, where one would in turn, expect lower returns. Between A and B we have medium levels of risk, where returns begin to increase. Levels of risk that lie between points B and C are where the highest returns can be made. Points to the right of C represent project risks that are just too high to contemplate. Huge returns would be required for just the smallest increments in risk.

There are a number of similarities amongst our sample of investees, in terms of the ways in which they chose to handle and manage risk. Whilst not all would admit to attaching a risk premium (in the technical sense), in reality, that is what they would do. This might be by means of an arbitrary 'add-on', or it might be more formally based, for example, by reference to the company's cost of capital.

At the start of a project, they might find it difficult to define a payback period but, in general, they were looking to show some sort of return within about two to three years. The consensus seemed to be that VC investors wanted, or needed, to see a good return on their investment. Given the uncertainty of high-technology investments, we might have expected to find that sensitivity analysis was important to our firms. Indeed, this was the case, with most using NPV calculations, and testing the company's reaction to changes of up to plus or minus ten per cent on certain key variables. Innovative companies often find that their most important asset is their intellectual property, including the people who create that intellectual property (i.e. their intellectual capital). So we often find that human resources embody their core competence, and that sensitivity analysis is therefore performed on variables relating to staffing.

Costs and revenues were sometimes treated as being dependent on one another, and sometimes as being independent. Where companies spend a long

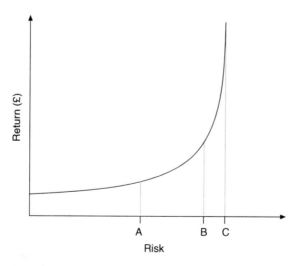

Figure 7.1 Risk and return.

period of time on development, then the major costs being incurred are on people, for example on scientists, or patent agents. So when it comes to marketing and selling the product, many major costs have already been incurred. Revenue, then, depends upon what price the company thinks the market will bear. By this stage, costs are so far divorced from revenues that it can be almost impossible to say that there is any clear link. This obviously has implications for pricing; from an accountant's point of view, what are the relevant costs of the goods sold?

We observe that all of these companies perform some sort of quantitative estimation of the worth of a project, whether it be very specific, and involving probable outcomes, or more vague. However, most would also want to make additional qualitative assessments, as a NPV alone is not, in itself, seen to be a good enough reason to pursue a project. This presents accountants and financial analysts with a problem as, typically, theory recommends that we accept projects with positive NPVs when they are discounted at the company's opportunity cost of finance (e.g. McLaney and Atrill, 2002).

8 Further illustrative case studies

Introduction

This further set of cases uses the same general framework as in Chapter 7. They have three significant features. First, they were constructed on the same basis of fieldwork evidence using face-to-face interview with entrepreneurs, employing an agenda that ran from Risk Premium through to Qualitative Appraisal (see Chapter 3 and Appendix 2). Second, two of the cases provide new perspectives on the same technology sector. Thus Case E and Case H both relate to the use of light emitting polymer technologies, but E relates to conformable 'macro' displays (e.g. moving posters on a metro station wall) and H relates to 'micro' displays (e.g. on digital cameras, mobile phones, etc.). To further illustrate, both Case D and Case J relate to e-commerce, but the focus in D is on encrypting and enciphering to make e-transactions secure, whereas the focus in J is on the retailing end of e-commerce, like selling groceries and household consumables. Third, there are two US case studies included in the set of cases in this chapter. This is done, again, for triangulation purposes. In the previous point, the triangulation arose through viewing the same technological sector (LEP technology) through the lenses of firms involved in different applications area (namely, the 'micro' and 'macro'). Now, the triangulation arises because we are viewing the VC investment process in high-technology enterprises from the standpoints of two different investment 'cultures', the UK in Cases A to H, and the US in Cases I and J.

As in Chapter 7, we first develop each case seriatim. A common terminology and framework are used in both Chapters 7 and 8 (see Appendix 2).

Case F – Laser and infrared detectors

This business, a university spin-out based in Glasgow, had been going for two and a half years when its director, a qualified engineer, was interviewed. It described itself in its literature as 'a world leader in the application of quantum cascade lasers'. Trace gas detection was now its main line of business. Essentially, the technology uses lasers and infrared detectors to sense changing light intensity as the laser beam passes through gases. It had applications in fields such as range finding, for military aircraft, and environmental monitoring and defence, for chemical weapon detection. The company employed nine full-time workers and had an annual turnover of £60,000, with net assets of £200,000. The three founders of the business retained a controlling ownership of 54 per cent.

The director depended very much on judgement when it came to making decisions about investment. No risk premium was attached to discount rates, he said, as 'we use a lot of judgement, seat of the pants things, as an early-stage company'. Cost of capital was not, therefore, a prime consideration. Rather, this company thought of investments as lying in risk classes, which were used as reference points in setting the risk premia.

The stages of investment that this director thought to be the most risky were seed and start-up, followed by other early-stage and turnaround propositions. Replacement capital investments were thought to hold least risk. He thought very carefully about the shape of the risk–return trade-off in his business, as 'we mitigate risks all the time'. For example, certain areas of investment were low risk, for example as regards health and safety development. On the other hand, the risk for product development in the area of explosive detection was thought to be high. As he explained, 'in how we've chosen to drive our product forward, we've looked at product risk, market risk and the ease of looking for funding'. Thus risk evaluation was a key factor in this organisation. Probing further on which aspects were important when assessing risk, the director identified market opportunities, the global environment, type of exit route and employee capabilities as being key. Here, the greater focus is on factors important to the agent, i.e. the entrepreneur. Of least importance were the IS capabilities and the scale of the business, which are arguably more the concern of the principal, the VC investor.

This company used payback, but did not discount cash flows; its main purpose was to identify the point at which the project would breakeven. The current planning horizon was two-and-a-half years, as the company was 'looking at raising £3.5 million to spend over two years, then generating significant growth in the marketplace'.

A target rate of return was set for the company at the point of exit. Rather than a fixed sum or a given percentage, this was defined in terms of multiples of investment, and was 'a very big number'. The director expressed a preference for earlier payback, the greater the risk: 'the sooner the better – one year if we can manage it'.

Breakeven was very important to this director. Sensitivity analysis looked at things like: the direct cost of the project; potential markets at two, three and four years ahead in time; the potential size of specific markets; which new markets might be expected to appear; and which markets that are currently on the horizon will disappear. The director added that 'even within each market, you can segment into railway, port, airport security and so on. Each market has different solutions that you can apply'. The variables included in the firm's sensitivity analysis were subject to 'massive' variation, with one of its key markets being worth £2 billion in Europe alone.

As elsewhere, breakeven was crucial when it came to sensitivity analysis. Costs and revenues were treated as being dependent: 'costs could go up and risks could go down'. However, projections were based on volume production and margin was the key driver. Sensitivity analysis was based around a reference point: 'we wrote a business plan and did three scenarios, including dropping sales volume by 50 per cent, and delaying a project, to see what happens.'

The director of Case F had used EVs in making decisions, but had found it difficult to persuade investors that their projections were realistic. He explained further:

> at £10,000 per instrument, we expected to sell 100 in year 1, then 400 in year 2. The numbers were so scary at that level that nobody believed us, so we stopped. You've got to be bullish, but not so bullish that you're going to take over the world.

Consideration made when determining EVs included competitors and other technologies in the market. They would be based on revenue models, rather than capital purchase models as the company was particularly interested in 'customer take-up – what drives them to invest money?'

The way in which risk varies from year to year was a consideration made by this director, as 'the longer you're not in the market, the better chance there is that a competitor or a new technology will get into the market'. With this company, risk on a particular project was reduced as the years progressed, and was factored into decision making. Revenues and costs were treated differently because 'you can predict costs very closely and you can manage that. With revenue, you're very dependent on customers believing in you, trusting the technology and then putting their hand in their pocket'. Cash flow projections were made, but informally. If there were only a slight chance that a project might run at a loss, then that would be considered to be too high a risk to take.

This company produced three to five year financial projections for balance sheets, profit and loss accounts and cash flow statements. The labour and research and development plans were reviewed every six to nine months. The model of the firm was scenario-based rather than optimising, but they would 'do a few iterations before we decide that's the one to go for'. Financial modelling was undertaken to enable the company to understand different cash flow requirements at different points in time. But it included 'base information, to create a valuation for the company', enabling them to discount sales, increase costs and see what was needed in order to breakeven.

A key requirement for the firm's financial modelling was having money in the bank. They tried to avoid stage payments from venture capitalists because of this: 'you plan on having money in the bank; you do things differently [if the money is not there]'. The variables used in financial modelling included cash, margin and revenue. Labour costs were said to be the largest, but also important were research and development, licence revenue, sales revenue, grant revenue and timing of, for example, product to market, and market entry.

The principles behind decision trees were used to help with decision making in this organisation: 'we have never had a decision-tree on the board, but we've gone through the gist of it'. Probabilities were based on expected risk, timing and costs. Very often, the company's best action might involve delay or waiting:

> we work in high technology, using a laser developed in 1995 – 10 years ago. Manufacturing is limited. We want to get into medical diagnostics, but the price must be low. It costs £7,000 for a laser. For example, we use the same laser as is in a DVD player. If we wait long enough, the costs will come right down and we'll get into the market.

Score-carding was unimportant in this organisation. Quality of the product was thought to be key when it came to undertaking risk appraisals. Of slightly lower importance were the company's public image, legal considerations and staff morale. Customer service was less important in this regard. In terms of innovation, it was most important to this company to measure: new product introduction compared to competitors; the number of key items in which the company was first or second to market; and breakeven time. The extent to which product introduction matched plans was relatively unimportant. As the director explained,

> it's to do with opportunity recognition. Our business plan did not even mention the marine emissions market of £2.1 billion. If something comes out, we are reactive to the market. The venture capitalists criticise us for being reactive, but why wouldn't you be? That's entrepreneurial.

Case G – Animal robotics

The company was based on the outskirts of Edinburgh, in a science park with strong connections to the University of Edinburgh. It produced advanced sensor systems and automation technologies to assist in the management of livestock. It had been formed from a merger of two Scottish companies, both of which had received SMART[1] awards for their innovative products. The company described its own activities as follows:

> [We take] inspiration from biology to develop biometric sensors and actuators for robots designed to operate in complex "real world" environments. [Our] devices are being adopted in new generation robot systems, particularly service robots that interact directly with people or animals.

In particular, the company was involved in developing and manufacturing products to cope with the three main problems encountered by cows: namely, mastitis, fertility and lameness. This is where the company identified their 'value-added' to the end user, the farmer.

The director interviewed was a research scientist with a PhD. He said that there was 'no official or formal method for evaluating the risk in a project' and would not, therefore, attach a risk premium to the discount rates used in making decisions about new products. Likewise, although the cost of capital would certainly be a factor in decisions, 'in the main, capital costs barely register' and the key factors in decisions about new projects were those relating to salaries and wages.

Informally, investment opportunities were considered to lie in risk classes: 'We are aware that some projects have a higher risk associated than others.' If relevant, these classes would be used in setting risk premia. This respondent thought that seed and start-up investments were the most risky, followed by other early-stage and replacement capital investments. MBO and MBI investments, traditionally less risky, were thought to be associated with only a low degree of risk. If an investment opportunity were thought to be high risk, this director would not necessarily refuse to go ahead, as 'there would be a point at which you needed investment to go ahead and do something'.

The most important factor identified by this director when it came to making a risk appraisal in the company were the potential market opportunities. Of slightly lower importance were also the global environment, the compelling nature of the proposition, the business and sales models and the extent of motivation, empowerment and alignment within the company. The local environment and scale of the business were considered to be unimportant, and the management team and employee capabilities only of low importance. The rankings are exactly what one would expect from an agency perspective, with early attributes being especially relevant to the entrepreneur (as agent) (e.g. market, global environment) and later attributes more relevant to the VC investor (as principal) (e.g. management team, employee capabilities).

The investor was at the back of this respondent's mind, when he admitted that the payback period method of investment appraisal was used: 'we certainly have to bear it in mind, because we have venture capital funds behind us'. The period used would vary from three months to two years, depending on the nature of the project concerned. When asked how these time horizons were determined, he explained:

> a lot comes down to how things play within the portfolio we've got. Our primary objective is to make money. We want to be number one in precision farming technologies. We make decisions that will enable us to keep that portfolio going. We're on target for our revenues this year, and certainly next year.

This company was not scared by risky or complex propositions; on the contrary, they had 'made a decision to drop some technologies because it was too simple. We're seeking complexity, because that gives us market advantage'.

Although this company was still in its development stage, it had already launched its first product, and so considered it important to maintain regular cash flows and produce monthly statements. Discount rates, however, were not incorporated into such analysis. The director explained that the company expected to make a minimum of a 50 per cent profit margin on everything that they sold: 'that should be enough to cover the wage bills, which are really the same as development costs,' he added.

As discount rates were not used, it is unsurprising that NPV methods were also not employed. Sensitivity analysis played a low importance, and was based on 'what we believe the market to be, what sort of price the farm would accept [and we] attach probabilities on individual sales; if they request a quote, we attach a probability to that'. The variation in sensitivity analysis would be very much product dependent. For example, 'We have a number of cows and a farm. If it's the farmers with 50 cows or more, [we would hope to] achieve 50 per cent penetration.'

Breakeven was irrelevant to this business, but they did consider costs and revenues to have a dependence upon one another. They focused particularly on keeping the cost of materials as low as possible:

> we allocate a percentage in our projections that we consider to be the cost of sales, [which] includes the cost of selling it. We have some equations that cover how we expect our build costs to decrease as the numbers we make increase.

In other words, their financial projections incorporated a learning curve effect, and considered economies of scale.

When it came to decisions about accepting projects, this director pointed out that projections were either 'likely' or 'pessimistic'. A positive projected return would mean that they would accept a project, without any further qualitative assessment. They would also allow for the fact that cash inflows might turn out to be more than the project cost: 'we have three main products in our business plan. We expect one to be very successful and the other two to trundle along or disappear.'

Financial models were produced for this business to 'avoid being in a damaging position'. Having anything less than three months' worth of cash in the bank would be 'unacceptable' because the company was keen to remain solvent. Further constraints on the company's financial modelling included one-off spends of capital, which required consent from their investors. According to the shareholders' agreement, 'anything over £25,000 needs consent. In reality, it's closer to £100,000.'

The company used SAGE[2] forecasting software to help them model inter-relationships between variables in their financial modelling, insofar as they connected volumes to costs of goods sold. They did this to create their 12-month rolling budget. It also enabled them to consider adjustments up or down by 50 per cent. The only thing that they were unsure about in such modelling was the number of units that they might sell; everything else was 'quite knowable'. From the investor's point of view, the main target, perhaps surprisingly, was said to be revenue, rather than profit, with a three-year time period of interest in performance.

This director would never use decision trees, and indeed his decision making appeared to be more intuitive than based on probabilities and predicted outcomes. The best action, in his opinion, would never depend upon delay or waiting: 'Our approach is to get something out sooner, rather than later, even if the product has less functionality. There are a lot of research farms around [and] they are early adopters of products.' However, the best action might be contingent upon a particular event; for example, the company had just obtained the exclusive licence of a particular technology, without which, they could not do what they were doing.

Scenario analysis was effectively the way this company operated, with a focus on 'worst' and 'middle' case scenarios. However, they tended to rely upon hard information, specifically the sales volume: 'we know exactly how many farms, the size of the farm, volumes, and size of the herd'. The percentage of sales expected to come from new products was therefore important, as was the time taken to develop the next generation of new products. However, whether the introduction of new products compared to the plan was unimportant, with the director explaining, 'it should be important to follow the plan, but I really don't care so long as it's going to make us money'.

Case H – Electronic micro-displays

This company was based in a science park, at Edinburgh University. It had been going for five years when approached, and had a staff of 37 full-time employees. The main line of business was described as the development, design, manufacture and sale of micro-displays. Essentially, this meant delivering TV quality pictures through the means of personal electronic products. For example, this might be applied to digital cameras, video cameras, cell phones, personal video players and hand-held computer games. Thus the target product markets for Case H were different from Case E, although both used LEP technology. Typically, they would apply a discount factor of 12.5 per cent to capital investment decisions, with additional flexibility for identified risk factors. Management and staff held 1 per cent of the ordinary share capital, and held an additional eight per cent options.

The chief financial officer (CFO) of the company, a university graduate and chartered management accountant, was interviewed about the company, and responded to the AQs as if for a specific project. Risk premia were not attached to discount rates when making decisions about product development, although the company would 'recognise the risks', and the cost of capital was considered. This particular director had built up his experience in high-risk companies, and so did not recognise opportunities as lying in risk classes: 'at the end of the day, many of our decisions are quite binary. You don't use risk premia for excluding competing opportunities.'

This respondent considered the most risky types of investment to be those requiring seed capital, followed by start-up and then other early-stage investments. Expansion was moderately risky, he thought, but other stages of investment were of low risk. He did not consider there to be a shape to any 'risk–return' curve in his business, as 'I almost think it's binary; it's either do it or don't do it. It's a hurdle, if you like.' He cited a current example of a decision, where the primary concern was of where to locate a new project: 'Right now, the investment is likely to be located in Asia, so I'm factoring risks like loss of intellectual property rights set off against what is more logical. We know we'll source our silicon wafers in Asia. Do we manufacture here or in Asia? It's likely to be in Taiwan. It's how we make the transition from technology development to product development to volume manufacturer.'

The most important factors considered when making a risk appraisal within this firm were: market opportunities; the global environment; the compelling nature of the proposition; the management team, and the business model. IS capabilities were of the lowest importance. These results are consistent with agency theory, with the entrepreneur focusing on markets and the investor on the management team and ISs.

This company used the payback period of investment appraisal, with a maximum two-year time horizon. This period was chosen because 'without being able to say precisely how we will change, the nature of our technology *will* change within two years'. Discounted cash flows were calculated using two separate rates: 'they model both our own considerations and what I consider the funding provider's considerations to be. The funding provider's discount rate is based on the published cost of capital, mainly in the banking area.' On occasion, investments could become too risky or too complex to make them worth pursuing further. However, the company would not require payback to be earlier if the technology were considered to be highly risky.

Sensitivity analysis was very important to this company but, rather than apply NPV calculations, it would be based on a 'what if?' analysis. Sensitivity analysis was generally done on future projections of the average selling price of the company's goods, and the analysis was allowed to vary widely:

> it's a very broad range, but it's not done in percentage terms. If I sell at a particular selling price, what effect would it have on the company? Being an early-stage company, we do deals on a customer by customer basis. The first customer has a 'sweet deal', thereafter it's market price. We want to offer better features from our technology, compared to LCD,[3] at the same price.

Breakeven was an important reference point in the sensitivity analysis of this company, and values were assigned independently to costs and revenues. As the director said, 'I assume we can sell everything we produce'. Probabilities were also applied to costs and revenues. The director expanded upon his previous 'what if?' comment by explaining that 'the probabilities apply to exchange rates as well as selling price. If the exchange rate dropped by x, what would the effect be?'

The company's sensitivity analysis was based around the existing market, which would then form part of the business model. The closest example to such a decision was given by the CFO: 'We sell to an OEM/ODM[4] environment. There is an opportunity to sell directly to ODM, rather than going through OEM.' Thus various scenarios had to be considered when the company was trying to determine what was expected to happen.

Expected values were used in this company when making decisions about developing and launching new technology products. For the current project under consideration, the actual value and the probability of it occurring were calculated separately: 'For example, in predicting what [our] share price might be in two years' time, all you can do is apply probabilities.' Expanding upon this, the CFO had a fairly sophisticated view of how risk varied in the company year by year: 'I'm trying to show that the covenant improves over time. It's a scenario where [we] acquire at point zero, but a volume manufacturing partner might acquire the asset in the future.'

This CFO did not estimate the distribution of prospective cash flows and would make further qualitative assessments of projects which showed a negative expected NPV, from an internal perspective. Their current project had a negative expected NPV, but they pursued it anyway 'because it's cheaper to fund from a dilution point of view, in terms of protecting our current shareholders; and it's a means to an end, from a strategic point of view.' He elucidated that 'I'm more interested in presenting a high NPV for the potential funder.'

The company constructed an explicit, non-optimising financial model of the firm's financial objectives. It was a 'flexible model' that could incorporate different scenarios. It was intended to present an 'achievable' situation, and the forecast would therefore always be 'conservative'. The objectives of the firm's financial modelling were 'to help run our own business and model scenarios very quickly, [because] we have to provide forecast information to analysts and brokers, [as] that is an expectation of being on AIM.'[5]

Decision trees were used in the company, but not in a formal way. Instead, the CFO tried 'to quantify consequential aspects' of decisions. They might, for example, attach probabilities to market outcomes. These probabilities were assigned 'by discussion with the senior management group ... [and were] not stochastic in any way'. They were conscious that certain actions might best be delayed, and had held back on the release of a product in order to incorporate further technological advances: 'it's better to do it now, before volume manufacture,' explained the CFO.

The quality of the product was a very important aspect of qualitative risk appraisals in this company. Public image, legal considerations and staff morale were also considered to be fairly important, but customer service was given low importance. The reason for this was given as follows: 'customer service is difficult [because] you're either providing a product to spec[ification], or you're not.'

Scenario analysis was another important way of assessing the potential performance of new high-technology products in this organisation. It was based primarily on 'hard' information. As the CFO said, it should be 'something I could model, [like] market assumptions, price assumptions, and semi-conductor yields [as] yield is equivalent to profitability'. And it is hardly surprising, given his previous responses, that all features of innovation on the given list (see semi-structured questionnaire in Appendix) were of moderate or very high importance to this company.

Case I – Automated baggage security inspection

This company was based in the Massachusetts high-technology corridor, USA, and had been going for two and a half years when approached for interview. It employed 43 full-time workers. The main line of business was in producing automated baggage inspection systems, and the company had developed an explosives detection system (EDS) that had passed the rigorous demands of the Transportation Safety Administration (TSA), giving its products valuable accreditation. Its latest model was space efficient and cheap enough to enable even the smallest regional airport to integrate security scanning through existing check-in desks, or elsewhere in the checked baggage system. The company had enjoyed support from a number of top VC investors, and was looking forward into breaking into the larger market for airport security.

The CFO was interviewed about his attitudes to and methods of accounting for risk in the organisation. He would make a 'very much judgmental' decision about how to attach a risk premium to the discount rates used to assess the potential development new technology products, and would use risk classes as a reference point in setting the risk premia. Reference was also made to the cost of capital. However, the CFO pointed out that:

> we look at *what does it do in terms of creating value in the enterprise?*, more than just in financial terms. Investors want to see the value of the company increase [so] we're only going to look at opportunities with very high multiples.

This CFO thought that seed, start-up and turnaround funding were the riskiest types of investment to make; and that replacement capital and/or follow-on investments were much safer, with a very low degree of risk. In terms of the risk inherent in his own company, he was looking for 'lots of multiples and lots of risk', explaining that 'a massive risk would be taking on a project and not getting it done before we run out of cash'. Therefore, the aspects that were most important to him when assessing risk were: the potential market opportunities or the compelling nature of the proposition (both market risk), and the management team and employee capabilities (both agency risk).

Payback was not a method used by this particular company, but there would be a point in time at which the development and launch of a new high-technology product became too risky to proceed. Cash flow was considered, but not discounted; and a target rate of return was not used, because everything was based on a multiple return on the investment made. If the technology under development was considered to be increasing in riskiness, then this

CFO would not require an earlier return, but would instead require the return to be larger.

Sensitivity analysis was something that this company found very useful, and they looked particularly at revenue projections, including the point at which they might expect to see sales. However, they did not incorporate NPV calculations in this analysis, possibly because the time horizon that was important to the CFO was no longer than one year ahead. Rather, scenario planning was seen to be important, and the CFO gave the example of four potential sales projections, each requiring the same cash investment. He had provided the Board with a summary, objectives and assumptions made, along with graphs of revenue, cash, change in cash, and low points (namely, potential cash flow crises) for each scenario. He based his sensitivity analysis on expected sales to determine 'when we hit the low point', and was therefore able to build in a cushion to support the company through that period. Following on from this, he added that breakeven analysis was 'very important': 'it's the number one thing that we look at'.

Costs and revenues were assigned values independently when the company conducted its sensitivity analysis. The CFO explained:

> I don't think they're linked. There are some scale economies, but it's not a lot … maybe 10 per cent. Right now we have no revenue. If we get to a point where we're making or losing $50,000 a month, in the short term, it's trivial. If we're near breakeven, until we start seeing some revenue, our most important job is to sell machines. We have it built into our model that we will reduce costs next year by ten per cent, as we ramp up quantities.

This company was unable to assign probabilities to costs and revenues as a key supplier was based in Germany and supplied goods in euros. If the company were able to agree on a fixed delivery charge, then they thought that they *could* attach probabilities. Sensitivity analysis was conducted around a reference point, which was usually based on a 'slightly better than worse case' scenario, but which was definitely 'not in the middle'.

The CFO of this organisation was not in favour of the use of EVs in making decisions about developing and launching new high-technology products. However, he did acknowledge that there were circumstances where small businesses might do such a thing. For example, it might be possible to predict the level of sales, but he explained that 'I'm not a big believer in expected value in terms of sales forecast.' He also admitted that 'our sales guys keep trying to do it, but I don't trust their math'. This organisation did take into consideration how risk might vary year by year, and would use different methods of assigning EVs, depending on whether a cost or a revenue was involved.

When it came to predicting cash flow, this company would 'put together one cash flow model', which was 'a conservative view of the world, not a worst case view'. However, a positive NPV alone was not enough to make this CFO adopt a risky project. All projects were expected to make money, as the company only took on a very small number. They would not, therefore, estimate the probability that a project might run at a loss.

Financial modelling was scenario based, which included an explicit model of the firm's financial objectives, but was not an optimising model. The main aim of this model was to predict cash flow, to manage expenses and to identify any general cash flow issues ahead of time. The main components of the financial model were staffing plans, expenses and unit sales, from which they would extrapolate revenue and cost. The CFO explained that 'most of the expenses are related to staffing [and] there are economies of scale; as revenue doubles, our engineering group may only increase by 40 or 50 per cent.'

Decisions in this company were made with the help of explicit decision trees which distinguished clearly between decision points and outcomes. The company's best action might sometimes require delay or waiting for something. For example, if they managed to clinch an anticipated deal, in a couple of months' time, from the TSA, then they would not need to raise money for research and development.

Score-carding techniques were not used to appraise the prospect of developing and launching a new product, and quality of the product was seen to be the most important non-financial indicator when undertaking risk appraisals within the company. Public image and customer service were also important considerations, whereas legal considerations were almost irrelevant.

Scenario analysis regularly used 'soft' information to create alternative outcomes for new high-technology products. This would focus primarily on 'how long is it going to take us to do it?' The company, however, was clearly focused on the extent to which they introduced new products compared to their competitors. Of next greatest importance were the percentage of scales that they might expect from new products, the number of key items in which the company is first or second to market, and the breakeven time of a particular project.

Case J – E-commerce retailing

This final interviewee, also based in Massachusetts, was in a slightly different situation. He had held a number of senior executive positions in a variety of businesses before his current role as a principal with a large investment banking organisation. His current role was to provide advice and banking solutions to both public and private middle market companies in targeted technology and manufacturing industries. However, he agreed to answer our questionnaire from the standpoint of a high-technology investee company; he had been the CFO of six companies, four of which were venture-backed. His responses, therefore, were based, in particular, on his experience of developing a company that was to become a market leader in the e-commerce retailing of groceries, household consumables and related services. While Case J, like Case D, involved e-commerce, company operations seemed to be quite different. Indeed, Case J seemed to most resemble Case A (drug development) in terms of business practice.

The respondent would attach a risk premium to discount rates, which was based on judgement, but also used the cost of capital and an assessment of risk class as a reference point:

> In general, you try to get a sense of what the market is at any point in time. A lot of it is gut feel. Investors will never tell you specifically, 'I'm going to get three times my money.' Venture money is, by definition, the riskiest.

This comment was supported by his identification of the riskiest types of investment. Seed capital and turnaround investments were thought to have inherently higher risks than others, closely followed by start-up and early-stage investments. Replacement capital and follow-on investments were not thought to be particularly risky; and expansion, MBO and MBI investments were associated with only moderate risk.

This CFO was able to visualise a risk–return locus for specific investments, stating that 'it's incremental; it's a progression'. He further explained that 'It's multiple factors, and that's part of the problem.' In addition, there was 'the risk of market expansion', and timing was crucial. In specific relation to the risk–return trade-off, he elaborated that 'the further you get out on the curve, the more risks you have. You over- or under-estimate the market size, the time to market, how customers perceive their market versus others. I assume a degree of risk for everything because there is no such thing as a risk-free product.'

Again, these comments were supported by his responses to a question on which factors he considered to be most important when making a risk appraisal. He identified the most important factors as being market opportunities; the local environment; the compelling nature of the proposition; the management team; the business model, and the extent of motivation, empowerment and alignment. Of least importance were the global environment and the type of exit.

This CFO used payback to appraise investments, and the time period considered would depend upon the type of investment under consideration. For example, if it were to involve capital expenditure, then he would expect a 36-month payback, but 24 months to exit. As he explained, 'people in the US are now much more focused on exit at the time of entry, [and] when we do think we'll get to exit, who will be willing to buy it?'

Time had changed this respondent's view on risk and return. Now, he would consider certain technological investments as being too risky, whereas in the past he might have pursued them regardless. He elaborated on the changing views of American investors as follows: 'with the dot.com boom in the USA, people lost sight of the risk–return. With time, you know that sticking your finger in the light socket hurts. Younger people don't know what they don't know.'

Decisions based on payback were influenced by cash flow considerations, and discount rates were assigned using cost of capital and rule of thumb, as 'it's as much art as it is science'. Target rates of return were set using a number of different factors. For example, 'if I use debt, the target rate is my cost of capital'. The 'hard' costs of, for example, equipment, were rarely thought to be significant in technology investments. Instead, 'soft' costs, as they relate to people, for example, were much more significant when evaluating competing opportunities. This, he explained, is why outsourcing has become much more popular.

Sensitivity analysis was important to project decisions, and was based on figures using NPV calculations. Breakeven was 'just another element of NPV', but was again important. The respondent would calculate a best and worst case scenario for investments, and thought that the base case he provided for investors might be a little lower than the base case kept for his own purposes, explaining that 'there's a bit of horse-trading that goes on behind the scenes'.

Values and probabilities were attached to costs and revenues in sensitivity calculations, the latter being assigned on 'gut feel'. He explained his thinking as follows: 'If I sell at six or seven figures, I can afford to have direct sales force. If I'm selling at six or seven hundred dollars, I can't.' He would also consider how the risk–return curve changed if his assumptions changed, adding 'what if I assume 20 per cent/80 per cent? Pareto's Law – the 80/20 rule – comes into business all the time.' He tried to calculate an ROI for each investment, explaining that 'it's not scientific, but I think about it from an end-user's perspective and work back from that'.

Expected values were calculated 'all the time' with values and probabilities multiplied together in the conventional way. Where possible, this CFO would use external references or historical evidence to assess expected value, as 'I don't like guessing'. He gave an empirical example to explain the way he thought about expected values:

> we had a $10,000 contingent liability and a 50/50 chance of it arising. The lawyers wanted to spend $20,000 to mitigate or protect against the risk. I only valued it at $5,000, because of the fifty per cent probability. I wouldn't spend $20,000 to save $10,000.

This CFO would estimate cash flows and use them to calculate NPVs on a given project: 'we put together one cash flow model. We have various budget scenarios with an individual cash flow result. It's a conservative view of the world, not a worst case view.' A positive NPV alone would not encourage him to accept a project, although 'a negative one might kill it – we use a best case, worst case and base case. If best is the only one that produces a positive NPV, then we are unlikely to follow it.' Further qualitative assessments were always undertaken.

As we might expect from his earlier responses, this CFO would construct an explicit financial model of the firm's objectives, based on alternative scenarios, and with an aim of testing the validity of the business plan. His plans would incorporate expected revenues, expenses, timing, volume and the wage bill, unless it was a manufactured product, in which case materials and associated expenses would assume more importance. Inter-relationships between these variables would be considered explicitly. For example, he would consider 'the costs of carrying compared to cost of delivery [knowing that] I can afford to carry inventory for three months.'

Decision making for this CFO was done partly with the aid of decision trees and partly much more informally. A distinction would be made between decision points and outcomes, and 'in more cases than not' the best action would be chosen on the basis of the highest expected return. Occasionally, it was important to delay a decision to implement a new project, for example 'when the market is not mature enough and the costs are not sure'. In this case, the CFO would prefer to be the 'second mover' in the marketplace.

As well as the detailed quantitative analysis of financial forecasts, qualitative assessment was also important to this respondent. He had developed what he called the 'Opportunity Evaluation Matrix', in order to have an objective score-card that he could use repeatedly. The following considerations were important when undertaking risk appraisals within his organisation: public image, customer service, quality of product ('you cannot afford to lose your public perception') and staff morale. Legal considerations were only moderately important.

Finally, the following features of innovation were considered to be important when the company was considering developing and launching a new high-technology product: the extent of new product introduction, compared to rivals; new product introduction versus the company's plan; the time it takes to develop new generation products. Of next greatest importance was the number of key products with which the company managed to be first or second to market. Of less importance were the percentage of sales expected from new products and the breakeven time of a new high-technology product.

Conclusion

Overall, there was considerable similarity between the cases of this Chapter and those of Chapter 7. In particular, the relative emphasis on risk factors was consistent with agency theory, in that the respondents (as agents) gave lesser emphasis to matters which were largely the concern of the investor as principal, like motivation, quality of management team, and information systems.

Generally, most areas of operations we examined, from risk premia to qualitative appraisal, were relevant to our respondents. On examination, there were some differences which are worthy of note. Table 8.1 summarises responses from the entrepreneurs (labelled A to J), across our areas of investigation, from risk premia to qualitative appraisal. An element of judgement was used in constructing this table, which (to resolve matters) sometimes involved reference to further evidence not reported upon in the written up versions of the cases.

What Table 8.1 tells us is generally reassuring, about the level of skill and expertise that the entrepreneur brings to a high-technology firm. Indeed, it suggests that entrepreneurs do not conform to the stereotype of being largely technology driven. They are technologically informed, but still businessmen. As such, profits, costs, returns, finance and decision making are the bread and butter of their daily existences.

One point that does show up clearly is that the use of risk premia is not very popular (though it is used in both the US cases, I and J). Here, we are asking about what percentage must be added to the risk-free rate to determine the

Table 8.1 Cross-site analysis of all case studies

	A	B	C	D	E	F	G	H	I	J
Risk premia	✓	✗	✗	✓	–	✗	✗	✗	✓	✓
Investment time horizon	✓	✓	✗	✓	✓	✓	✓	✓	–	✓
Sensitivity analysis	✓	✓	✗	✓	✓	✓	✓	✓	✓	✓
Expected value	✓	✓	✗	✓	–	✓	–	✓	–	✓
Predicted cash flow	✓	–	✗	–	–	✓	–	✓	✓	✓
Financial modelling	✓	✓	✓	✓	✓	✓	✓	✓	✓	✓
Decision making	✓	✓	✓	–	✓	✓	✗	✓	✓	✓
Qualitative appraisal	✓	–	✓	✗	✓	✓	✓	✓	✓	✓

Notes
✓ Technique used; ✗ Technique not used; – Technique not mentioned.

required rate of return (Quiry *et al.*, 2005, Ch. 22). However, the notion of a risk premium will only be meaningful if risk is spread over multiple (indeed, one would suggest, many) investment opportunities. In this sense, the idea of a risk premium would be more relevant to the VC investor, rather than to the entrepreneurs we have reported upon in Chapter 7 and 8. Even so, there are firms that do have multiple, and indeed, sometimes many investment projects being undertaken within the umbrella of the firm. To them, no doubt, the idea of a risk premium is useful.

Another area in which practice differs, as indicated by Table 8.1, is in cash flow prediction. Only one firm (C) admitted to definitely not using cash flow methods. However, this firm is something of a maverick within the set of ten cases as a whole. It was described by its entrepreneur as being 'cash rich', which maybe obviated the use of explicit cash flow prediction methods. Other firms, for which case flow prediction was not mentioned (firms B, D, E and G) did, no doubt, pay attention to cash flow, but did not put this into an explicitly predictive framework. Finally, the use of EVs was not universally endorsed, dissenters being firms C, E, G and I, though only C explicitly did not use this technique. With one exception (J), they also could not assign risk premia, suggesting the two are related. In 'one-off' situations it is hard to assign probabilities, so risk premia and expected values cease to be relevant (or even meaningful) concepts.

Looking again at entrepreneurs now, and their firms (A to J), it is quite clear that firm C is a maverick, though firm G too is a bit of an odd-ball. Recall that firm C specialises in copyright protection. It was a successful firm. However, its modus operandum was quite different from the other firms considered in Chapters 7 and 8. Firm C was apparently run on a highly intuitive basis (at least in a relative sense). It was, however, highly competitive in stance. Its main focus was on profit margins and growth. It was very technically oriented, and emphasised the critical importance of being first to market. In order to grasp market opportunities, it shunned internally generated growth as being too slow – so growth was by acquisition. The entrepreneur of firm C claimed it was so 'cash rich' that, for example, formal techniques like DCF, and less formal ones like payback period, 'didn't count'. In fact, firm C was very US influenced. As the entrepreneur said, 'every six months, a guy in the States provides us with a list of possible investments'. So, although this entrepreneur was one of the most aware of technology and of innovation risk, his 'entrepreneurial style' was towards the qualitative end, focusing too on decision making and finance. In short, this entrepreneur was in business to do business.

A connection can be made here with the US case study of firm I (which was developing, and selling, new technologies for the security inspection of baggage, notably at airports). Although this firm (like its compatriot US firm) ticked most of the boxes under our eight headings, the evidence of the case shows some similarity to case C discussed above. Thus the entrepreneur of firm I said he did not use techniques like NPV or payback, and could not compute probabilities or EVs. In fact, he was generally unimpressed with forecasting methods (rather like a Misean entrepreneur[6]). When it came to sales forecasting, he said he permitted it, but 'I don't trust their math!' His financial 'modelling' was scenario based, rather than formally based (e.g. using spreadsheets, or more specialised software). This entrepreneur was highly technologically orientated, but tended to use 'soft' information, and qualitative methods, much as in Firm C.

One can see advantages in the more intuitive approaches of Firms C and I, but they do run into problems if business conditions are not buoyant. A firm may not always be 'cash rich', and if acquisition targets dry up, and internally led growth becomes the prime alternative, then a lot of the more prosaic methods of financial economics and financial analysis may come into their own.

To conclude, the case study evidence is generally consistent with the more systematic statistical and econometric evidence developed elsewhere in this book. However, the cases do provide an indispensable explicit verification, on a firm by firm basis, of the ubiquity of the agency frame of evidence, and furthermore richly illustrate the complexity and variety of high-technology business functions in a way that equations and graphs cannot do.

Part V

Reporting and investment

9 Reporting, risk and intangibles

Introduction

The general purpose of this chapter, and the one to follow (Chapter 10), is to examine the conduct of UK investors (Murray and Lott, 1995; Murray and Marriott, 1998; Bushrod, 2002), in their provision of finance capital (in venture capital or private equity form (Robbie, 1998; Campbell, 2003). As in previous chapters in this book, the firms in question are producing or developing high-technology products. The specific focus of this chapter is on the valuation of such companies (Brown and Cliff, 2005) on the evidence base of financial reporting, risk reporting (Kothavala, 2003) and information on internally developed intangible assets (Brynjolfsson *et al.*, 2002; Mueller and Supina, 2002; Brown and Cliff, 2005). The ultimate purpose of these, we shall see in the next chapter, is to determine the level of provision of funds to investees.

The key features of our approach in this, and the next, chapter involve the following. First, in Chapter 9: (a) the extraction and use of new primary source data (compare Bailes *et al.*, 1998; Wong, 2003, on use of survey data and investor sentiment) on UK investor behaviour; (b) the detailed exploration of investor attitudes (Ruchala, 1999) in terms of perceived utility of the structure of reporting (e.g. risk disclosure) in seeking to value high-technology firms (Eckstein *et al.*, 1998). Then, in Chapter 10, we look at: (c) explicit statistical analysis of factors which contribute to perceived superior investor conduct (compare Engel, 2004) (e.g. financial accounts, location in science parks, control over investees' AIS); and (d) the impact of investor attitudes (Barkham and Ward, 1999; Fisher and Statman, 2000; Brown and Cliff, 2005) on the level of private equity they are willing to provide to investors.

Whilst our approach is provisional, we believe it is of some novelty, and that it can lay the basis for a broader and more general adoption of our methodologies and techniques. In turn, this academic development may have the potential for a positive impact on the practitioner side. Since events like the dot.com meltdown of 2000, when investors hung back from high-technology investments (Poynder, 2001), we have been more acutely aware of how a change in investor attitudes – what might be called 'investor sentiment' – can be to the detriment of commercialising products from the science base. Behind such sentiment, as we shall aim to demonstrate, are quite specific (and malleable or controllable) features of AIS. In turn, these attitudes drive investment levels, as our econometric analysis demonstrates.

The academic points of departure for this chapter are the extant literature on VC investing (e.g. Robbie, 1998; Khurshed, 2000; Weber and Willenborg, 2003; Florou, 2005; Jelic *et al.*, 2005), financial and risk reporting (Sahlman, 1994; Ruchala, 1999), intellectual property (Eliasson and Wihlborg, 2003), intangible asset valuation (Gelb and Siegel, 2000; Holland, 2001; Hand, 2002; Garcia-Ayuso, 2003; Mueller, 2004); and investment decision making (see Schroeder and Gibson (1990) for analysis of comprehension of management discussion and analysis (MD&A), and Zacharakis and Meyer (2000), in an explicitly VC investment context). These different strands of thought are combined in an interdisciplinary way to create a new view on investment decisions and their predication on reporting protocols. Of especial concern to us is the valuation of internally generated intangible assets, typical assets – for high-technology firms – being protected through devices like patents (Hall *et al.*, 2005), copyrights and brands, or simply through trade secrecy.

The methodology we adopt combines the questionnaire analysis of this chapter with statistical and econometric analysis of Chapter 10. Briefly, new primary source data were generated by a postal questionnaire (with call-back) to the UK's most active investors in high-technology firms. The data gathered concerned investment type and sector; utility of financial reporting; disclosure of risk (Kothavala, 2003); and management accounting and performance (Engel *et al.*, 2002; Florou, 2005; Jelic *et al.*, 2005). Statistical analysis is used to examine the utility of financial reporting in assessing company risk. Finally, econometric analysis involves estimating a multiple regression model which explains the level of investment in high-technology firms by investors' attitudes. The dimensions of the latter involve attitudes to: extent of disclosure (Maines *et al.*, 2003); standardised risk reporting; and compulsory information provision (Schroeder and Gibson, 1990).

The chapter develops its ideas in the following way. It has two substantive sections: methodology, covering the sample and questionnaire; and evidence, covering key features of the new data gathered. Statistical and econometric evidence, covering correlation analysis and multiple regression analysis, are deferred to Chapter 10.

Briefly, our key findings in this chapter are as follows: investors prefer to rely on their own procedures and processes, do not find financial reporting particularly useful, yet do not favour (for competitive reasons) greater provision of financial information.

Methodology

More broadly, the work of this chapter provides insights into the problems that investors in high-technology firms face, when using such firms' financial accounts, prepared in accordance with Generally Accepted Accounting Principles (GAAP), especially as regards the valuation of intangible assets (Peneder, 2002) and good-will (Canibano *et al.*, 2000; Meuller and Supina, 2002; Statement of Financial Accounting Standard No. 142). Against this background, we next consider how the sampling frame of UK investors was constructed, how sampling was per-formed, and how the questionnaire was designed and administered.

Sample

A sampling frame was created by drawing upon two sources: first, the member-ship list of the BVCA; and second, the listing of UK investors provided by the VCR. Given the theme of our research, we screened for investors who had an expressed interest in backing high-technology companies. Using web site resources for these two organisations, a sample of 114 investors was identified who satisfied our criteria. A response rate of 27 per cent was achieved, which is quite typical for postal surveys of this sort.

Figure 9.1 indicates the sectoral representation of the sample. Investors were asked to identify their five most favoured high-technology sectors, out of a set of nineteen, and then to rank these five in order of preference (coded as 1=low to 5=high) (See Q.1.3 of Postal Questionnaire, Appendix 4). Using these scores, mean responses over the nineteen sectors were computed, as indicated in Figure 9.1. Essentially, each bar height indicates the average desirability of investment involvement in a specific sector (e.g. biotechnology, software) (compare for example the analysis of the energy sector in Perdue, 2004). Desirability scores can drop below an average of unity, as sectors which were not nominated had an assigned score of zero. Taking unity as a threshold value, we see that seven sectors stand out as being most desirable, in terms of the perceptions of UK investors, namely: biotechnology, medical/health related, communications, information technology hardware, software and computer services, internet technology, and electronics. Of these, software and computer services was by far the most pre-ferred. Some of the surprising 'ugly sectors' included chemicals and materials, industrial automation, and energy. Although patenting is traditionally high in these technologies, they may be perceived as older generation investment types, com-pared to the knowledge intensive products currently finding favour.

The preference of investors by stage of investment is indicated in Figure 9.2. For high-technology contexts, investors were asked to rank their five most common stages of investment involvement (e.g. start-ups, MBO) (See Q.1.4 in Postal Questionnaire, Appendix 4). Coding of responses was 0=irrelevant; 1=low through to 5=high). It is of great interest that seed-corn, start-up, early-stage, and expansion are by far the most common investment involvements. UK VC is legendary for favouring development capital opportunities, with a focus on company turnaround, MBO and MBI investment involvements. These are, certainly, forms of private equity provision, but arguably, not properly classified as true business venturing. However, so far as high-technology is concerned, the clear picture is that UK investors behave like true 'adventurers', and commonly go in at the high-risk end of equity provision, with early-stage (other than

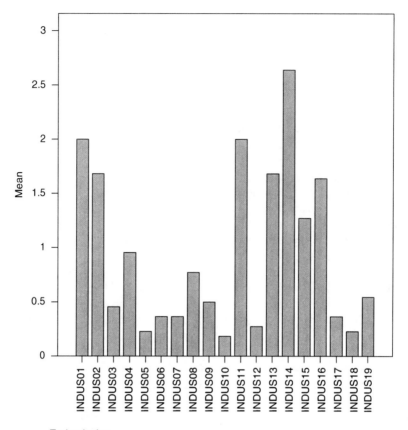

Technologies

01 Biotechnology	11 Communication
02 Medical/health related	12 Media and photography
03 Chemicals and materials	13 Information technology hardware
04 Energy	14 Software and computer services
05 Construction and building products	15 Internet technology
06 Financial services	16 Electronics
07 Industrial automation	17 Leisure and entertainment
08 Industrial products and services	18 Other consumer related
09 Manufacturing	19 Services
10 Transportation	

Figure 9.1 Investment preference by technology.

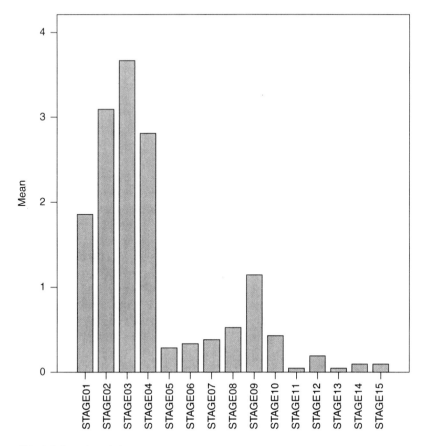

Principle investment stages

01 Seed
02 Start-up
03 Other early stage
04 Expansion
05 Bridge financing
06 Refinancing bank debt
07 Secondary purchase/replacement equity
08 Rescue/turnaround
09 Management buy-out (MBO)
10 Management buy-in (MBI)
11 Institutional buy-out (IBO)
12 Leveraged build-up (LBU)
13 Mezzanine finance
14 Public to private
15 Purchase of quoted shares

Figure 9.2 Investment preference by stage.

seed-corn and start-up) being the commonest type of investment involvement. Of the remaining wide range of investment involvements, the MBO is the most common; but it is relatively unimportant compared to the broad range of early-stage involvements that UK venture capitalists in high-technology areas now favour. The evidence on investor preference here can be usefully contrasted with that on investor attitude to risk in Chapter 4–6. As risk and return are positively related, the preferences stated in Figure 9.2 make sense. However, to achieve portfolio balance investors will mix high and low risk opportunities.

Within the class of early-stage investments, one does find a ranking of prevalence which corresponds to well known rankings of high-risk investment propositions (see, for example, the introductory chapters to the *Venture Capital Report*). Thus seed-corn backing is less common than other early-stage, indicating a reverse ranking by risk exposure. However, there does seem to be a de-coupling of risk attitude when it comes to the remaining wide range of investment types by stage, ranging from mezzanine financing to replacement equity. The latter are all, more obviously, the domain of private equity investing and are much less prevalent investment forms when it comes to high-technology backing. In sum, investors are bullish about the prospects of high-technology firms and are bold in seeking high-risk investment involvements, in their pursuit of high investment returns. Within this broad category of investment (namely, high-technology) this represents a welcome change of UK investor sentiment, in contrast to the aversion to the 'bleeding-edge' of technology so fearfully stylised ten to 15 years ago.

Finally, Figure 9.3 reports on UK investors' preferences by market extent. The data were generated by a question asking investors what geographical preference they had when deciding whether or not to make an investment. Five options were allowed, ranging from local to worldwide (See Q.1.1 in Postal Questionnaire, Appendix 4). In effect, these options comprise a nesting of the desired extent of the market for the dispensing of investible funds. Thus the pie-chart denotes preference for market extent, rather than allocation of funds by regions. Surprisingly, the preferences of UK investors over market extent are quite diverse. In particular, proximity does not appear to play as large a role as one might suspect, with preferences, on balance (52.6 per cent), being for investments beyond the local or regional area. As contrasted with US experience, where proximity does seem to be important, UK investors appear to be willing to go to wherever the deal is favourable. This is not just because the UK is geographically small, as over one quarter of investors (27.4 per cent) have preferences for investing internationally (either in Europe, or in the rest of the world).

Questionnaire

The investors of our sampling frame, as described above, were approached directly (using addresses from the VCR) by post, using a pre-letter (explaining the scope and purpose of the study) and a hard copy of an eight-page questionnaire (see Appendix 4). Briefly, this questionnaire investigated: the general

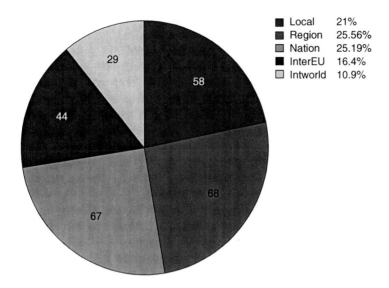

■ Local	21%
■ Region	25.56%
☐ Nation	25.19%
■ InterEU	16.4%
☐ Intworld	10.9%

Figure 9.3 Preference for investment by market extent.

background of investors (e.g. desired investee location, sector, stage, type); ways of assessing, managing and accounting for intangible assets in high-technology companies; and investor influence on investees' internal management and reporting. Most questions were qualitative in purposes, and measured importance, extent of agreement, significance, etc. from an investor standpoint, using a Likert scale. In the event of non-response, a follow-up copy of the questionnaire was sent by email. After both mailings had been concluded, our raw response was 31 investors, which included the great bulk of the leading UK investors in high-technology companies.

Table 9.1 provides summary statistics on key attributes of the investors who

Table 9.1 Summary statistics on investor conduct

	Minimum	*Maximum*	*Mean*
Minimum investment (£)	5,000	10,000,000	856,818
Maximum Investment (£)	100,000	50,000,000	4,459,091
Average investment (£)	80,000	30,000,000	2,565,714
Percentage who invest in technopoles			18%
Percentage who invest a lump sum			64%
Percentage who use staged finance			91%
Percentage who value intangibles at current replacement cost			25%
Percentage who value intangibles at estimated market value			75%

made returns. Several points are noteworthy. First, very high levels of funding are being allocated, even at the small end of the market, to high-technology enterprises. The average minimum investment across investors was £857k and the average maximum investment was £4,459k. Overall, the average investment in a high-technology firm was £2.6 millions. Typically (91 per cent), staged financing was used in disbursing these funds, but lump sum payment was a common alternative (64 per cent), where, as we shall see below, the willingness to take this simpler route being predicated on the information and control systems to which investees were subject. We see that high-technology investing is by no means intrinsically a science park or technopole phenomenon, with less than one-fifth of investors (18 per cent) specifically targeting such geographic clusters. When technopoles or science parks were named, they were diverse, ranging from Oxford, Cambridge and Manchester to East Midlands, Merseyside in the UK, and from Bavaria to Boston and Bay Area, CA, outside the UK. Finally, intangibles are much more likely (75 per cent) to be valued at estimated market value, rather than at current replacement cost (25 per cent), suggesting some refinement in the valuing of intangibles, and perhaps also a need to prove the worth of the firm (e.g. as a development company, creating intellectual property (Lewis and Lippitt, 1999), but with no product to market, as yet) to potential VC backers and other possible funders (e.g. local, regional or central governments).

Turning now from key results elicited by the questionnaire, we shall briefly consider elements of its design. The general approach to instrument design was to create questions which would reveal things about investor attitudes or preferences that would not be available in any other way, using regular data resources.

Table 9.2 indicates the three main components of the postal questionnaire: (a) background information on location, size and stage of investment; (b) the utility of reporting (Schroeder and Gibson, 1990; Gelb and Siegel, 2000; Hand, 2002; Mueller, 2004); and (c) information systems (Mitchell *et al.*, 1995; Wright *et al.*, 2004a, 2004b), especially as regards company valuation and its risk sensitivity (Ruhnka and Young, 1991; Fiet, 1995a, 1995b; Uher and Toakley, 1999). Full details are given in Appendix 4, which sets out the complete postal questionnaire in its original layout. The typical question design elicits information on *attitudes* (e.g. preferred investee location, preferred industrial sector), *utility* (e.g. of score-carding for risk appraisal), or *preference* (e.g. of method for valuing intangible assets). In that sense, the focus of this instrument is also on eliciting qualitative information about patterns of investor behaviour. By scoring the responses (e.g. typically on a five-point scale) they can be converted into quantitative data (e.g. of the type used to construct Figures 9.1, 9.2 and 9.3).

Evidence

In this section, we shall consider the substantive evidence obtained from the questionnaire described above, as it relates to financial reporting, risk disclosure and intangible assets. Here, the main purpose is to establish the general behavioural features of UK investor conduct. It will be left to the 'Intangible assets'

Table 9.2 Outline of postal questionnaire

1 Background
- Geographical preference
- Science park investing
- Preferred high-technology sector
- Most common investment stage
- Size of investment
- Preference for lump-sum vs staged investment

2 High Technology and Financial Accounting
- Utility of standard financial accounts
- Required valuation information on internally developed intangible assets
- Adequacy of investee information for company valuation
- Current replacement cost vs estimated market value of intangible assets
- Significance of costs in evaluating investment worth
- Extent of requirements of risk disclosure
- Qualitative vs quantitative risk information
- Use of score-carding for risk appraisal
- Necessity of required elements in financial accounts
- Degree of agreement on risk reporting and disclosure

3 Management Accounting and Performance
- Extent of influence on firm's internal management
- Extent of contact with high vs low performing firms
- Required reporting frequency in firm's AIS
- Problems of measuring and managing risk

(p. 143) to consider how this behavioural evidence can be put into an inferential framework.

Financial reporting

First, investors were asked the extent to which the standard financial accounts they received from potential investees, active in the high-technology area, were useful in assessing their company's value (see Q.2.1 in Appendix 4). Scoring was from zero ('completely useless') to four ('very useful'), thus creating the *FinAcUse* variable. As the value of high-technology companies is difficult to assess, given that much of their prospective value is tied up in intangible assets, typically based on intellectual property, like patents and brands, investors were asked how they assessed, managed and accounted for such intangible assets. Figure 9.4 presents a histogram of the responses. This indicates that the modal response by investors was that standard financial accounts were fairly useless for assessing the value of investee companies. The mean response was 1.4, which is only slightly better than 'fairly useless'.

This finding might be indicating a potential 'market failure', due to the information asymmetry (Chen *et al.*, 2003; Wong, 2003) arising from investors having inferior access to value relevant information, compared to investees. However, if the prime purpose of financial reporting is to satisfy statutory

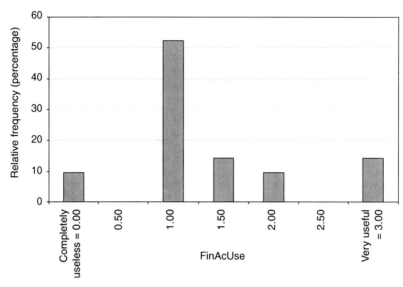

Figure 9.4 Usefulness of financial reports in assessing the value of high-technology firms.

reporting requirements, representing, in some sense, information deemed suitable for accountability and exterior audit, rather than investible value calculation, then this critique has less force. Indeed, investors themselves appear fairly sanguine about the lack of utility of financial reporting for value estimation, and are inclined to focus on their own skills in performing their own due diligence, or in buying-in relevant third-party due diligence. Looked at in this way, they regard their performing of such financial intermediation functions as resolving problems of information asymmetry. Explicit statements made by investors, mentioned below, support this conclusion.

Risk reporting and disclosure

Figure 9.5 reports on the answers to a question about risk reporting and disclosure (see Q.2.10, Appendix 4). A range of options had to be calibrated, in terms of investor agreement. As the caption to Figure 9.5 indicates, this covered adequacy of financial accounts, need for more information, adequacy of due diligence, and risk reporting. Degree of agreement was calibrated from unity (complete disagreement) to five (complete agreement). Taking 3.0, the central point of our scale, as indicating neutrality on the issue, investors were approximately neutral about 'the information currently provided in financial accounts is sufficient for our purposes' (*Risk1* = 2.95) and 'requiring more disclosure in published information would provide too much information to rivals' (*Risk3* = 3.11). So, sufficiency of information and excessive disclosure are not issues. However, there was general disagreement of views on the desirability of more compulsory

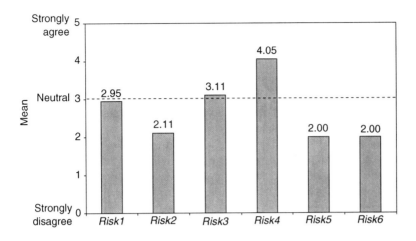

Variable	Statement
Risk1	The information currently provided in financial accounts is sufficient for our purposes
Risk2	More information should be provided compulsorily
Risk3	Requiring more disclosure in published accounts would provide too much information to rivals
Risk4	Our own due diligence is enough to enable us to assess high-technology investments
Risk5	Standardised risk reporting would facilitate the comparison of potential investees
Risk6	Standardised risk reporting would facilitate the allocation of risk capital

Figure 9.5 Risk reporting in financial accounts.

information (*Risk2*=2.11), the supposed benefits of risk reporting for comparing investees (*Risk5*=2.00), and on the potential for improving risk capital allocation (*Risk6*=2.00). To illustrate, one investor said 'I do not feel standardised risk reporting would help. It might do the opposite, as it is almost impossible to achieve accuracy.' Finally, it is clear that there was general agreement with the view that investors' 'own due diligence is enough to enable us to assess high technology investments' (*Risk4*=4.05). Overall, reinforcing the above analysis of information asymmetry, the picture emerging is of considerable confidence by investors in their own capabilities, and a general aversion by them to further regulation (including extended statutory requirements) of information provision. Given the sharp behavioural picture provided by this evidence, the principal and, we believe, novel question we ask in the econometric part of this chapter is: what impact does behavioural attitude have on actual investment provision by investors?

Benefit from required publishing of financial accounts

The evidence of Figure 9.5 prompts the question, what particular aspects of financial accounts *do* investors think would benefit from required publishing? We address this issue in Figure 9.6. Responses to the question (see Q.2.9, Appendix 4) relate to the categories of financial risk (*ReqFinR*); people risk (*ReqPeopR*); technology risk (*ReqTechR*); market risk (*ReqMktR*); and valuation of intangible assets (*ReqIntR*) (see an example of its impact on the cost of replacing assets in the semi-conductor industry (Megna and Klock, 1993)). Attitudes to the question were measured on a five-point scale, from unity (not at all important) to five (crucial). Figure 9.5 displays barcharts of response categories against mean responses. Again, the value 3 is neutral. Taking that as a benchmark value, marked with the dotted horizontal line in Figure 9.6, we see that investors generally were of the view that it was not important to have risk disclosure of several attributes (notably of markets, of people, and of intangible assets) in financial reports. They were neutral, on average, about there being required reporting on technology.

Thus, in terms of agency theory, investee (namely, agent) knowledge (e.g. of markets, people, intangibles) of an insider nature, which is a prime source of information asymmetry (Barkham and Ward, 1999), is not something investors

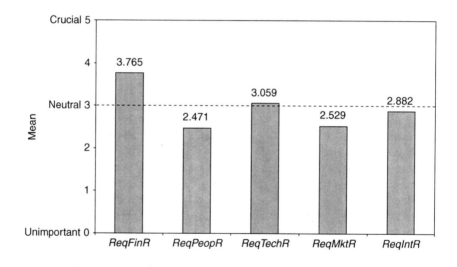

Variable	Risk disclosure should be required as it relates to:
ReqFinR	Finance
ReqPeopR	People
ReqTechR	Technology
ReqMktR	Marketing
ReqIntR	Intangible assets

Figure 9.6 Importance of disclosure in financial reports.

want to see resolved by compulsory financial reporting. Presumably, they feel that resolving this information asymmetry by their own due diligence (e.g. with respect to markets, people and intangibles), or by third party due diligence (e.g. with respect to technology) is part of their financial intermediation function. Essentially, this is part of their competitive advantage as allocators of risk capital, and it is this which would be diminished by more extensive risk reporting requirements. This is reinforced by the finding (far left column, Figure 9.6) that the only area in which investors are likely to be quite well informed (namely, on the financial side) is also the sole one that they would rate as important to risk disclosure, in terms of more detailed publishing.

This view of investor conduct and behaviour is reinforced by our qualitative evidence. Emphasising the relatively neutral attitudes displayed in Figure 9.6, one investor said, 'I have no view – the companies we invest in won't have published any accounts at that time. We sit on the Boards of all investees and so have exposure/visibility of the broad range of activities, and can exert influence across that range.' This quotation precisely characterises the monitoring and control function of the investor, as principal, and suggests how this function can attenuate information asymmetry. Another relevant investor quotation is: 'I seem to disagree with your basic premise. The sort of businesses we deal with are mainly concerned with market risk – they've invented the world's best mouse-trap, now can they sell it? I don't see how you can account for that.' This quotation emphasises that investors feel that investees too would rather communicate market sensitive information to entrusted insiders (like the investor, post-contract) rather than to the wider world (including other investors) through more extensive financial reporting. Indeed, the general investor aversion to calibration of the sort envisaged by more extensive risk reporting is perfectly captured in the comment: 'It's more an art than a science, and should be kept that way for private companies.'

Intangible assets

Finally, we turn to the evidence in Figure 9.7. This was generated from a question (see Q.2.2 in Appendix 4) which asked about internally developed assets (see Hand, 2002; Maines *et al.*, 2003; Mueller, 2004; and the literature review of Canibano *et al.*, 2000) which may have been valued by a potential investee company in a way which was less than transparent. Specifically, it asked of investors: for which of a set of internally developed intangible assets would they require a comment to provide valuation information? This set included patents, franchises, licences and so on, as listed in Figure 9.7 (Hall *et al.*, 2005). Responses were coded as unity if companies requested valuation information, and zero if it was thought that the valuation information in financial statements was adequate. The bar chart of Figure 9.7 has bar heights based on average responses across investors' mean responses, and they range from zero to unity.

The evidence of this figure is particularly revealing. Investors are unanimous in their view that financial statements do not provide adequate valuation

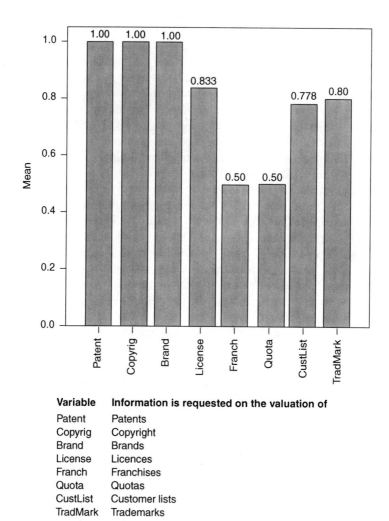

Variable	Information is requested on the valuation of
Patent	Patents
Copyrig	Copyright
Brand	Brands
License	Licences
Franch	Franchises
Quota	Quotas
CustList	Customer lists
TradMark	Trademarks

Figure 9.7 Requirement for valuation information.

information about patents, copyrights and brands, and that therefore they would ask investee companies specifically to provide such valuation information. A clear majority view was also in favour of receiving such information about customer lists and trademarks. Investors were equivocal concerning franchises and quotas.

The interpretation of Figure 9.7 should be done in the light of the evidence in Figure 9.5, that investors do not generally favour more information regulation, and in Figure 9.6, that investors relish information asymmetries that make their own due diligence skill more valuable. This suggests that it would be wrong to interpret the data of Figure 9.7 as suggesting an investor desire for more *public* information on key intangible assets like patents, copyrights and brands. Rather, they are admitting that they would prefer to pursue such information, as and when needed, from investees, during the due diligence process, and probably post-investment as well. Thus, at least as far as private (rather than public) gains and losses are concerned, the investor view is somewhat conservative and not likely to be a driver of change in financial reporting. This view is influenced, at least in part, by the fact that many high-technology companies will still be in their early start-up or development phases, and may not, as yet, have produced any financial accounts.

Conclusion

This chapter aims to advance the methodology of analysing investment practice, using the setting of UK VC investing in high-technology companies. It summarised the sampling methodology used, and then explored evidence on investment preference (by technology, stage, market) and on investor conduct (as regards use of financial reports, risk reporting, disclosure and valuation information). Its key conclusions are:

- investors prefer to rely upon their own procedures and processes (rather than those of investees) when evaluating potential investments in high-technology companies
- financial accounts appear to have little to offer to investors, in terms of risk disclosure or the valuation of intangible assets such as intellectual property
- it does *not* seem that investors would welcome compulsory risk disclosure, as they judge that this is likely to provide too much information to rival investors.

10 Behavioural variables and investment

Introduction

This chapter moves from the illustrative descriptive and analytical concerns of Chapter 9 to explicit inferential methods. It has essentially two parts. First, it uses correlation analysis to investigate links between: usefulness of financial accounts, and stage of investment and performance; technopole investment, and disclosure of risk over various attributes (e.g. finance, markets, health and safety); and influence by investors on investees' information systems (Wright and Robbie, 1996a; Mitchell *et al.*, 1997) and stage, sector, risk reporting, etc. (Reid *et al.*, 1997; Uher and Toakley, 1999). Second, it uses multiple regression analysis to examine the impact that investor opinion has on willingness to allocate greater or lesser volumes of funding to high-technology firms. Both approaches are unusual in that they focus on investor opinion (elsewhere, as in financial journalism, known as 'investor sentiment') as determinants (or correlates) of 'real' outcomes, like return on investment, or level of funds allocated. The contribution of this work is therefore to make outcomes directly behaviourally determined, rather than indirectly determined (e.g. intermediated by financial structure, such as gearing) (see Fisher and Statman, 2000; Wong, 2003; Brown and Cliff, 2005), which focus on investor sentiment).

Statistical analysis

What follows is a set of revealing correlations between behavioural variables (like the usefulness of financial accounts) and objective variables (like return on capital employed, ROCE). The measure of association we report is the conventional Pearsonian product-moment correlation coefficient, though the findings are similar if the nonparametric Spearman rank correlation coefficient is used. Although these correlations are associative, rather than causal relationships, they are suggestive of what might be consistent with causal reasoning, and therefore lead us logically to the more causal modelling of the following section, on econometric analysis.

As in Chapter 9, the data are based on a sample frame of 114 leading UK investors, who are active in backing high-technology firms. The sampling frame was drawn from BVCA and VCR sources, and the instrument used for data collection was a postal questionnaire (Appendix 4 to this book). The sample of investors (27% response rate) complements that used in Parts II, III and IV.

Usefulness of financial accounts

Table 10.1 presents Pearson correlation coefficients, their statistical significance, and the sample size (N). Given no a priori knowledge, two-tailed tests are reported. The key variable is the usefulness of standard financial accounts *(FinAcUse)*, as appraised by investors, in evaluating the value of high-techno-logy investments. This variable (which is the larger, the more the usefulness) was correlated with three measures of potential value, *Staged,* return on share-holder's funds (ROSF) *ROSF* and *ROCE.*

Staged measures investor preference for staged (=1) over lump sum (=0) investments. Thus the higher is *Staged* for the sample average, the greater is investor preference for this investment mode. Furthermore, the lesser the value of *Staged*, the greater is the implied value of the investee firm, because a prefer-ence for lump-sum investing implies greater confidence that an investment will work out, without the precaution of the staging of financial support for it. *ROSF* is, as usual, return on shareholders' funds; and *ROCE* is return on capital employed. Both *ROSF* and *ROCE* are conventional performance measures, each looking at investors' returns in slightly different ways.

We find that Table 10.1 presents a consistent picture: the more useful are financial accounts, the better is company performance. All three correlations are significant at the 5 per cent level with, as expected, positive correlations with *ROCE* and *ROSF*, and negative correlations with *Staged*. It may be that better run firms both perform well and report more usefully. Reverse causality is also possible, with more useful financial accounts leading to a better allocation of investible funds, and thereby better performance.

Technopoles: investment stage and risk disclosure

The correlations of Table 10.2 relate to another key variable, *Technopole* (see Q.1.12 in Appendix 4). This asks whether investors do (=1) or do not (=0) specifically target investments in science parks or technopoles. About 18 per cent of investors replied in the affirmative. Our interest is in whether such an

Table 10.1 Correlations with the usefulness of financial accounts

FinAcUse	Staged	ROSF	ROCE
Pearson correlation	−0.449*	0.509*	0.553*
Prob. value	0.041	0.044	0.028
N	21	16	16

Note
*Correlation is significant at the 0.05 level (2-tailed).

Table 10.2 Correlations with investment in technopoles

Techpole	Indus07	Stage11	Stage13	TechFin
Pearson correlation	0.547*	0.463*	0.463*	0.494*
Prob. value	0.008	0.030	0.030	0.044
N	22	22	22	17

Techpole	PeopFin	MarkFin	FinQual	HnSFin
Pearson correlation	0.789**	0.494*	0.566*	0.658**
Prob. value	0.000	0.044	0.018	0.004
N	17	17	17	14

Notes
**Correlation is significant at the 0.01 level (2-tailed).
*Correlation is significant at the 0.05 level (2-tailed).

intention correlates with particular sectors, stages of finance, or requirements on risk disclosure. The results of Table 10.2 are clear and revealing. From a sectoral standpoint, only in the case of industrial automation (*Indus07*) is there significant evidence of targeting by technopole investors (prob. = 0.008). In terms of stage of investment, both institutional buyouts (*Stage11*) and mezzanine finance (*Stage13*) were significantly (positively) correlated with targeting technopoles (prob. = 0.030 and 0.030, respectively). These two are amongst the less common forms of investment types, certainly not associated with early-stage investing, and typically falling within a prudential investing category.

Finally, Table 10.2 reports on the targeting of technopoles and requirements on risk disclosure in terms of hard (namely, quantitative) reporting, over the dimension of technology (*TechFin*), people (*PeopFin*), markets (*MarkFin*), finance (*FinQual*), and health and safety (*HnSFin*). The correlations were significant (and positive) for four out of five of these categories, namely technology (prob. = 0.004), people (prob. = 0.000), markets (prob. = 0.044) and health and safety (prob. = 0.004). Although *quantitative* risk disclosure was not significant for finance, *qualitative* assessment (*FinQual*) of financial risk *was* significantly correlated with targeting technopoles (prob. = 0.018).

The picture that emerges here is of limited special requirements for technopole targeting by sector and mode of finance, but a highly structured (and comprehensive) approach in this case to risk reporting, with an emphasis on quantitative reporting, except in the case of financial risk alone, for which qualitative reporting is preferred.

Influence over internal management

To conclude our discussion of correlations with key variables, consider Table 10.3, which focuses on investors' influence on investees' internal management. The key variable here is information flow (*InflInfo*). It is based on a question which asks how strong an influence investors have on entrepreneurs internal

Table 10.3 Correlations with influence over management accounting

InflInfo	Indus12	Indus19	Stage09	Stage10
Pearson correlation	−0.447*	−0.667**	−0.577**	−0.478*
Sig. (2-tailed)	0.037	0.001	0.005	0.025
N	22	22	22	22
InflInfo	**Stage12**	**Stage14**	**MarkSens**	**Risk4**
Pearson correlation	−0.426*	−0.481*	0.590*	0.656**
Sig. (2-tailed)	0.048	0.023	0.013	0.002
N	22	22	17	19
InflInfo	**Risk6**	**InflMgt1**	**InflDec**	**InflStaff**
Pearson correlation	−0.516*	0.593*	0.567**	0.458*
Sig. (2-tailed)	0.024	0.004	0.006	0.032
N	19	22	22	22
InflInfo	**Inflmgt2**	**InflProd**		
Pearson correlation	0.593*	0.436*		
Sig. (2-tailed)	0.004	0.043		
N	22	22		

Notes
**Correlation is significant at the 0.01 level (2-tailed).
*Correlation is significant at the 0.05 level (2-tailed).

information systems (see Q.3.1 in Appendix 4). Strength of influence was cali-brated from little influence ($=0$) to complete control ($=5$).

It should be noted that the extent of control by investors is not generally cor-related with industrial sector, though there is slight evidence of negative correla-tions with sectors such as media and photography (*Indus12*; prob.$=0.037$) and services (*Indus19*; prob.$=0.001$), which, by their nature, are sectors in which person-to-person, creative and low authority milieus prevail.

On stage of investment, several negative impacts of control were found, specifi-cally from MBOs (*Stage9*; prob.$=0.005$), MBI (*Stage10*; prob.$=0.025$), LBOs (*Stage12*; prob.$=0.048$), and public to private investments (*Stage14*; prob.$=0.023$). The characteristic of all these investment forms is that the investor has necessarily an attenuated influence, because of other persons (e.g. management teams) or insti-tutions. On the other hand, a strong positive influence ($r=0.590$; prob.$=0.013$) was found between extent of investor control and the use of quantitative risk disclosures (e.g. using sensitivity or probability analysis) as it relates to markets (*MarkSens*).

Turning to risk, Table 10.3 has two very revealing results. First, there is a positive ($r=0.656$) and highly statistically significant (prob.$=0.002$) correlation between investor control and their confidence in their own due diligence (*Risk4*). This reinforces the finding of Chapter 9 ('Evidence'), on 'Risk Reporting and Disclosure', as it relates to the quantitative evidence of Figure 9.3 (on 'Risk

Reporting in Financial Accounts') and qualitative comments like 'our own due diligence is enough'. Given a free hand, investors are confident in their ability to value companies. Second, there is a negative ($r=-0.516$) and statistically significant relationship (prob.$=0.024$) between investor control and the view that standardised risk reporting facilitates the allocation of risk capital (*Risk6*). In a sense, this is the reverse side of the coin, as regards the *Risk4* variable on due diligence. It too is buttressed by the evidence of Figure 9.5 above, and by qualitative comments like 'I do not feel standardised risk reporting would help. It might do the opposite.' The overall picture that emerges is of proactive, self-confident investors who, if they have good control, are able to find what information they require, and are not convinced that standardised financial accounts can meet their information needs.

Finally, Table 10.3 was insightful on the relationship between investor influence on entrepreneur's IS and the exerting of control over specific features of internal management. Thus there are high (and significant) positive correlations between investor influence on IS in general and influence on other factors like management accounting (*InflMgt1*; prob.$=0.004$); decision-making processes (*InflDec*; prob.$=0.006$); control of staff (*InflStaff*; prob.$=0.032$); control of management (*InflMgt2*; prob.$=0.004$) and product development (*InflProd*; prob.$=0.043$). Thus, in relatively unfettered settings (e.g. free of the likes of MBO and MBI settings) the strength and scope of investor influence over the entrepreneur is considerable.

Econometric analysis

Although the evidence above provides insight into investor behaviour towards the entrepreneur in high-technology settings, and provides important interpretative clues about the relationship between investor influence and the investee firm's internal structure, it provides little guidance on cause and effect. It may be, as we have indicated, that there is often a situation of mutual causality. This is often so when performance is involved (compare Jain and Kini, 2000). Thus better information systems can improve performance; and better performance allows information systems to be enhanced.

However, in some cases, the causal connections are more clear-cut, and it is to one such instance that this last substantive section turns: the determination of the level of investment that an investor is willing to commit to a business. Our approach is direct, which is only made possible by two unique features of our work: our use of new primary source data; and utilisation of this data in a new way. Our view (based on the evidence of earlier chapters) is that, ultimately, it is 'investor sentiment', or investor judgement (Luft and Shields, 2001), that determines the allocation of investible funds to high-technology enterprises. The key component to that key decision, we would further argue, is judgements about risk (see Bhattacharyya and Leach, 1999), in a capital budgeting context, and Hardman and Ayton, 1997, in the context of qualitative risk assessment).

We return, therefore, to the evidence of Figure 9.5 in Chapter 9 (on risk reporting) to use it inductively in a new explanatory framework (see Q. 2.10 in

Appendix 4). To recap, in Figure 9.5, the evidence related to investor opinion (on a spectrum of complete disagreement to complete agreement) about matters like information provision, due diligence and risk reporting. We will now use these underlying opinions (embodied in variables *Risk1* to *Risk6*), per se, to explain the level of funds allocated to a high-technology entrepreneur. This behavioural approach by-passes more traditional measures of investment intention (e.g. those that are financial ratio- or capital structure-based).

The dependent variable chosen takes two forms. It is either: an investor's average investment (*Average*); or it is his minimum investment (*Minimum*) in a high-technology enterprise (see Q.1.4 in Appendix 4). The independent variables are *Risk1* to *Risk6*. Models 1 and 2, respectively, in Table 10.4, refer to the use of either the *Average* or *Minimum* level of investment made, respectively. Essentially, the underpinning of each model is the control relationship:

$$\text{Level of investment funds allocated} = f(\text{investor attitude to risk}) + \varepsilon \qquad (10.1)$$

where ε is a random error term. The model of equation (10.1) is estimated by multiple linear regression, using least squares on our cross-section of data on investors, as reported in Table 10.4.

We observe, first, that both models explain over 50 per cent of the variation in level of funds allocated (either average or minimum). Each regression is highly statistically significant, with F values of 4.098 (prob. = 0.018) and 4.830 (prob. = 0.010), respectively (for $k = 6$, $n-k = 12$ degrees of freedom). Table 10.4 gives estimated coefficients, and their corresponding t-statistics and prob. values. Not surprisingly, given the small sample size, high significance levels are hard to achieve for individual coefficients, given the sample size and limited degree of freedom.

Even so, the results are of interest. Most reassuring, all coefficients have the same sign in each model, with the exception of that attaching to the variable *Risk6*. Indeed, this variable, and that of *Risk5* too (both on standardised risk reporting), must be considered insignificant, on any reasonable interpretation of probabilities. That is, investors' views on risk reporting do *not* determine levels of investment. This result is robust across the two models. Note this evidence is consistent with the finding of Figure 9.5, that investors generally (namely, on average) disagree with the view that standardised risk reporting could either facilitate the comparison of potential investees (*Risk5*) or facilitate the allocation of risk capital (*Risk6*).

Of the other independent variables, the interpretation of *Risk2* ('more information should be compulsory') and *Risk4* ('our own due diligence is enough') are equivocal, given the probability levels. Perhaps the only interpretation one could reasonably confidently lean upon is that minimum investment is lower (Model 2) the greater is the confidence in due diligence (*Risk4*). This suggests that investors' due diligence does not, on average, favour the investible position of UK high-technology firms. Given that the fixed costs of due diligence are considerable, this may be filtering out the prospects of smaller companies.

Table 10.4 Regressions explaining levels of investment

Dependent variables	Model 1		Model 2	
	Average investment		Minimum investment	
Independent variables	Coefficients	t-statistic (prob. value)	Coefficients	t-statistic (prob. value)
Risk1	$1,506.10^3$	1.875 (0.085)	$5,637.10^2$	2.163 (0.051)
Risk2	$1,201.10^3$	1.598 (0.136)	$4,020.10^2$	1.646 (0.126)
Risk3	$2,566.10^3$	2.635 (0.022)	$9,269.10^2$	2.932 (0.013)
Risk4	$-2,657.10^3$	-1.652 (0.124)	$-9,656.10^2$	-1.849 (0.089)
Risk5	$4,282.10^2$	0.171 (0.867)	$6,138.10^2$	0.755 (0.465)
Risk6	$3,372.10^2$	0.125 (0.903)	$-4,373.10^2$	-0.499 (0.627)
Constant	$2,952.10^3$	-0.399 (0.697)	$-9,092.10^2$	-0.378 (0.712)
Adjusted R^2	0.508		0.561	
F-Statistic	4.098		4.830	
Probability value	0.018		0.010	

Variable	Statement
Risk1	The information currently provided in financial accounts is sufficient for our purposes
Risk2	More information should be provided compulsorily
Risk3	Requiring more disclosure in published accounts would provide too much information to rivals
Risk4	Our own due diligence is enough to enable us to assess high-technology investments
Risk5	Standardised risk reporting would facilitate the comparison of potential investees
Risk6	Standardised risk reporting would facilitate the allocation of risk capital

Finally, we turn to the independent variables *Risk1* ('current provision of financial information is adequate') and *Risk3* ('more disclosure would provide too much information'). These variables both calibrate conservative investors' positions. They are both positively correlated with higher levels of investment, both average and minimum. The strongest result related to *Risk3*. The finding is consistent with what we know of investment practice. If investors know more about target investees than rival investors, and due diligence is (on average) rigorous, they will allocate higher levels of investible funds, both in minimum terms and on average, over deals directed at such targets. The behaviour implied by the *Risk1* variable is, arguably, consistent with that of the *Risk3* variable, as it suggests that investors who perceive themselves to be capable of eliciting greater deal-sensitive information from investees than rivals will be willing to invest more, and will not want current financial accounting practice to be enhanced.

Overall, these results, and their interpretation, suggest the potential fruitfulness of an approach to explaining levels of investment by focusing on behavioural variables (attitudes to information, risk disclosure, etc.), rather than on structural variables (e.g. gearing, assets and so on).

Conclusion

This chapter concludes the empirical investigation into the ways in which venture capitalists value (and invest in) high-technology firms, focusing on financial reporting, risk behaviour and intangible assets. Using questionnaire returns from UK investors in diverse sectors, varying from biotechnology, through software/computer services, to communications and medical services, it examined: (a) the usefulness of financial accounts; (b) the implications of technopole investment; (c) the extent of investor control over the entrepreneur's AIS; and (d) the role of investor opinion (e.g. on disclosure, due diligence and risk reporting) in determining the level of equity provision. Finally, two alternative econometric models were used to provide explanations of the level of investment in high-technology companies, using risk-based behavioural variables.

The two main conclusions reached were: (a) that investors' attitudes do correlate with their overt practice, which may be summarised as being proactive, information intensive and risk-managing; and (b) that investors' attitudes to information provision and risk reporting have a significant (and measurable) impact on the volume of funds they will allocate.

Part VI
Concluding material

11 Conclusion

Overview

Our original motivation for writing this book had been the observed increase in interest in backing high-technology ventures by UK venture capitalists. On the one hand, this might have been more driven by a desire for long-term commitment in funding, such as would arise from a setting in which exit markets were illiquid, and therefore VC investors would display a relative preference for high-technology and early-stage investees, as they help to postpone exit, (Cumming *et al.*, 2005). Clearly there could be a cycle in enthusiasm for such investment involvements, with, for example, VC investors' preference for later-stage involvements like MBOs emerging as exit markets become more liquid.

On the other hand one has the finding that, under yardstick comparisons (e.g. with the USA) (Waites and Dies, 2006), there was a *relative* under-investment in high-technology ventures in the UK (Lockett *et al.*, 2002). This suggested (positively) that creative evolution was occurring in improving methods of risk appraisal, in the high-technology investment arena; and (negatively) that further progress in increasing VC involvement in high-technology was still desirable. We therefore aimed to examine current methods of risk appraisal in high-technology situations, in the setting of investors' and entrepreneurs' techniques and methods, with a view to examining their rationality and efficacy in specific investment contexts. We did so by determining a broad framework (compare Frigo *et al.*, 2005) for risk analysis. One central aspect of that was to recognise the ubiquity of agency effects (compare Baiman, 1982; Reid, 1998) from which we determined three main categories of risk, *business*, *innovation* and *agency*, which we found to have a wide range of applications.

For example, market opportunities (an aspect of business risk), and the management team (an aspect of agency risk) were regarded as important by VC investors. Naturally, agency risk was ranked lower as a factor in risk appraisal by entrepreneurs, because they are the 'agents' in the principal–agent relationship between investor and entrepreneur. Thus agency risk is borne more by the investor than the investee. However, factors like the sales and business model (aspects of business risk) were ranked as highly by entrepreneurs as by investors.

When it came to innovation risk (compare Lerner, 2002; Moore and Wüstenhagen, 2004; Cumming *et al.*, 2005), we found that its importance was considerable for both VC investors and entrepreneurs. However, a somewhat different attitude was taken by VC investor and entrepreneur to the contracting. Regarding overall risk, VC investors generally attached more importance to the full range of innovation features than did entrepreneurs. Examining attitudes by individual innovation features, there were clear differences of approach between investors and entrepreneurs. Investors tended to emphasise novelty, timeliness and sales revenue. Entrepreneurs were more interested in the technology, as such, and in winning the technological race against rivals. As a broad generalisation, although entrepreneurs had more concern for business risk than investors, they showed a lesser awareness than did investors of the importance of marketing a new innovation effectively.

Although this generic insight on agency effects is pivotal to the analysis and conclusions of our book, we found much more besides that, which was new and analytically important, could be derived from our work. The structure of the book indeed suggests this: conceptual framework; sampling and evidence; statistical analysis; case study analysis; and reporting and investment. That is to say, the book is also about models and methods, and has aimed to be innovative in both these areas. To illustrate, it has introduced new models for calibrating risk (Chapters 4 and 10); and has expounded new methods for comparing risk, across economic agents (Chapter 5), and between economic agents (Chapter 6).

The contents of this book

A brief review of the contents of the book is as follows. In Part I (Conceptual Framework) the scene was set from the standpoint of VC investors and entrepreneurs in the UK who were involved in developing and selling high-technology products. The key features of the UK venture capital market were reviewed and related to the policy context (notably a desire to reduce business risk in technology sectors). The research methods to be utilised were briefly expounded, focusing on fieldwork methods and instrumentation. The important distinction between qualitative and quantitative risk assessment was made, and problems of measuring risk under each heading were broached. It became clear that the distinction between quantitative and qualitative was more a matter of position on the spectrum of riskiness than of measurement per se, as even qualitative risk is amenable to some form of calibration (e.g. by risk class). Then the relationship between risk and decision making was considered, with especial reference to the decision of fund allocation to a high-technology project. Principal–agent modelling was reviewed, with the principal as investor and the entrepreneur as the agent. Finally, IP was seen as the main bargaining chip on the table between investor and entrepreneur: the potential value of new ideas, as embodied, for example, in patentable high-technology products.

Part II (Sampling and Evidence) was largely inductively based. It explained how evidence was gathered, and then focused on exploring what that evidence said about the two key economic agents of this book, the VC investor and the entrepreneur. We explained how one gained access to the field, and how evidence was gathered, stored and analysed. That evidence was then subjected to what some have called 'exploratory data analysis' (Tukey, 1977). This emphasises the use of schema, rather than formal inferential methods, for exploring the 'shape' of your data, i.e. what the evidence is telling us, before we come to questions like: how probable is this, or how are these effects connected? From this perspective, attitudes to risk of the VC investor and the entrepreneur were explored, and then this approach was extended to consider factors important to risk appraisal, innovation risk, and non-financial factors impacting on risk (e.g. legal considerations, public image). Even without explicit use of inferential techniques, it was found that the evidence could confirm the main categories of risk implied by principal–agent analysis (namely, business, innovation and agency risk) and further, suggested how these might be linked.

Having cleared the ground, in terms of conceptual framework and evidence, Part III (Statistical Analysis) took us into formal hypothesis testing, both in terms of the relationship between investor and entrepreneur, and in terms of what we have called 'industry consensus'. The latter is a measurable concept of concordance of approach, as adopted, for example, by VC investors when making decisions about the level of funding to be allocated to a high-technology project being steered by an entrepreneur. This approach bolstered the exploratory data analysis of the previous section of the book, pinning down very precisely (by using the W test) the degree of confidence one could have in patterns detected, by statistical means, in the data. Further, it greatly extended the analysis by making detailed reference to key decision-making tools for investment analysis, and by getting behind the process of risk appraisal itself, to ask what the key influences upon it were (e.g. commercial and non-commercial factors). Amongst other things, this section set out quite explicitly (in this sense paralleling the exposition of the central model of the principal and agent in Part I) the methods used to check whether investors' and entrepreneurs' views were statistically significant, and whether one could say that there was an 'industry consensus'. As it turned out, investors' views on risk were not unsystematic – they were coherently patterned. Further, their views were largely in agreement. This was despite evidence, like that provided by Reid (1998), that 'house styles' of investors can differ greatly from house to house. That may be true, but when it comes to techniques of risk analysis, there is considerable consensus on how to proceed. To put it metaphorically, there may be differences in what goes on the menu, but all are agreed on the recipes.

Thus far, what we have considered about the content of this book has focused on models (e.g. of risk, of principal and agent) and methods (e.g. of data acquisition, of statistical analysis of evidence). The next section of the book, Part IV ('Case Study Analysis'), turned to what might be called 'illustration'. It is one thing to formalise the relation between investor and entrepreneur (e.g. as principal and agent), but that tells you surprisingly little about what they do. This detail is lost, because of the level of generalisation used, and as much is true of many parts of statistical testing, though not all (e.g. see the detailed exploration of investor evidence in the latter part of Chapter 6). To move from the general to the specific, illustrative case studies were presented in Chapters 7 and 8. Whilst these case studies illustrate, in their detail and diversity, the wide variety of forms of investor and investee conduct, they do also illustrate a unity of principle, in that business risk, agency risk and innovation risk emerge as common categories, across all case studies.

Finally, we came to Part V ('Reporting and Investment'), the last substantive part of the book. The foundation of this part was primary data source based, but this time the evidence was gathered by a postal questionnaire, rather than by fieldwork methods. Again, the focus of discussion was on information asymmetry (Healy and Palepu, 2001), and risk appraisal, but this time the information asymmetry was addressed more directly in terms of financial reporting (Hand, 2005), and the role of risk was embodied explicitly in a behavioural econometric model, explaining level of funds allocated to a high-technology firm by a set of VC investor attitudes to risk. We have not aimed to justify these attitudes to risk – rather, we have taken them as behaviourally given (as measured by an instrument), and we have used them (successfully) to explain the volume of funding given to entrepreneurs.

Overall, the structure of the book, though diverse and often detailed, is actually quite simple. We expound key principles, develop appropriate models and methods, and apply these to new bodies of primary source data. As ever, the devil is in the detail, and we have aimed to provide both detailed analysis and yet a general framework, applicable to a wide range of high-technology investment settings. We turn now to areas for further development, especially in the practitioner domain.

Discussion of main findings

The difference between the received approach, and the findings we refer to above, may be explained by reference to Figure 11.1 (see Carey and Turnbull, 2000); Reid and Smith, 2005). This is intended to display the main determinants of total company risk. They are seven in number: goods markets; factor markets; taxes; finance; law; regulation; and operations. Of these, only goods markets and markets for factors of production lie logically within one of our risk classes (namely, business risk, Goodman, 2003; Frigo and Sweeney, 2005). Most of the other risk factors in that figure are institutional (e.g. law, taxes, regulation) and in that sense cannot be part of risk management strategies. Thus, in our high-technology context (compare Norman, 2004), in which the role of the venture capitalist and of innovation play a crucial part in the risk exposure of a company, a standard diagram like Figure 11.1 omits a lot. An important overall finding of our work is that this standard picture of Figure 11.1 does not suffice in a high-technology world. To it must be added innovation risk (Lerner, 2002; Moore and Wüstenhagen, 2004; Cumming *et al.*, 2005); and agency risk (Hyytinen and Toivanen, 2003).

A principal aim of our research work was to examine the extent to which our evidence 'mapped into' our three risk categories (business, agency, innovation).

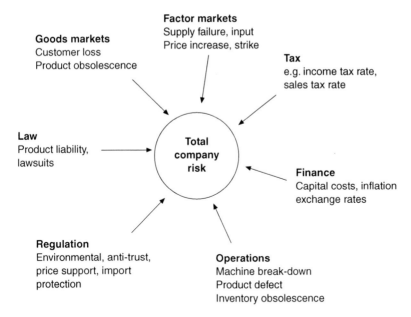

Factor markets
Supply failure, input
Price increase, strike

Goods markets
Customer loss
Product obsolescence

Tax
e.g. income tax rate,
sales tax rate

Law
Product liability,
lawsuits

**Total
company
risk**

Finance
Capital costs, inflation
exchange rates

Regulation
Environmental, anti-trust,
price support, import
protection

Operations
Machine break-down
Product defect
Inventory obsolescence

Figure 11.1 Determinants of total company risk.

Such evidence was gathered by fieldwork methods and was both qualitative and quantitative in nature. Our general finding was that these three categories of risk captured many attitudes to risk of investors and entrepreneurs involved in high-technology companies.

In reaching this conclusion we generated a wide variety of additional specific findings. These related, for example, to the differing degrees of risk aversion generally displayed by investors and entrepreneurs, and their different judgements on key factors affecting risk. We found that entrepreneurs were typically more risk-averse than investors. However, they tended to agree on the key factors which affected risk. This was especially true of commercial factors, less true of non-commercial factors, and scarcely true of innovation factors.

We found that investors and entrepreneurs both think of risk within the same framework. This can be conveniently encapsulated in our threefold division into business, innovation and agency risk. However, investors and entrepreneurs attach different importance to these risk categories. Thus the investor focuses on agency risk, being particularly worried about issues like delegation of responsibilities, incentives for effort, risk sharing and the use of information systems. On the other hand, entrepreneurs recognise, but downplay, agency risk, and emphasise business risk. This suggests that the relationship between both parties is positive, in that risk is being shifted from investee to investor, allowing the former to focus on exploiting business opportunities. There was a kind of apportioning of responsibility between investor and entrepreneur, with the entrepreneur focusing on achieving technology milestones, with a view of getting to market, and the investor focusing on the perceived novelty of a high-technology product in the marketplace, and its potential to generate sales.

In terms of investor conduct, we found that a general pattern emerged. Investors use a lot of the devices familiar from textbooks, like IRR, NPV, DCF and payback, but neglect a variety of more sophisticated methods which could improve investment appraisal.

Some neglected areas

We found that these neglected areas include simulation (Monte Carlo), VaR, and decision tree methods. To illustrate, whilst most investors use sensitivity analysis, the parameter variations used in such analysis are chosen systematically and predictably. This is unlikely to generate surprises. On the other hand, the related Monte Carlo methods throw random shocks at different parts of the firm's system, with a view to unmasking surprising effects. From a prescriptive standpoint, we would hope that practitioners might turn to these neglected techniques, to see what they might offer in the area of risk appraisal.

The Monte Carlo approach (see Dupire, 1999; Quiry *et al.*, 2005) allows you to consider chance configurations which can – just by accident – have relatively strong consequences for good or bad within the small firm. Such configurations are rarely discovered by standard forms of sensitivity analysis, because they are only discovered in a serendipitous way. They are never revealed in most sensitivity studies, as they often vary just one parameter at a time (e.g. discount rate) over a grid of values, without considering possible interactions with other parameters. In the Monte Carlo approach, the whole system (i.e. model of the business) is subject to random shocks, which allows relatively unusual coincidental situations to be generated. They can indicate how crisis points can appear by chance within the structure of the firm. Quite often, these points of vulnerability exposed by Monte Carlo analysis can be nullified by relatively inexpensive 'circuit breaking' or 'firewall' devices. To illustrate, intrinsic cycles within the firm, for example, salary payment, research milestones, inventory replenishment, debt servicing, license fees, can, by chance, coincide in a destabilising way. This can be offset or forestalled by a variety of low cost rescheduling devices.

VaR (see KPMG, 1997; Jorion, 2000, Ch. 14; Quiry *et al.*, 2006, Ch. 48) is defined as the maximum loss that a firm can incur over a specific time horizon within a given confidence interval. It can be interpreted in a variety of ways. One of the most useful is to look at it as the minimum equity required to support a risky business. There are three reasons why the VaR methodology is important. First, diverse risky positions can be compared and aggregated. Second, the required financial capital to support a given level of risky activity can be measured. Third, the performance of diverse risky projects, on a risk-adjusted basis, can be directly compared for management purposes. The evolution of the VaR methodology started with a meeting of the Bank for International Settlements in Basle in 1995. Its focus was on how much capital institutions should hold to guard against exposure to market risk.

A ready-made technique for solving such VaR problems is to hand. It takes the shape of the *RiskMetrics*™ software of JP Morgan, which became available on the internet at no cost, in a variety of forms, from 1994 onwards. Briefly, the method provides a measure of the market risk of a firm's 'book', i.e. its position in terms of investments which expose it to financial risk (see Duffie and Pan, 1997). Using the method requires the ability to define correlations between company assets, which may need the entrepreneur to provide information about probabilities, in a numerical sense. These can be directly assigned using 'rational beliefs', rather than estimated using statistical time series (compare 'Qualitative and quantitative uncertainty' on p. 19). Once done, for a given holding period horizon, it is possible to quantify the downside risk. Thus the value at risk of a portfolio is the loss in market value over a given time period (e.g. a month) that is exceeded with a small probability, like 0.01. This has the merit of providing a lower downside estimate than the VC investor would get if only the full equity exposure were considered. Our general finding is that the latter is most commonly considered. However, it is really too pessimistic a view, in terms of risk assessment. VaR analysis emphasises what you are likely to lose, not what you would only lose in the very worst scenario. Needless to say, it follows from the above that potentially promising high-technology investments may fail to be backed because of pessimism of the latter sort.

Decision trees can be used by investors as a valuable form of decision support, when considering alternative investments. The purpose of a decision tree is to display clearly the choices confronting an investor, and to illustrate the possible consequences of each choice (Quiry *et al.*, 2006, p. 381). Intrinsic to the way a decision tree is constructed is to lay out consequences of actions as a kind of branching process. Going down different branches involves irreversible choices over time, which lead to different payoffs. A decision tree is made up of decision nodes and branches. At each decision node, the investor must make a choice as to which branch he will select. The whole decision tree starts from an initial node, and proceeds by a branching process to terminal nodes, at which payoffs are collected. In logic, the decision tree should be solved by a process known as 'backward induction' or 'rollback' (Dixit and Skeath, 1999, Ch. 3). Starting from the highest expected payoff across the various terminal nodes, one works backwards selecting the best payoff action (i.e. branch) at every decision node, until the initial node is reached. This defines a route through the decision tree, which is optimal, in the sense of being payoff maximising.

On a practitioner level, the full logic of the above is not usually followed through, and the implementation of the decision tree approach can have a great variety of forms, involving various degrees of informality. However, as investing is done for profit, the above mode of thinking should be intrinsic to profitable investment selection. We found that the use of decision trees was widespread, with over three-quarters of investors using this technique for evaluating different project scenarios. Furthermore, most investors (nearly 90 per cent) were aware of technical aspects of creating decision trees, like the distinction between decision points (or nodes) and outcomes. However, it was less common to think in terms of *expected* payoffs as opposed to *certain* payoffs. This does seem a weakness in the utilisation of this form of decision support. After all, we know that elsewhere in decision making, it is quite common to assign probabilities, so why not for decision trees?

When it came to rollback arguments, we found that this line of reasoning was rarely employed. Only a quarter of investors decided on their best actions using the highest expected payoff. More often, the use of decision trees seemed to be to give more explicit content to scenario analysis. Thus different routes through the decision tree were seen to involve alternative scenarios. However, investors generally have not yet taken the next logical step of going from scenarios to the best investment alternative. What seems to be dissuading them is the frequent presence of waiting or time-shifting moves that make them abandon the decision tree perspective. In fact, this is not necessary. Investors might learn that 'proceed' and 'wait' do themselves present alternative branches, with different payoff consequences, at any given decision node (providing a link between decision trees and real options reasoning). Clearly this complicates the construction of decision trees. However, by focusing on payoff, rather than scenarios, the increased complication is worth contemplating. As improved software for decision support in this area emerges, so one would expect investors to become increasingly sophisticated in their use of devices like decision trees.

Conclusion

Many aspects of our work have led to a coherent view of how investors and entrepreneurs interact in high-technology contexts. For example, we found that the diversified risk specialist, the investor, was less risk averse than the more risk exposed entrepreneur; and we found that the entrepreneur paid more attention to business risk than did the investor. In terms of weaknesses of current practice, as we observed it, we have singled out three areas where the embracing of new technical developments could be fruitful: Monte Carlo analysis; VaR analysis; and decision tree analysis. There are other developments too, that we think should be considered as standard tools for investors in high-technology firms, like real options analysis (Triantis and Hodder, 1990; Bowman and Hurry, 1993; Quiry *et al.,* 2006, Ch. 20).

However, we also found that score-carding methods (Kaplan and Norton, 1996; Mendoza *et al.*, 2002), and a variety of tabular displays, serve as adequate, and sometimes highly efficient, guides to sound risk appraisal. This is certainly true if these methods are to be compared with traditional methods like intuition, and 'playing a hunch'. Essentially, most rational formalisations, be they ever so simple, do dominate the intuitive approach in terms of quality of decision making. For example, a very simple schema like Figure 11.2 can provide a good way of prioritising risk (Carey and Turnbull, 2000). It could be used as part of the background analysis for risk reporting of the sort recommended in the Turnbull Report (1999). On the horizontal axis is risk, which only requires that the broad categories of high and low risk be ascertainable. Thus only qualitative, rather than statistical, risk assessment is required in this case. On the vertical

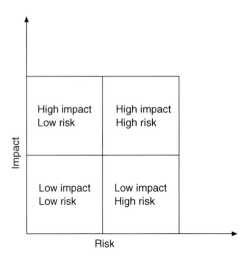

Figure 11.2 Risk and impact categories.

axis is impact on the company of risk factors. Again, the schema only requires that high impact and low impact be distinguishable. This simple schema will often outperform 'playing a hunch', simply because it requires the decision maker to formalise a gut feeling by reference to attributes (impact and risk) which can be openly discussed in terms of evidence and judgement. Before introducing sophisticated risk management tools, like Monte Carlo analysis, it would be important to ensure, first of all, that the more prosaic methods of schemas like Figure 11.2 have been fully explored and exploited.

That having been said, there clearly is a role for explicit modelling, both at the practitioner and academic level. We have suggested above what models might be of use to the practitioner. From our own point of view, that of researchers in the areas of risk, investment and high-technology enterprise, there is a clear place for new models and methods. As to methods, our novelty, we would claim, lies in the utilisation of new primary source data, where part of the innovation lies in instrument design (see Appendices). As regards models, there are several aspects of our work that come to mind as involving novel insight and techniques, including the use of the new 45° diagrams in Chapter 5 to display the extent of agreement between VC investors and entrepreneur; and the regression model of Chapter 10, which (for the first time) uses behaviourally-based 'attitudes to risk' variables to explain the level of fund allocation. As ever, our research endeavour involves the search for new ways to do things. This has applied as much to the entrepreneurial, high-technology firms we have examined as it has (by inspiration drawn from their own creative endeavours) to our own research agenda. Likewise, we hope that others in our field might be inspired to build on part of what he have expounded above to build new and better models, and to devise novel and insight-generating methods.

Appendices

Appendix 1: Pre-letter

Address

Date

Dear ***

RISK APPRAISAL IN HIGH-TECHNOLOGY VENTURES

The rapid growth of the venture capital industry has been one of the success stories of the British economy over the last decade. However, the pace of change has been so fast that many areas of business practice, including accounting methods, have not yet adapted to the new problems that innovative enterprises and their backers encounter.

Against this background, we have been asked by the Chartered Institute of Management Accountants (CIMA) to examine methods of managing risk in high-technology ventures. We aim to do this by direct meetings with UK venture capital investors. Briefly, our proposed framework of enquiry will split total risk into innovation risk, business risk and agency risk. It is the expectation that this study will contribute to the evolution of best practice in the management of risk. We have discussed our proposed framework with David Thorp, Chairman of the British Venture Capital Association (BVCA), who has given our work his positive endorsement.

We would therefore seek your cooperation in agreeing a face-to-face interview, which would involve working through the attached agenda. Our experience is that this exercise can in itself be of benefit to you, in that it takes you through the conduct of your business from the perspective of an objective outsider's standpoint. On the reverse of the agenda outline is a basic data sheet. It would be very helpful, and would save time, if this could be completed before the interview.

The interview will be conducted on the basis of confidentiality and, in our final report to CIMA, we will not identify any firms or individuals by name. At the end of our research, we will provide you with a summary report of our findings.

We do hope you will be willing to be interviewed. One of us will be contacting you by telephone in the near future.

Yours sincerely

Professor Gavin C Reid   Dr Julia A Smith
Director, CRIEFF   Cardiff Business School

Encs:

Appendix 2: Administered questionnaire

[Respondent's Copy - Pink]

Administered Questionnaire

'Risk Appraisal in High-Technology Ventures'

CI*m*A

A Project Sponsored by the
Chartered Institute of Management Accountants
And the Carnegie Trust for the Universities of Scotland

Interviewer _____

Respondent _____

Company Name _____

Address _____

_____

_____

_____

Telephone _____

Date _____

Time _____

Professor Gavin C Reid
Director, Centre for Research into Industry,
Enterprise, Finance and the Firm (CRIEFF)
Department of Economics
University of St Andrews
St Salvator's College
St Andrews
Fife KY16 9AL

Tel: 01334 462431
Email: gcr@st-andrews.ac.uk

Dr Julia A Smith
Cardiff Business School
Aberconway Building
Colum Drive
Cardiff
CF10 3EU

Tel: 029 2087 6652
Email: SmithJA5@cardiff.ac.uk

AGENDA

Risk Premium

Time Horizon

Sensitivity Analysis

Expected Values

Cash Flow

Financial Modelling

Decision Making

Qualitative Appraisal

PREAMBLE

This interview looks at ways in which high-technology firms, that are actively patenting and have attracted venture capital funding, appraise risk. The rapid growth of the venture capital industry has been one of the success stories of the British economy over the last decade. However, the pace of change has been so fast that many areas of business practice, including accounting and economic methods, have not yet adapted to the new problems that innovative enterprises and their backers encounter.

We have been asked by the Chartered Institute of Management Accountants (CIMA), with additional support from the Carnegie Trust for the Universities of Scotland, to examine methods of managing risk in high-technology ventures. We aim to do this by direct meetings with people like you, following the agenda that we sent you earlier. We hope that this study will contribute to the evolution of best practice in the management of risk and would like to thank you, in advance, for agreeing to help us in our work.

RISK PREMIUM

In this context, a risk premium is that additional return which a risky new product development and launch must offer you in compensation for accepting the additional risk.

1. Do you attach a risk premium to the discount rates which you use in making a decision about developing and launching a new high technology product?

    Yes   ☐   Go to question 1.1

    No   ☐   Go to question 2

    1.1   How do you calculate the size of the risk premium?

    1.2   In this context, the cost of capital is that rate of return required on a high technology project which will induce you to go ahead and invest in it. It is used as the discount rate when evaluating one of your firm's new capital projects.

    Do you use the cost of capital as a reference point in adjusting the discount rate by a premium?

    Yes   ☐

    No   ☐

2.   Risk classes are sets of similar degrees of risk into which projects can be grouped for effective risk management without too much violence to reality. Typical classes are, for example, high, medium and low risk.

Do you recognise investment opportunities as lying in risk classes?

Yes   ☐   Go to question 2.1

No   ☐   Go to question 3

2.1   Do you use such classes as reference points in setting the risk premia?

Yes   ☐

No   ☐

3.   In high-technology firms, the timing and type of investment made in them can vary in form. Examples include the 'start-up' and the 'MBO'. On the attached sheet, could you please indicate how risky you believe each form of investment to be, on a scale which runs from high to low.

[Hand respondent sheet 3]

[Retrieve sheet 3 after completion]

4.   The so-called 'risk-return' curve is the increasing relationship between risk
       and expected return, which indicates that additional risk will only be borne
       if it carries with it an additional expected return.

       Do you have in mind a certain 'shape' (e.g. slope) for this locus when you
       assess the risk of high technology opportunities in which you might invest
       the firm's resources?

       Yes   ☐   Go to question 4.1

       No   ☐   Go to question 4

4.1   In your view, what factors influence its shape?

5.   Could you please indicate on the attached sheet how important the
       following factors are when you make a risk appraisal.

                        [Hand respondent sheet 5]

                   [Retrieve sheet 5 after completion]

INVESTMENT TIME HORIZON

In this context, the payback period is defined as the length of time it takes you to recover your initial cash outlay, in investing in a new high technology product, from its cash flow returns.

6. Do you use the payback period method of investment appraisal?

Yes ☐ Go to question 6.1

No ☐ Go to question 7

6.1 How many months do you look forward in using the payback period method?

6.2 Briefly, why do you have this time horizon?

7. Is there a certain point beyond which you would regard the development and launch of a new high technology as having outcomes which are either too risky (or too complex) to make it worth pursuing further?

Yes ☐

No ☐

8. Are decisions you base on the payback period influenced by cash flow considerations?

Yes ☐

No ☐

9. Do you use discounted cash-flow methods?

Yes ☐   Go to question 9.1

No ☐   Go to question 10

9.1   Briefly, how are discount rates assigned?

10. Do you set a target rate of return?

Yes ☐   Go to question 10.1

No ☐   Go to question 11

10.1   Briefly, how is it set?

11. Do you require the payback period to be earlier, the riskier the high technology you are developing?

Yes ☐

No ☐

12. Do you regard your target rate of return and your payback period as being dependent or independent?

Dependent ☐

Independent ☐

SENSITIVITY ANALYSIS

In this context, sensitivity analysis tests how a new high technology's project's expected commercial outcome (e.g. NPV, IRR) changes in response to changes in project variables (e.g. sales, price). It aims to identify the variables which have most effect on the expected outcome.

13.   How important is the use of sensitivity analysis to your project decision, on a scale of 1 to 5, where 1 is unimportant, and 5 is very important?

[circle below, 0 being irrelevant]

Unimportant   Very Important

0 ————1 ————2 ————3 ————4 ————5

14.   Do you apply NPV calculations in your sensitivity analysis?

Yes   ☐

No   ☐

15.   Briefly, what variables (e.g. costs) do you use in your sensitivity analysis?

16. Briefly, how widely do you let those variables range in your sensitivity analysis?

17. How important is breakeven as a reference point in your sensitivity analysis, on a scale of 1 to 5, where 1 is unimportant, and 5 is very important?

[circle below, 0 being irrelevant]

Unimportant   Very Important

0 ————1 ————2 ————3 ————4 ————5

18. Do you independently assign values to costs and revenues in your sensitivity analysis, or do you treat them as being dependent?

Independent   ☐ Go to question 19

Dependent   ☐ Go to question 18.1

  18.1 Briefly, what form does this dependence take, and can it be quantified?

19.   Do you attach probabilities to costs and revenues in your sensitivity calculations?

Yes   ☐   Go to question 19.1

No   ☐   Go to question 20

19.1   How do you assign them?

20.   Do you construct your sensitivity analysis around a reference point viz. what you expect to happen?

Yes   ☐   Go to question 20.1

No   ☐   Go to question 21

20.1   Briefly, what factors do you take into account in determining what is expected to happen?

EXPECTED VALUES

In this context, an expected value is a weighted average of all prospective commercial value generated by a new high technology product development. It represents your estimate of the long-run average value of this investment, assuming no unforeseen changes in circumstances.

21.   In this sense, do you use expected values in making decisions about developing and launching new high technology products?

Yes   ☐   Go to question 21.1

No   ☐   Go to question 22

21.1   Do you determine actual value and the probability of it occurring separately, and then do you calculate expected values. Or do you determine expected values directly?

Separately   ☐ Go to question 22

Directly   ☐ Go to question 21.2

21.2   Briefly, what factors do you bear in mind in determining expected values?

22.   Do you consider how risk varies, year by year, over the prospective life time of your new high technology product development and launch?

Yes   ☐

No   ☐

23. Do you recognise dependence when you assign expected values (e.g. across years, with higher risk attached to later years)?

Yes ☐

No ☐

24. Do you use different methods of assigning expected values in any given year, depending on whether a cost or a revenue is being considered?

Yes ☐ Go to question 24.1

No ☐ Go to question 25

24.1 Briefly, how (or why) do you do this?

PREDICTING CASH FLOW

25. Do you explicitly estimate how probable your cash flows are?   (i.e. in effect, can you estimate the distribution of probabilities of prospective cash flows)?

Yes   ☐   Go to question 25.1

No   ☐   Go to question 26

25.1 Do you use these estimates in calculations of the NPV of a high technology project?

Yes   ☐

No   ☐

26. Would an expected positive NPV alone lead you to adopt a risky project? Or would you moderate your decision by further qualitative risk assessment?

Just adopt project   ☐

Make further qualitative assessment   ☐

27. Do you estimate the chances that the present value of cash inflows might be less than the project cost (i.e. the probability that the project will run at a loss)?

Yes   ☐   Go to question 27.1

No   ☐   Go to question 28

27.1 How poor do your chances have to be for you to regard the risk as unacceptably high?

[circle below]

Chance of success

minimal —slight —very low —quite low —below average

FINANCIAL MODELLING

Here, it will be assumed that you do undertake at least some sort of financial modelling, be it informal (even simply in your head) or formal (e.g. spreadsheet based).

28.   Do you construct an explicit model of your firm's financial objectives?

Yes   ☐   Go to question 28.1
No   ☐   Go to question 29

28.1   Is it an optimising model?

Yes   ☐
No   ☐

29.   Briefly, what are the objectives of your financial modelling?

30.   Briefly, what are the constraints, if any, on your financial modelling?

31. Briefly, what variables do you use in your financial modelling?

32. Are inter-relationships between these variables considered explicitly in your financial modelling?

    Yes ☐

    No ☐

33. Do you use your financial modelling to plan ahead?

    Yes ☐

    No ☐

34. Can you estimate the future profitability of your firm?

    Yes ☐

    No ☐

35.   Are the predictions you make about your firm used to influence its long-run strategy?

Yes   ☐

No   ☐

36.   Are simulation methods (e.g. Monte Carlo techniques) used by you to examine possible performance paths of your firm over time?

Yes   ☐   Go to question 36.1

No   ☐   Go to question 37

36.1   What is your time frame of interest, and what parameters and decision rules do you vary across simulation runs?

DECISION MAKING

A decision tree is a way of illustrating the choices facing a decision-maker and the possible consequences of each choice.

37.   Do you construct explicit decision trees to evaluate different project scenarios within your firm?

Yes   ☐   Go to question 37.1

No   ☐   Go to question 38

37.1   In a decision tree, do you distinguish between decision points and outcomes?

Yes   ☐

No   ☐

38.   Do you attach probabilities to outcomes?

Yes   ☐   Go to question 38.1

No   ☐   Go to question 39

38.1   On what basis do you assign these probabilities?

39.   Do you decide upon your best action on the basis of the highest expected value generated by one of the set of alternative high technology product opportunities open to you?

   Yes   ☐

   No   ☐

40.   Might your best action, involving a new high technology development within your company, involve delay or waiting?

   Yes   ☐

   No   ☐

41.   Might your best action, concerning a new high technology development within your company, sometimes be contingent on something (e.g. information acquired over a waiting period)?

   Yes   ☐

   No   ☐

QUALITATIVE APPRAISAL

The aim of a scorecard is to provide a framework for translating a company's strategic objectives into a set of performance measures.

42. Do you use any type of 'Scorecarding' when appraising the prospect of developing and launching a new high technology product?

Yes ☐ Go to question 42.1

No ☐ Go to question 43

42.1 Briefly, what form does this take?

43. How important are the following non-financial indicators to you in your appraisal of new high technology product opportunities?

[Hand respondent sheet 43]

[Retrieve sheet 43 on completion]

44.   Do you use scenario analysis to create a 'best', 'middle' (most likely) and 'worst' case scenario for your new high technology product?

Yes   ☐   Go to question 44.1

No   ☐   Go to question 45

44.1   If so, does this rely more on 'hard' or 'soft' information?

Hard   ☐

Soft   ☐

44.2   Specifically, what might this include?

45.   How important are the following measures of innovation, when you are thinking about developing and launching a new high technology product?

[Hand respondent sheet 45]

[Retrieve sheet 45 on completion]

END OF QUESTIONNAIRE

Sheet 3

With reference to your knowledge of the high-technology area, how risky do you think the following types of investment are?

[Please circle one number in each case]

Type of investment	Degree of Risk

Low .... High

(a)	Seed	0 —— 1 —— 2 —— 3 —— 4 —— 5
(b)	Start-up	0 —— 1 —— 2 —— 3 —— 4 —— 5
(c)	Other early-stage	0 —— 1 —— 2 —— 3 —— 4 —— 5
(d)	Expansion	0 —— 1 —— 2 —— 3 —— 4 —— 5
(e)	MBO	0 —— 1 —— 2 —— 3 —— 4 —— 5
(f)	MBI	0 —— 1 —— 2 —— 3 —— 4 —— 5
(g)	Turnaround	0 —— 1 —— 2 —— 3 —— 4 —— 5
(h)	Replacement capital	0 —— 1 —— 2 —— 3 —— 4 —— 5
(i)	Follow-on investments	0 —— 1 —— 2 —— 3 —— 4 —— 5
(j)	Other _____ [Please specify]	0 —— 1 —— 2 —— 3 —— 4 —— 5

Thank you.

Now please hand this sheet back to the interviewer.

Sheet 5

Could you please circle below the importance to you of the following factors when you make a risk appraisal within your firm.

Factor		Degree of Importance Low .... High
(a)	Market opportunities	0 —— 1 —— 2 —— 3 —— 4 —— 5
(b)	Global environment	0 —— 1 —— 2 —— 3 —— 4 —— 5
(c)	Local environment	0 —— 1 —— 2 —— 3 —— 4 —— 5
(d)	Compelling nature of the proposition	0 —— 1 —— 2 —— 3 —— 4 —— 5
(e)	Management team	0 —— 1 —— 2 —— 3 —— 4 —— 5
(f)	Business model	0 —— 1 —— 2 —— 3 —— 4 —— 5
(g)	Sales model	0 —— 1 —— 2 —— 3 —— 4 —— 5
(h)	Scale of the business	0 —— 1 —— 2 —— 3 —— 4 —— 5
(i)	Commitment to bring in others	0 —— 1 —— 2 —— 3 —— 4 —— 5
(j)	Funding structure	0 —— 1 —— 2 —— 3 —— 4 —— 5
(k)	Type of exit	0 —— 1 —— 2 —— 3 —— 4 —— 5
(l)	Comparable investments	0 —— 1 —— 2 —— 3 —— 4 —— 5
(m)	Employee capabilities	0 —— 1 —— 2 —— 3 —— 4 —— 5
(n)	Information system capabilities	0 —— 1 —— 2 —— 3 —— 4 —— 5
(o)	Extent of motivation, Empowerment & alignment	0 —— 1 —— 2 —— 3 —— 4 —— 5
	Other _____ [Please specify]	0 —— 1 —— 2 —— 3 —— 4 —— 5

Thank you.

Now please hand this sheet back to the interviewer.

Sheet 43

Could you please indicate below the importance to you of the following factors when you undertake risk appraisals.

Factor	Degree of Importance
	Low .... High

(a)	Public image	0 —— 1 —— 2 —— 3 —— 4 —— 5
(b)	Customer service	0 —— 1 —— 2 —— 3 —— 4 —— 5
(c)	Quality of product	0 —— 1 —— 2 —— 3 —— 4 —— 5
(d)	Legal considerations	0 —— 1 —— 2 —— 3 —— 4 —— 5
(e)	Staff morale	0 —— 1 —— 2 —— 3 —— 4 —— 5
(f)	Other _____	0 —— 1 —— 2 —— 3 —— 4 —— 5
	[Please specify]	

Thank you.

Now please hand this sheet back to the interviewer.

Sheet 45

Could you please indicate below the importance to you of the following features of innovation when you are considering developing and launching a new high-technology product.

Feature   Degree of Importance

                                       Low .... High

(a)   Percentage   0——1——2——3——4——5
      of sales from new
      products

(b)   New product introduction 0——1——2——3——4——5
      versus competitors'

(c)   New product introduction 0——1——2——3——4——5
      versus plan

(d)   Time to develop next   0——1——2——3——4——5
      generation of products

(e)   Number of key items   0——1——2——3——4——5
      in which your company is first
      or second to market

(f)   Breakeven time   0——1——2——3——4——5

(g)   Other _____   0——1——2——3——4——5
      [Please specify]

Thank you.

Now please hand this sheet back to the interviewer.

Sheet 3

With reference to your knowledge of the high-technology area, how risky do you think the following types of investment are?

[Please circle one number in each case]

Type of investment	Degree of Risk

Low .... High

(a)	Seed	0 ——— 1 ——— 2 ——— 3 ——— 4 ——— 5
(b)	Start-up	0 ——— 1 ——— 2 ——— 3 ——— 4 ——— 5
(c)	Other early-stage	0 ——— 1 ——— 2 ——— 3 ——— 4 ——— 5
(d)	Expansion	0 ——— 1 ——— 2 ——— 3 ——— 4 ——— 5
(e)	MBO	0 ——— 1 ——— 2 ——— 3 ——— 4 ——— 5
(f)	MBI	0 ——— 1 ——— 2 ——— 3 ——— 4 ——— 5
(g)	Turnaround	0 ——— 1 ——— 2 ——— 3 ——— 4 ——— 5
(h)	Replacement capital	0 ——— 1 ——— 2 ——— 3 ——— 4 ——— 5
(i)	Follow-on investments	0 ——— 1 ——— 2 ——— 3 ——— 4 ——— 5
(j)	Other _____ [Please specify]	0 ——— 1 ——— 2 ——— 3 ——— 4 ——— 5

Thank you.

Now please hand this sheet back to the interviewer

Sheet 5

Could you please circle below the importance to you of the following factors when you make a risk appraisal within your comapny.

Factor		Degree of Importance
		Low .... High

(a)	Market opportunities	0 —— 1 —— 2 —— 3 —— 4 —— 5
(b)	Global environment	0 —— 1 —— 2 —— 3 —— 4 —— 5
(c)	Local environment	0 —— 1 —— 2 —— 3 —— 4 —— 5
(d)	Compelling nature of the proposition	0 —— 1 —— 2 —— 3 —— 4 —— 5
(e)	Management team	0 —— 1 —— 2 —— 3 —— 4 —— 5
(f)	Business model	0 —— 1 —— 2 —— 3 —— 4 —— 5
(g)	Sales model	0 —— 1 —— 2 —— 3 —— 4 —— 5
(h)	Scale of the business	0 —— 1 —— 2 —— 3 —— 4 —— 5
(i)	Commitment to bring in others	0 —— 1 —— 2 —— 3 —— 4 —— 5
(j)	Funding structure	0 —— 1 —— 2 —— 3 —— 4 —— 5
(k)	Type of exit	0 —— 1 —— 2 —— 3 —— 4 —— 5
(l)	Comparable investments	0 —— 1 —— 2 —— 3 —— 4 —— 5
(m)	Employee capabilities	0 —— 1 —— 2 —— 3 —— 4 —— 5
(n)	Information system capabilities	0 —— 1 —— 2 —— 3 —— 4 —— 5
(o)	Extent of motivation, Empowerment & alignment	0 —— 1 —— 2 —— 3 —— 4 —— 5
	Other _____ [Please specify]	0 —— 1 —— 2 —— 3 —— 4 —— 5

Thank you.

Now please hand this sheet back to the interviewer.

Sheet 43

Could you please indicate below the importance to you of the following factors when you undertake risk appraisals within your company.

Factor	Degree of Importance
	Low .... High

(a)   Public image $0 — 1 — 2 — 3 — 4 — 5$

(b)   Customer service $0 — 1 — 2 — 3 — 4 — 5$

(c)   Quality of product $0 — 1 — 2 — 3 — 4 — 5$

(d)   Legal considerations $0 — 1 — 2 — 3 — 4 — 5$

(e)   Staff morale $0 — 1 — 2 — 3 — 4 — 5$

(f)   Other _____ $0 — 1 — 2 — 3 — 4 — 5$

    [Please specify]

Thank you.

Now please hand this sheet back to the interviewer.

Sheet 45

Could you please indicate below the importance to you of the following features of innovation when you are considering developing and launching a new high-technology product.

Feature   Degree of Importance

Low .... High

(a)   Investee's percentage   0———1———2———3———4———5
      of sales from new
      products

(b)   New product introduction   0———1———2———3———4———5
      versus competitors'

(c)   New product introduction   0———1———2———3———4———5
      versus plan

(d)   Time to develop next   0———1———2———3———4———5
      generation of products

(e)   Number of key items   0———1———2———3———4———5
      in which your company is first
      or second to market

(f)   Breakeven time   0———1———2———3———4———5

(g)   Other _____   0———1———2———3———4———5
      [Please specify]

Thank you.

Now please hand this sheet back to the interviewer.

Appendix 3: Basic data sheet for entrepreneurs

Risk Appraisal in High-Technology Ventures	The Carnegie Trust for the Universities of Scotland

Basic Data Sheet: Investees

1. How many years have you been in business?

2. Define your main line of business

3. At what time intervals do you recalculate your key budgets?

4. What discount rate do you use in capital investment appraisal?

5. What payback method do you use in capital investment appraisal?

6. How many full-time employees do you have?

7. What is your annual turnover?

8. What are your net assets (i.e. fixed assets + current assets - liabilities)?

9. What were your latest net profits?

10. What is your recent history of equity holding in the firm (e.g. high, low and current values)?

11. What was your debt/equity ratio before and after involvement with the venture capital investor?

12. What proportion of ordinary share capital do you own?

13. What is your current rate of return (i.e. net profit after tax divided by total owners' capital employed, including reserves and retained profits)?

14. What rate of return does your investor require?

Appendix 4: Postal questionnaire

Accounting for Risk in UK Venture Capital Contexts
A project sponsored by the Carnegie Trust for the Universities of Scotland

1. Background

1.1   What geographical preferences do you have when deciding whether or not to make an investment? Please rank your preferences below, from 1 to 5 (where 1 is most important, 5 is least important).

Geographical Preference	Rank (1 to 5, with 1 most important)
Local	
Regional	
National	
International (Europe)	
International (world wide)	

1.1   Do you specifically target investment in science parks or technopoles?   Yes ☐ No ☐

If yes, please identify which:

_____

_____

1.2   Please identify below your five preferred industrial sectors for investment, ranked from 1 to 5 (where 1 is most important, 5 is least important).

Industry	Top five rank (1 most important)
Biotechnology	
Medical/health related	
Chemicals and materials	
Energy	
Construction and building products	
Financial services	
Industrial automation	
Industrial products & services	
Manufacturing	
Transportation	
Communications	
Media and photography	
Information technology hardware	
Software and computer services	
Internet technology	
Electronics	
Leisure and entertainment	
Other consumer related	
Services	

1.3   Please identify below your five most common stages of investment, from 1 to 5 (where 1 is most important).

Stage of Investment	Most common (from 1 to 5)
Seed	
Start-up	
Other early stage	
Expansion	
Bridge financing	
Refinancing bank debt	
Secondary purchase/Replacement equity	
Rescue/turnaround	
Management buy-out (MBO)	
Management buy-in (MBI)	
Institutional buy-out (IBO)	
Leveraged build-up (LBU)	
Mezzanine finance	
Public to private	
Purchase of quoted shares	

1.4   What are the minimum, maximum and average size of investments you make in a year?

Minimum	£
Maximum	£
Average	£

1.5   Do you have a preference for lump sum or staged investments, or a combination of the two? [please tick relevant box below]

Lump sum   ☐

Staged investment   ☐

Combination   ☐

2. High Technology and Financial Accounting

High-technology companies are difficult to assess, because much of their value is tied up in so-called intangible assets, such as intellectual property, brands, patents, and so on. This section therefore examines the ways in which you assess, manage and account for intangible assets in high-technology companies.

2.1   To what extent are the standard financial accounts you receive from potential high-technology investees useful in assessing their value?

Completely Useless	Fairly Useless	Neutral	Useful	Very Useful

2.2   Certain internally developed assets may have been valued by the company in ways which are not transparent.

In this context, for which of the following ***internally developed intangible assets*** do you ask investees to provide such valuation information?

	[Please tick one box for each case below]		
Intangible Asset	**We request information on how these have been valued**	**The financial statements provide sufficient information**	**Not relevant**
i. Patents			
ii. Copyright			
iii. Brands			
iv. Licenses			
v. Franchises			
vi. Quotas			
vii. Customer lists			

2.3   To what extent is the following information you receive from potential high-technology investees adequate for the purposes of assessing the value of their company?

Category	On a scale from 1 to 5, where 1 is insufficient and 5 is full and complete information, please tick the relevant box for each item. Insufficient .... Full/complete				
	1	**2**	**3**	**4**	**5**
i. Training					
ii. Marketing					
iii. Strategy					
iv. Development costs					
v. Concessions					
vi. Patents					
vii. Licenses					
viii. Trademarks					
ix. Goodwill					
x. Payments on account					

2.4   When assessing the value of intangible assets in high-technology companies, do you favour valuation at current replacement cost or at estimated market value? *[tick one]*

We favour current replacement cost   ☐

We favour estimated market value   ☐

2.5   How significant are the following costs to you, when evaluating the worth of a high-technology investment.

Category	On a scale from 1 to 5, where 1 is insignificant and 5 is highly significant information, please tick the relevant box for each item. Insignificant .... Highly Significant				
	1	**2**	**3**	**4**	**5**
i. Time our own workforce spends on assessing the technology					
ii. Employment of technology foresight specialists					
iii. Use of other external consultants [please give examples]					

2.6.   How extensive are your requirements on disclosure of risk under the following categories?

Category	On a scale from 1 to 5, where 1 is not at all and 5 is very extensive, please tick the relevant box for each item. Not at all ....Very Extensive				
	1	**2**	**3**	**4**	**5**
i. Technology					
ii. People					
iii. Market					
iv. Financial					
v. Health & Safety					

2.7.   Is the risk information that you require from investees quantitative, qualitative, or both? *[Please tick all that apply]*

Category	Risk disclosure must be .... *[tick all that apply]*		
	Quantitative (in monetary terms)	**Quantitative (in % terms, or with sensitivity or probability analysis)**	**Qualitative**
i. Technology			
ii. People			
iii. Market			
iv. Financial			
v. Health & Safety			

2.8   Do you use score-carding methods to appraise the risk in potential investee companies?

Yes ☐ No ☐

If yes, how important are each of the following items?

Category	On a scale from 1 to 5, where 1 is not at all important and 5 is crucial, please tick the relevant box for each item. Not at all important .... Crucial				
	1	2	3	4	5
i. Technical skills					
ii. Operations					
iii. Production					
iv. Support					
v. Cost estimating					
vi. Benefit estimating					
vii. Scheduling					
viii. Management					
ix. Funding					
x. Stakeholders					
xi. Information security					
xii. Human factors					
xiii. Safety					
xiv. Other *[please specify]*					

2.9 In your view, how important is it that the following be **required** in published financial accounts?

Category	On a scale from 1 to 5, where 1 is not at all important and 5 is crucial, please tick the relevant box for each item. Not at all important .... Crucial				
	1	2	3	4	5
i. Financial risk					
ii. People risk					
iii. Technology risk					
iv. Market risk					
v. Valuations of intangible assets					

2.10 To what extent do you agree with the following statements about risk in high-technology investee companies?

	On a scale from 1 to 5, where 1 is completely disagree and 5 is completely agree, please tick the relevant box for each item. Completely.......Completely disagree agree				
	1	2	3	4	5
i. The information currently provided in financial accounts is sufficient for our purposes					
ii. More information should be provided compulsorily					
iii. Requiring more disclosure in published accounts would provide too much information to rivals					
iv. Our own due diligence is enough to enable us to assess high-technology investments					
v. Standardised risk reporting would facilitate the comparison of potential investees					
vi. Standardised risk reporting would facilitate the allocation of risk capital					

3. Management Accounting and Performance

3.1   How strong an influence do you have over your investee companies' internal management, under the headings below?

	On a scale of 1 to 5, where 1 is little influence and 5 is complete control, please tick the relevant box for each item. Little influence..............Complete control				
	1	2	3	4	5
i. Information systems					
ii. Management accounting					
iii. Financial reporting policies					
iv. Decision-making processes					
v. Control of staff					
vi. Control of management					
vii. Product development					
viii. Marketing					

3.2   On average, how often are you in contact with both low and high performing investee companies? [please tick relevant box for each of low and high performers below]

Frequency of Contact	Low Performers	High Performers
Several times a day		
Daily		
Weekly		
Monthly		
Quarterly		
6-monthly		
Annually		

3.3   How regularly do you require reports from your investee companies on each of the following items?

	daily	weekly	monthly	quarterly	annually
i. Information systems					
ii. Management accounts					
iii. Financial accounts					
iv. Decision-making processes					
v. Control of staff					
vi. Control of management					
vii. Product development					
viii. Marketing					

3.4   Please use the space below to provide us with any further comments you may have on the problems of measuring and managing risk in high-technology ventures.

Many thanks for your cooperation in completing this questionnaire. If you are interested in receiving summary results from our project, in due course, please tick the box.	

	Dr Julia A Smith *Cardiff Business School* *Tel: 029 2087 6652*		*Professor Gavin C Reid* *University of St Andrews* *Tel: 01334 462431*

Please return completed questionnaire to:

Dr Julia A Smith
Cardiff Business School
Aberconway Building
Colum Drive
Cardiff CF10 3EU

Office use only: _____

Notes

8 Further illustrative case studies

1 UK government-funded awards which aim 'to stimulate the creation of new, innovative businesses and to help existing small businesses improve their competitiveness by developing new products and processes to the benefit of the national economy' (Scottish Enterprise, 2006).
2 Sage plc is the UK's leading Accounting Software company with over 3.6 million users worldwide.
3 Liquid Crystal Display.
4 Original Equipment Manufacturer/Original Design Manufacturer.
5 Alternative Investment Market.
6 Named after the Austrian writer on entrepreneurship, Ludwig von Mises, who in his *Human Action* (1949) developed a subjectivist view of entrepreneurship, which emphasised the nimbleness and adaptability of the entrepreneur in the face of uncertainty, rather than his predictive ability. See Moss (1974).

References

Arnold, J. and S. Turley (1996) *Accounting for Management Decisions* (3rd edn), Prentice Hall, New York.

Atrill, P. (2006) *Financial Management for Decision Makers*, Pearson Education, Harlow.

Bacon, C.J. and B. Fitzgerald (2001) A systematic framework for the field of information systems, *Database for Advances in Information Systems*, 32(2), 46–67.

Bailes, J., J. Nielsen and S. Lawton (1998) How forest product companies analyze capital budgets, *Management Accounting*, 80(4), pp. 24–30.

Baiman, S. (1982) Agency research in managerial accounting: a survey, *Journal of Accounting Literature*, 1, 154–209.

Barkham, R.J. and C.W.R. Ward (1999) Investor sentiment and noise traders: discount to net asset value in listed property companies in the UK, *Journal of Real Estate Research*, 18(2), 291–312.

Beetsma, R.M.W.J. and P.C. Schotman (2001) Measuring risk attitudes in a natural experiment: data from the television game show Lingo, *Economic Journal*, 111, 821–48.

Bhattacharyya, S. and J.C. Leach (1999) Risk spillovers and required returns in capital budgeting, *Review of Financial Studies*. 12(3), 461–79.

Bowman, E.H. and D. Hurry (1993) Strategy through the option lens: an integrated view of resource investments and the incremental-choice process, *Academy of Management Review*, 18(4), 760–82.

Bricker, R. and N. Chander (2000) Where Berle and Means went wrong: a reassessment of capital market agency and financial reporting, *Accounting, Organizations and Society*, 25, 529–54.

Brigham, E.F. (1992) *Fundamentals of Financial Management* (6th edn), Dryden Press, Fort Worth, TX.

Brouwer, E. and A. Kleinknecht (1999) Innovative output, and a firm's propensity to patent: an exploration of CIS micro data, *Research Policy*, 28, 615–24.

Brown, G.W. and M.T. Cliff (2005) Investor sentiment and asset valuation, *Journal of Business*, 78(2), 405–40.

Brynjolfsson, E., L.M. Hitt, S. Yang, M.N. Baily, and R.E. Hall (2002) Intangible assets: computers and organizational capital, *Brookings Papers on Economic Activity*, 1, 137–98.

Burgess, R.G. (1984) *In the Field: An Introduction to Field Research*, London, Allen and Unwin.

Bushrod, L. (2002) Regional VC funds come into action, *European Venture Capital Journal*, March, p. 15.

BVCA (2001) at: www.bvca.co.uk.

Campbell, K. (2003) *Smarter Ventures: a survivor's guide to venture capital through the new cycle*, FT Prentice Hall, London.

Canibano, L. Garcia-Ayuso, M. and Sanchez, P. (2000) Accounting for intangibles: a literature review, *Journal of Accounting Literature*, 19, 102–28.

Carey, A. and N. Turnbull (2000) The boardroom imperative on internal control, in *Mastering Risk Financial Times*, 25 April.

Chan, Y.-S. (1983) On the positive role of financial intermediation in the allocation of venture capital in a market with imperfect information, *Journal of Finance*, 38(5), 1543–68.

Chan, Y.-S., D. Siegel, and A.V. Thakor (1990) Learning, corporate control and the performance requirements in venture capital contracts, *International Economic Review*, 31(2), 1543–81.

Chen, J.-H., C.X. Jiang, J.-C. Kim and T.H. McInish (2003) Bid-ask spreads, information asymmetry, and abnormal investor sentiment: evidence from closed-end funds, *Review of Quantitative Finance and Accounting*, 21(4), 303–21.

Coopey, R. and D. Clarke (1995) *3i: Fifty years investing in industry*, Oxford University Press, Oxford.

Cumming, D.J. (2006) The determinants of venture capital portfolio size: empirical evidence, *Journal of Business*, 79(3), 1083–126.

Cumming, D., G. Fleming and A. Schwienbacher (2005) Liquidity risk and venture capital finance, *Financial Management*, 34(4), 77–105.

Damodaran, A. (2006) *Applied Corporate Finance* (2nd edn), Wiley, New York.

Dauterive, J. and W. Fok (2004) Venture capital for China: opportunities and challenges, *Managerial Finance*, 30(2), 3–15.

Dixit, A. and S. Skeath (1999) *Games of Strategy*, Norton, New York.

Duffie, D. and J. Pan (1997) An overview of value at risk, *Journal of Derivatives*, Spring, 7–49.

Dupire, B. (1999) *Monte Carlo: methodologies and applications for pricing and risk management*, Risk Books, London.

Eckstein, C., P. Kyviakidis and D. Tinkelman (1998) Resolving audit issues in a high-tech environment: a case study, *Issues in Accounting Education*, 13(3), 595–612.

Eliasson, G. and C. Wihlborg (2003) On the macroeconomic effects of establishing tradability in weak property rights, *Journal of Evolutionary Economics*, 13(5), 607–32.

Engel, D. (2004) The performance of venture-backed firms: the effect of venture capital company characteristics, *Industry and Innovation*, 11(3), 249–63.

Engel, E., E.A. Gordon and R.M. Hayes (2002) The roles of performance measures and monitoring in annual governance decisions in entrepreneurial firms, *Journal of Accounting Research*, 40(2), 485–518.

Ezzamel, M. and H. Hart (1987) *Advanced Management Accounting: An Organizational Emphasis*, Cassell, Gillingham.

Fielding, N.G. and J.L. Fielding (1986) *Linking Data*, Sage, Beverley Hills, CA.

Fiet, J.O. (1995a) Risk avoidance strategies in venture capital markets, *Journal of Management Studies*, 32, 551–74.

Fiet, J.O. (1995b) Reliance upon informants in the venture capital industry, *Journal of Business Venturing*, 10, 195–223.

Fisher, K.L. and M. Statman (2000) Investor sentiment and stock returns, *Financial Analysts Journal*, 56(2), 16–23.

Florou, A. (2005) Discussion of performance of private to public MBOs: the role of venture capital, *Journal of Business Finance and Accounting*, 32(3–4), 683–90.

Francis, J. and A. Smith (1995) Agency costs and innovation: some empirical evidence, *Journal of Accounting and Economics*, 19, 383–409.

Frank, M.Z. (1988) An intertemporal model of industry exit, *Quarterly Journal of Economics*, 103, 333–44.

Frederickson, J.R. (1992) Relative performance information: the effects of common uncertainty and contract type on agent effort, *Accounting Review* 67(4), 647–69.

Freel, M.S. (1999) The financing of small firm product innovation within the UK, *Technovation*, 19, 707–19.

Fried, V.H. and R.D. Hisrich (1995) The venture capitalist: a relationship investor?, *California Management Review*, 37(2), 101–13.

Frigo, M.L. and J.P. Sweeney (2005) A holistic approach to venture capital investment decisions, *Strategic Finance*, 86(8), 8–10.

Garcia-Ayuso, M. (2003) Factors explaining the inefficient valuation of intangibles, *Accounting, Auditing and Accountability Journal*, 16(1), 57–69.

Gelb, D.S. and P. Siegel (2000) Intangible assets and corporate signaling, *Review of Quantitative Finance and Accounting*, 15(4), 307–23.

Ghemawat, P. (1991) *Commitment*, Free Press, New York.

Gibbons, J.D. (1985) *Nonparametric Statistical Inference* (2nd edn), Marcel Dekker, New York.

Gifford, S. (1995) Endogenous opportunity costs and first-best outcomes in a principal–agent model of venture capital, Working Paper, Boston University.

Glaser, B.G. and A.L. Strauss (1967) *The Discovery of Grounded Theory*, Aldine, Chicago.

Gompers, P. and J. Lerner (2001) The venture capital revolution, *Journal of Economic Perspectives*, 15(2), 145–68.

Gompers, P.J., Lerner, M.M. Blair and T. Hellmann (1998) What drives venture capital fundraising? *Brookings Papers on Economic Activity: Microeconomics*, 1, 149–204.

Goodman, E.A. (2003) Before you invest in venture capital, *Strategic Finance*, 85(6), 20–3.

Green, J. (2004) Venture capital at a new crossroads: lessons from the Bubble, *Journal of Management Development*, 23(10), 972–6.

Green, M.B. (2004) Venture capital investment in the United States 1995–2002, *Industrial Geographer: Special Issue: Geography of Finance*. Part 1, 2(1), 2–30A.

Hall, B.H., A. Jaffe and M. Trajtenberg (2005) Market value and patent citations, *Rand Journal of Economics*, 36(1), 16–38.

Hand, J.R.M. (2002) Intangibles: management, measurement, and reporting, *Accounting Review*, 77(3), 696–7.

Hand, J.R.M. (2005) The value relevance of financial statements in the venture capital market, *Accounting Review*, 80(2), 613–48.

Hardman, D.K. and P. Ayton (1997) Arguments for qualitative risk assessment: the StAR risk adviser, *Expert Systems*, 14(1), 24–36.

Healy, P.M. and K.G. Palepu (2001) Information asymmetry, corporate disclosure and the capital markets: a review of the empirical disclosure literature, *Journal of Accounting and Economics*, 31, 405–40.

Holland, J. (2001) Financial institutions, intangibles and corporate governance, *Accounting, Auditing and Accountability Journal*, 14(4), 497–529.

Holmström, B. (1979) Moral hazard and observability, *Bell Journal of Economics*, 10, 74–91.

Hsu, D.H. and M. Kenney (2005) Organizing venture capital: the rise and demise of

American Research and Development Corporation, 1946–1973, *Industrial and Corporate Change*, 14(4), 579.

Hyytinen, A. and O. Toivanen (2003) Asymmetric information and the market structure of the venture capital industry, *Journal of Financial Services Research*, 23(3), 241–9.

Jaffe, A.B. (2000) The US patent system in transition: policy innovation and the innovation process, *Research Policy*, 29, 531–57.

Jain, B.A. and O. Kini (2000) Does the presence of venture capitalists improve the survival profile of IPO firms?, *Journal of Business Finance and Accounting*, 27(9–10), 1139–83.

Jankowicz, A.D. (2000) *Business Research Projects*, 3rd edn, Business Press, London.

Jelic, R., B Saadouni and M. Wright (2005) Performance of private to public MBOs: the role of venture capital, *Journal of Business Finance and Accounting*, 32(3–4), 643–82.

Jensen, M.C. and Meckling, W.H. (1976) Theory of the firm: managerial behaviour, agency costs and ownership structure, *Journal of Financial Economics*, 3, 305–60.

Jorion, P. (2000) *Value at Risk: the new benchmark for controlling market risk*, Irwin, Chicago.

Jovanovic, B. (1982) Selection and evolution of industry, *Econometrica*, 50, 649–70.

Kahneman, D. and A. Tversky (1979) Prospect theory: an analysis of decision under risk, *Econometrica*, 47, 263–91.

Kaplan, R.S. and D.P. Norton (1992) The balanced scorecard – measures that drive performance, *Harvard Business Review*, Jan/Feb, 71–80.

Kaplan, R.S. and D.P. Norton (1996) Using the balanced scorecard as a strategic management system, *Harvard Business Review*, 74(1), 75–85.

Kaplan, S.E. (1982) The effects of client risk, internal control evaluation and internal control strength on audit program planning: an empirical study, University of Illinois at Urbana-Champaign.

Kaplan, S.N. and P. Stromberg (2001) Venture capitalists as principals: contracting, screening and monitoring, *American Economic Review*, 91(2), 426–30.

Keuschnigg, C. (2004) Venture capital backed growth, *Journal of Economic Growth*, 9(2), 239–61.

Keynes, J.M. (1921) *A Treatise on Probability*, Macmillan, London.

Knight, F.H. (1921) *Risk, Uncertainty and Profit*, Chicago University Press (Stigler edition, 1971).

Kortum, S. and J. Lerner (1999) What is behind the recent surge in patenting?, *Research Policy*, 28, 1–22.

Kothavala, K. (2003) Proportional consolidation versus the equity method: a risk measurement perspective on reporting interests in joint ventures, *Journal of Accounting and Public Policy*, 22(6), 517–38.

KPMG (1997) *VaR – Understanding and Applying Value-at-Risk*, Risk Books, London.

Khurshed, A. (2000) Does the presence of venture capitalists improve the survival profile of IPO firms?, *Journal of Business Finance and Accounting*, 27(9–10), 1177–83.

Lefley, F. (1997) Approaches to risk and uncertainty in the appraisal of new technology capital projects, *International Journal of Production Economics*, 53, 21–33.

Lerner, J. (2002) Boom and bust in the venture capital industry and the impact on innovation, *Economic Review – Federal Reserve Bank of Atlanta*, 87(4), 25–39.

Lewis, E.E. and J.W. Lippitt (1999) Valuing intellectual assets, *Journal of Legal Economics*, 9(1), 31–48.

Lin, C. and C. Chou (2005) An empirical study on corporate governance mechanism and its antecedents: evidence from Taiwanese venture capital industry, *Journal of American Academy of Business*, 6(1), 155–60.

Lipe, M.G. (1998) Individual investors' risk judgements and investment decisions: the impact of accounting and market data, *Accounting, Organizations and Society* 23(7), 625–40.

Liu, C.-C. and S.-H. Chen (2006) The management of risk by Taiwanese venture capital firms operating in China: a process perspective, *International Journal of Management*, 123(3), 419–29.

Lockett, A., G. Murray and M. Wright (2002) Do UK venture capitalists *still* have a bias against investment in new technology firms? *Research Policy*, 31(6), 1009–30.

Lorenz, T. (1989) *Venture Capital Today: A practical guide to the venture capital market*, 2nd edition, New York, Woodhead-Faulkner.

Loft, J.L. and M.D. Shields (2001) Why does fixation persist? Experimental evidence on the judgement performance effects of expensing intangibles, *Accounting Review*, 76(4), 561–87.

McLaney, E. and P. Atrill (2002) *Accounting: an introduction*. Pearson Education Limited, Harlow.

Magee, R.P. (1998) Variable cost allocation in a principal–agent setting, *Accounting Review*, 63(1), 42–54.

Maines, L.A., E. Bartov, P.M. Fairfield, D.E. Hirst *et al.* (2003) Evaluation of the FASB's proposed accounting and disclosure requirements for guarantors, *Accounting Horizons*, 17(1), 51–9.

Manigart, S., K. de Waele, M. Wright, K. Robbie, P. Desbrières, H.J. Sapienza and A. Beekman (2002) Determinants of required return in venture capital investments: a five-country study, *Journal of Business Venturing*, 17(4), 291–312.

Mantell, E.H. (2003) Stochastic properties of the venture capital funding process, *Journal of Financial Management and Analysis*, 16(1), 1–13.

Mason, C.M. and R.T. Harrison (1997) Business angel networks and the development of the informal venture capital market in the UK: is there still a role for the public sector?, *Small Business Economics*, 9(2), 111–24.

Mason, C.M. and R.T. Harrison (2000) The size of the informal venture capital investor market in the United Kingdom, *Small Business Economics*, 15(2), 137–48.

Megna, P. and M. Klock (1993) The impact of intangible capital on Tobin's q in the semiconductor industry, *American Economic Review*, 83(2), 265.

Mendoza, L.E., A.C. Griman, M.A. Perez and T. Rojas (2002) Evaluation of environments for portals development: a case study, *Information Systems Management*, 19(2), 70.

Mueller, D.C. and D. Supina (2002) Goodwill capital, *Small Business Economics*, 19(3), 233.

Miles, M.B. and A.M. Huberman (1984) *Qualitative Data Analysis*, Sage, London.

Mirrlees, J. (1976) The optimal structure of incentives and authority within an organization, *Bell Journal of Economics*, 7, 105–31.

Mises, L. von (1949) *Human Action, The Scholars Edition*, Ludwig von Mises Institute, Auburn, Alabama.

Mitchell, F., G.C. Reid and J.A.S. Smith (2000) *Information System Development in the Small Firm: the use of management accounting*, CIMA Research Monograph, Chartered Institute of Management Accountants; London.

Mitchell, F., G.C. Reid and N. Terry (1995) Post-investment demand for accounting information by venture capitalists, *Accounting and Business Research*, 25(99), 186–96.

Mitchell, F., G.C. Reid and N. Terry (1997) Venture capital supply and accounting information system development, *Entrepreneurship Theory and Practice*, Summer, 45–62.

Mitchell, F., G.C. Reid and N. Terry (1999) Accounting information system development and the supply of venture capital. Chapter 12 in M. Wright and K. Robbie (eds), *Management Buyouts and Venture Capital: Into the Next Millennium*, Edward Elgar, Cheltenham, pp. 263–79.

Mitra, D. (2000) The venture capital industry in India, *Journal of Small Business Management*, 38(2), 76–9.

Moesel, D.D. and J.O. Fiet (2001) Embedded fitness landscapes – Part 2: Cognitive representation by venture capitalists, *Venture Capital* 3(3), 187–213.

Moesel, D.D., J.O. Fiet and L.W. Busenitz (2001) Embedded fitness landscapes – Part 1: How a venture capitalist maps highly subjective risk, *Venture Capital*, 3(2), 91–106.

Moore, B. and R. Wüstenhagen (2004) Innovative and sustainable energy technopoles: the role of venture capital, *Business Strategy and the Environment*, 13(4), 235.

Moss, L.S. (ed.) (1974) *The Economics of Ludwig von Mises*, Sheed and Ward, Lanham, MD.

Mueller, J.M. (2004) Amortization of certain intangible assets, *Journal of Accountancy*, 198(6), 74–8.

Murray, G. (1995) Managing investors' risk in venture capital-financed new technology-based firms, paper presented to the ESRC conference on Risk in Organisational Settings, The White House, London.

Murray, G. and J. Lott (1995) Have UK venture capitalists a bias against investment in new technology-based firms?, *Research Policy*, 24, 283–99.

Murray, G.C. and R. Marriott (1998) Why has the investment performance of technology-specialist, European venture capital funds been so poor?, *Research Policy*, 27, 947–76.

Mutch, A. (1999) Critical realism, managers and information, *British Journal of Management*, 10, 323–33.

Neujens, P. (1987) *The Choice Questionnaire: design and evaluation of instrument for collecting informed opinions of a population*, Free University Press, Amsterdam.

Norman, A. (2004) Venture capital contracting and the valuation of high-technology firms, *Journal of Economics Literature*, 42(3), 924.

Norusis, M.J. (1993) *SPSS Base System User's Guide 6.0*, SPSS Inc., Chicago.

Nouri, H. and R.J. Parker (1996) The effect of organizational commitment on the relation between budgetary participation and budgetary slack, *Behavioural Research in Accounting*, 8, 74–90.

Oppenheim, A.N. (2000) *Questionnaire Design, Interviewing, and Attitude Measurement*, Pinter, London.

Ouksel, A.M., K. Mihavics and P. Chalos (1997) Accounting information systems and organization learning: a simulation, *Accounting, Management and Information technology*, 7(1), 1–19.

Peneder, M. (2002) Intangible investment and human resources, *Journal of Evolutionary Economics*, 12(1–2), 107–34.

Perdue, J.C. (2004) Energy venture capital sector sees renewed interest, *Journal of Structured and Project Finance*, 9(4), 56–9.

Perez-Castrillo, D. and N. Riedinger (1999) Auditing cost overrun claims, mimeo, Department of Economics, Autonomous University of Barcelona.

Poynder, R. (2001) Getting back to basics, *Information World Review*, 49–50.

Proimos, A. and S. Wright (2005) A pilot study of venture capital investment appraisal in Australia, *Journal of Financial Services Marketing*, 9(3), 272–86.

Pruthi, S., M. Wright and A. Lockett (2003) Do foreign and domestic venture capital firms differ in their monitoring of investees? *Asia Pacific Journal of Management*, 20(2), 175–204.

Quiry, P., M. Dallochio, Y. Le Fur and A. Salvi (2005) *Corporate Finance: theory and practice (Pierre Vernimmen)*, Wiley, New York.

Radner, R. (1985) The internal economy of large firms, *Economic Journal*, 96, 1–22.

Rahl, L. (2000) *Risk Budgeting: a new approach to investing*, Risk Books, London.

Randjelovic, J., A.R. O'Rourke and R.J. Orasato (2003) The emergence of green value capital, *Business Strategy and the Environment*, 12(4), 240.

Reid, G.C. (1987) *Theories of Industrial Organization*, Basil Blackwell, Oxford.

Reid, G.C. (1989) *Classical Economic Growth*, Basil Blackwell, Oxford.

Reid, G.C. (1992) A note on the design and structure of a small firm's relational database, *Small Business Economics*, 4, 9–14.

Reid, G.C. (1993) *Small Business Enterprise*, Routledge, London.

Reid, G.C. (1996) Fast growing small entrepreneurial firms and their venture capital backers: an applied principal–agent analysis, *Small Business Economics*, 8, 1–14.

Reid, G.C. (1998) *Venture Capital Investment: an agency analysis of practice*, Routledge, London.

Reid, G.C. (1999) The application of principal–agent methods to investor–investee relations in the UK venture capital industry, *Venture Capital*, 1(4), 1–18.

Reid, G.C. (2007) *The Foundations of Small Business Enterprise: an entrepreneurial analysis of small firm inception and growth*, Routledge, London.

Reid, G.C. and C.J. Roberts (1996) Performance implications of patent family size, Chapter 8 in A. Belcher, J. Hassard and S.J. Procter (eds), *R&D Decisions: Strategy, Policy and Disclosure*, Routledge, London, pp. 169–88.

Reid, G.C. and J.A. Smith (2000) The impact of contingencies on information system development, *Management Accounting Research*, 11(4), 427–50.

Reid, G.C. and J.A. Smith (2001) How do venture capitalists handle risk in high-technology ventures? Some preliminary results, *Frontiers of Entrepreneurship Research*, Babson College, 565.

Reid, G.C. and J.A. Smith (2002) How do venture capitalists handle risk in high-technology ventures?, in M. Epstein (ed.), *Performance Measurement and Management Control*, Vol. 12, Elsevier Science Ltd, pp. 361–79.

Reid, G.C. and J.A. Smith (2003a) Venture capital and risk in high-technology enterprises, 2003, *International Journal of Business and Economics*, 2(3), 227–44.

Reid, G.C. and J.A. Smith (2003b) Is there an industry consensus on risk? Evidence from UK venture capital contracting in high-technology enterprises, *Frontiers of Entrepreneurship Research*, Babson College.

Reid, G.C. and J.A. Smith (2004) Investor and investee conduct in the risk appraisal of high technology new ventures in the UK, *Problemy Teorii i Praktiki Upravleniya* [*Problems of Management Theory and Practice*], 1, 48–56 (Russian).

Reid, G.C. and J.A. Smith (2005) When our chip comes in…, *Articles of Merit Award Program for Distinguished Contribution to Management Accounting*, Professional Accountants in Business Committee, International Federation of Accountants, New York (reprint).

Reid, G.C. and J.A. Smith (2006) Investment Strategy, *Financial Management*, February, 27–8.

Reid, G.C., P.A. Siler and J.A. Smith (1994) Intellectual property and patent quality, Department of Economics and Law, Dundee Institute of Technology, discussion paper.

Reid, G.C., P.A. Siler and J.A. Smith (1996) The quality of patenting in the UK scientific instruments industry, in A. Webster and K. Packer (eds), *Innovation and the Intellectual Property System*, Kluwer Law International, London, pp. 23–45.

Reid, G.C., N.G. Terry and J.A. Smith (1996) The quality of patenting in the UK scientific instruments industry, in A. Webster and K. Packer (eds), *Innovation and the Intellectual Property System*, Kluwer Law International, London, pp. 23–45.

Reid, G.C., N.G. Terry and J.A. Smith (1997) Risk management in venture capital investor–investee relations, *European Journal of Finance*, 3(1), 27–47.

Repullo, R. and J. Suarez (2004) Venture capital finance: a security design approach, *Review of Finance*, 8(1), 75–108.

Rice, M.P., G.C. O'Connor, R. Leifer, C.M. McDermott and T. Standish-Kuon (2000) Corporate venture capital models for promoting radical innovation, *Journal of Marketing Theory and Practice*, 8(3), 1–10.

Ricketts, M. (1986) The geometry of principal and agent: yet another use for the Edgeworth box, *Scottish Journal of Political Economy*, 33, 228–48.

Ricketts, M. (2002) *The Economics of Business Enterprise*, Edward Elgar, Cheltenham.

Robbie, M.K. (1998) Venture capital and private equity: a review and synthesis, *Journal of Business Finance and Accounting*, 25(5–6), 521–70.

Robnik, L. (2006) Venture capital development and its importance for Slovenian entrepreneurship, *Economic and Business Review for Central and South-Eastern Europe*, 8(2), 167–84.

Rosenberg, D. (2003) The two 'cycles' of venture capital, *Journal of Corporation Law*, 28(3), 419.

Ross, S.A. (1973) The economic theory of agency: the principal's problem, *American Economic Review*, 63, 134–9.

Ruchala, L.V. (1999) The influence of budget goal attainment on risk attitudes and escalation, *Behavioural Research in Accounting*, 11, 161–91.

Ruhnka, J.C. and J.E. Young (1991) Some hypotheses about risk in venture capital investing, *Journal of Business Venturing*, 6, 115–33.

Sahlman, W.A. (1994) Insights from the venture capital model of project governance, *Business Economics*, July, 35–7.

Salehizadeh, M. (2005) Venture capital investments in emerging economies: an empirical analysis, *Journal of Developmental Entrepreneurship*, 10(3), 253–69.

Salter, S.B. and D.J. Sharp (2001) Agency effects and escalation of commitment: do small national culture differences matter?, *International Journal of Accounting*, 36, 33–45.

Sapienza, H.J. (1989) Variations in Venture Capitalist-Entrepreneur Relations: antecedents and consequences, unpublished PhD thesis, University of Maryland at College Park, Ann Arbor, Michigan.

Sapienza, H.J., M.A. Korsgaard, P.K. Goulet and J.P. Hoogendam (2000) Effects of agency risks and procedural justice on board processes in venture-backed firms, *Entrepreneurship and Regional Development*, 12, 331–51.

Scapens, R.W. (1991) *Management Accounting: a review of recent development*, 2nd edition, Macmillan, London.

Schroeder, N. and C. Gibson (1990) Readability of management's discussion and analysis, *Accounting Horizons*, 4(4), 78–87.

Sekaran, U. (1992) *Research Methods for Business: a skill building approach* (2nd edn), Wiley, New York.

Sheu, D.-F. and H.-S. Lin (2006) A study on the information transparency of the involvements by venture capital – case from Taiwan IT industry, *Journal of American Academy of Business*, 10(1), 227–33.

Smith, J.A. (2005) Empirical study of a venture capital relationship, *Accounting, Auditing and Accountability Journal*, 18(6), 756–84.

Smolarski, J., H. Verick, S. Foxen and C. Kut (2005) Risk management in Indian venture capital and private equity firms: a comparative study, *Thunderbird International Business Review*, 47(4), 469.

Statman, L. (1990) How many stocks make a diversified portfolio?, in D.H. Miller and S.C. Myers (eds), *Frontiers of Finance: the Battermach Fellowship Papers*, Blackwell, Oxford.

Terry, N.G. (1994) Some thoughts on trends and maturity patterns in UK venture capital 1985–1993, Working Paper 94.3, Centre for Financial Markets Research, Department of Business Studies, University of Edinburgh.

Thompson, P.B. (1997) Evaluating energy efficiency investments: accounting for risk in the discounting process, *Energy Policy*, 25(12), 989–96.

Tremblay, M.A. (1982) The key informant technique: a non-ethnographic application, in R. Burgess (ed.), *Field Research: a Sourcebook and Field Manual*, Allen and Unwin; London.

Triantis, A.J. and J.E. Hodder (1990) Valuing flexibility as a complex option, *Journal of Finance*, 45, 549–65.

Tukey, J.W. (1977) *Exploratory Data Analysis*, Princeton University Press, Princeton, NJ.

Turnbull Report (1999) *Internal Control: Guidance for Directors on the Combined Code, (The Turnbull Report)*, Institute of Chartered Accountants in England and Wales, Accountancy Books, London.

Uher, T.E. and A.R. Toakley (1999) Risk management in the conceptual phase of the project, *International Journal of Project Management*, 17(3), 161–9.

VCR Guide (2000) *The Venture Capital Report Directory 2000/01: private equity and venture capital in the UK and Europe*, Financial Times/Prentice Hall (Pearson Education), London.

Waites, R. and G. Dies (2006) Corporate research and venture capital can learn from each other, *Research Technology Management*, 49(2), 20–4.

Wallsten, T.S. (1990) The costs and benefits of vague information, in R.M. Hogarth (ed.), *Insights in Decision Making: a tribute to Hillel J. Einhorn*, Chicago University Press, pp. 28–43.

Weber, J. and M. Willenborg (2003) Do expert informational intermediaries add value? Evidence from auditors in microcap initial public offerings, *Journal of Accounting Research*, 41(4), 681–720.

Webster, A. and K. Packer (1996a) Intellectual property and the wider innovation system. Chapter 1, in A. Webster and K. Packer (eds), *Innovation and the Intellectual Property System*, Kluwer Law International, London.

Webster, A. and K. Packer (eds) (1996b) *Innovation and the Intellectual Property System*, Kluwer Law International, London.

Werner, O. and M. Schoepfle (1987) *Systematic Fieldwork, vol. 1: Foundations of Ethnography and Interviewing*, Sage, Newbury Park, CA.

Wilson, J.W. (1985) *The New Ventures: inside the high-stakes world of venture capital*, Addison-Wesley, Reading, MA.

Wong, Shee Q. (2003) Investor sentiment and asymmetric earnings revisions, *American Business Review*, 21(1), 17–20.

Wonnacott, T.N. and R.J. Wonnacott (1977) *Introductory Statistics* (3rd edn), Wiley, New York.

Woolcott, H.F. (2005) *The Art of Fieldwork*, 2nd edition, Altimura Press, Wahaut Creek, CA.

Wright, M. and K. Robbie (1996a) Venture capitalists, unquoted equity investment appraisal and the role of accounting information, *Accounting and Business Research*, 26(2), 153–77.

Wright, M. and K. Robbie (1996b) *Management buy-outs 1986–1996 – Toward the next Millennium*, CMBOR Occasional Report, Centre for Management Buyout Research, Nottingham University Business School, University of Nottingham.

Wright, M., A. Lockett, S. Pruthi, S. Manigart, H. Sapienza, P. Desbrières, and U. Hommel (2004a) Venture capital investors, capital markets, valuation and information: US, Europe and Asia, *Journal of International Entrepreneurship*, 2(4), 305.

Wright, M.A., A. Vohora and A. Lockett (2004b) The formation of high-tech university spin-outs: the role of joint ventures and venture capital investors, *Journal of Technology Transfer* 29(3–4), 287–310.

Yin, R.K. (1984) *Case Study Research*, Sage, Beverley Hills, CA.

Yin, R.K. (1993) *Applications of Case Study Research*, Sage, Newbury Park, CA.

Zacharakis, A.L. and G.D. Meyer (2000) The potential of actuarial decision models: can they improve the venture capital investment decision?, *Journal of Business Venturing*, 15(4), 323–46.

Index

administered questionnaire 43–4, 167–96
advertising 82
agency: concerns 109; factors 77; optimal
  relationship 25; view of investor behaviour 92
agency risk 5, 22–7, 30, 121, 157; attenuation of
  4; definition of 3; management of 58
agency theory 64, 142
analysis: breakeven 104; of database 49–50;
  hard and soft 11; sensitivity 102, 104, 106,
  113, 122
animal robotics 114–18
Apax 38
applied principal-agent framework 18
appraisal: of investments 105; qualitative 47, 87
Asia 119
assets, intangible 143–5
automated baggage security inspection 121–3

backward induction 163
Bank for International Settlements in Basle 162
behavioural variables and investment 146–53
Bernoulli, D. 29
biotechnology 100
brands 145
breakeven 113, 119; analysis 104; expected time
  60
British Private Equity and Venture Capital
  Association (BVCA) 38
business angels 31
business risk 22–7, 30, 108; definition of 3, 5

California 108
Cambridge 105
Cambridge high-technology agglomeration 8
capital: cost of 113; intellectual 110
capital purchase models 114
cardinal numbers 33
cash flow: management of 83; predicting 46, 83
certain payoffs 164
certainty: effects 29; equivalents 12; line 26
classical frequency limit approach 21
coefficient of concordance 70
collateral evidence 21
colonial merchant adventuring 7
commercial factors influencing risk appraisal
  90–3

common interest, mutual assumptions of 63
company, public image 62
complexity and uncertainty 24
concordance: coefficient of 70; of investors' or
  entrepreneurs' opinion 71–2; Kendall W test
  of 75, 78, 90
conduct of venture capitalists and entrepreneurs
  53–64
conservatism of UK investors 16–17
contracting, the implications of effort for
  efficient contracting **26**
control and ownership 24
copy protection 103–5
Copyright, Director of 40
copyrights 145
cost overrun, problem of 5
cows 115–18
cross-site analysis in all case studies *127*
customer service 120, 126

Damodaran, A. 82
database: analysis of 49–50; construction 47–8
DCF 127–8; methods 104
deal-sensitive information 153
decision making 46, 86–7
decision systems, expert 14
decision tree methods 162
decision trees 103, 120, 163
degree of belief estimates 22
degree of incentivisation 24
delegation of responsibilities 161
Delphic method 33
Department of Trade and Industry (DTI) 9
direct payoff maximisation 86–7
Director of Copyright 40
disclosure and risk reporting 140–1
dot-com: boom 124; crash 108
drug development 99–101

e-commerce: acceleration 105–7; retailing
  123–6
early-stage investment 54, 109
Edinburgh, University of 115–21
effort, incentives for 161
eight-point agenda for administered
  questionnaire *44*

electronic micro-displays 118–21
employees' capabilities 57
empowerment 56
encryption 103
enciphering 103
entrepreneurs 40–3; attitudes to risk **54**; basic
    data sheet for 197; concordance with
    investors' opinion 71–2; conduct 53–64;
    difference from venture capitalists 19; first
    priority 64; importance of features of
    innovation **61**; importance of non-financial
    factors **63**; most important factors in risk
    appraisal **57, 75**; participating in fieldwork
    43; public image 63; ranking of risk of
    investment stage by mean rank **69**; statistical
    analysis 67–78
environment 93
equity, replacement 136
equity provision, high risk end of 133
ethical values 93
euros 122
exchange rate 119
exit: flop 59
exit strategies 59
expected payoffs 164
expected values 45–6, 82–3
expert decision systems 14
explosives detection systems (EDS) 121

factors in risk appraisal 56–9, 72–8
fee schedule 25
fieldwork 37–51; unstructured preliminary
    38–40
Fiet, J. 10
financial accounts: benefits from required
    publishing 142–3; correlations with the
    usefulness of *147*; usefulness of 147
financial modelling 46, 84–5, 107; scenario
    based 123
financial reporting 139–40; compulsory 143
financial reports: importance of disclosure in
    142; usefulness in assessing the value of
    high-technology firms **140**
flat panel displays 107
follow-on investments 124
formal modelling 58
Franklin, B. 13
frequency limit approach, classical 21
frequency limit principle 6, 20–1, 30
fund size, average 41
funding structure 92

gatekeepers 39
Generally Accepted Accounting Practice
    (GAAP) 132–3
Germany 122
Gibbons, J.D. 69–70
Glasgow 112
grant revenue 114

hard analysis 11
hard information 87
head room in risk management plans 53

high communicators 39

incentives for effort 161
incentivisation, degree of 24
individual investors' rankings of importance of
    factors for risk appraisal *91*
Industrial and Commercial Finance Corporation
    (ICFC) 7
informal investors 31
information: asymmetry 141, 142; deal-sensitive
    153; provision 141; soft 123, 128; soft or hard
    87
information systems 126, 161; benefits 26;
    capability 75, 92
infra-red microprocessors 101–3
innovation features; impact on high-technology
    investment 94
innovation risk 22–7, 158; definition of 3, 6;
    features of 59–61
instrumentation 37–51; design 43–4; designing
    new 11
intangible assets 143–5; valuation of 133
intangibles 131–45
intellectual capital 110
intellectual property 5, 32–3, 110; how to value
    9
internal management 148–50
internal rates of return (IRRs) 7
investee firm's internal structure and investor
    influence 150
investment: appraisals of 105; average
    maximum 138; average minimum 138; and
    behavioural variables 146–53; early-stage *see*
    early stage investment; monitoring 58;
    preference by stage **135**; preference by
    technology **134**; preference for investment by
    market extent **137**; riskiness of 88–90;
    seed-corn *see* seed-corn investment; startup
    see startup investment; time horizon 45, 81
investment stage and risk disclosure 147–8
investment types and individual investors'
    rankings of risk of investment types *89*
investor 40–3; agency view of behaviour 92;
    agreement 140–1; concordance with
    entrepreneurs' opinion 71–2; informal 31;
    judgement 150; major risk concern of 64;
    opinion 146; risk appraisal by 79–95;
    sentiment 146, 150; statistical analysis 67–78
Investors in Industry (3i) 38
investor influence and investee firm's internal
    structure 150
investor–entrepreneur venture capital 13
investors' and entrepreneurs' mean rank scores
    of riskiness by investment types **73**
investors' and entrepreneurs' mean ranks of
    importance of factors for risk appraisal **76**
Investors' most important factors in risk
    appraisal **74**

Japan 108

Kendall W test of concordance 75, 78, 90
key informants 39

Keynes, J.M. 20–1, 28
Knight, F. 11

laboratory research, initial 100
labour costs 114
laser detectors 112–15
legal considerations 120, 126
LEP technology 112
Lerner, J. 33
licence revenue 114
light emitting polymer (LEP) displays 107–9
lighting 107
Likert scale 49, 64, 90
liquidity risk 32
local environment 77
London Stock Exchange 100, 105
loss: maximum 162; maximum expected 84

M4 corridor 8, 43
macroeconomy 102
main determinants of total company risk 160
major restructuring 55
management 92; accounting system (MAS) 32;
    buy-in (MBI) 7, 55; buy-out (MBO) 7, 55; of
    cash flow 83; internal 148–50
management accounting 20; correlations with
    influence over management accounting *149*
management team 56, 157; quality of 126
market: entry 114; opportunities 77, 157; risk 121
Massachusetts 123–6; high-technology corridor
    121
maximisation, direct payoff 86–7
maximum expected loss 84
maximum loss 162
mezzanine financing 134
microprocessors, infra-red 101–3
Minister of Science 9
modelling, financial 84–5, 107
monitoring: investment 58; sophistication of 24
Monte Carlo: methods 162; techniques 85
moral hazard 23, 57
moral values 93
morale; staff 62
Morgan, J.P. 163
motivation 56, 126

National Association of Securities Dealers
    Automated Quotations system (NASDAQ)
    39, 100
net present value (NPV) 12
new products, sales from 61
new technological product, forecast
    development cost of 27
Newport Patent Office 40
non-commercial factors influencing risk
    appraisal 93–4
Norusis, M.J. 71
novelty, concept of 60
NPV calculations 106
null hypothesis 70
numbers: cardinal 33; ordinal 33

Opportunity Evaluation Matrix 126

optimal agency relationship 25
ordinal numbers 33
ownership; and control 24

Pareto's law 125
Patent 4, 145; grant of 34
Patent Office 40; database 99
payback period 81, 127–8
payoff: certain 164; expected 164; function 25
perks 23
perquisite consumption 23
portfolio balance 134
ports of access 10
postal questionnaire 198–205
pre-clinical trials 101
predicting cash flow 46, 83
premium, risk 110
principal-agent: approach 20; model 18;
    relationship 23; setting for investor and
    entrepreneur **23**
private equity 131
product to market 114
products, sales from new 61
project lifetime, risk variation over 83
property, intellectual 110
public image 80, 120, 126; entrepreneurs 63
public image of a company 62
publishing, financial accounts 142–3

qualitative appraisal 47, 87
qualitative methods 128
qualitative and quantitative uncertainty 19–22
qualitative risk assessment 13–14
quality: of management team 126; of product
    126
quantitative and qualitative uncertainty 19–22
quantitative risk assessment 12–13
questionnaire 167–96; administered 43–4,
    167–96; outline of postal questionnaire *139*;
    postal 198–205

rational beliefs 163
reflection effects 29
regression line 77
regressions explaining levels of investment *152*
Reid, G.C. 29
replacement capital 124
replacement equity 136
reporting, risk and intangibles 131–45
research: and development 114; principal stages
    37–8
residual claim 25
responsibilities, delegation of 161
restructuring, major 55
return: on capital employed (ROCE) 146–7; on
    shareholders' funds (ROSF) 147
revenue models 114
risk: agency *see* agency risk; attitudes to 53–6;
    average rankings 88; business *see* business
    risk; capital allocation 141; classes of 3; four
    degrees of 40; and impact categories **165**;
    innovation *see* innovation risk; liquidity 32;
    main determinants of total company risk 160;

risk *continued*
  non-financial factors 61–3; premia 45, 80–1,
    110; reporting in financial accounts **141**; and
    return **110**; and uncertainty 18–34
risk appraisal: by entrepreneurs 99–111; by
    investors 78–95; commercial factors
    influencing 90–3; factors in 56–9, 72–8; non-
    commercial factors influencing 93–4
risk assessment: qualitative 13–14; quantitative
    12–13; and uncertainty 27–9
risk disclosure and investment stage 147–8
risk management plans, headroom in 53
risk reporting: and disclosure 140–1; and
    intangibles 131–45
risk variation over project's lifetime 83
risk-return 81; curve 106; locus 124
riskiness of investment 88–90
RiskMetrics software 163
rollback 163

SAGE forecasting software 117
Sainsbury, Lord D.J. 9
sales revenue 114
sampling 37–51
scale of the business 92
scenario analysis 123
scenario based financial modelling 123
score-card 109, 115, 126; method 13
sectors, ugly 133
seed capital 124
seed investment 68
seed-corn investment 54, 109
sensitivity analysis 45, 82, 102, 104, 106, 113,
    122, 162
share price, collapse of 59
silicon wafers 119
simulation 162
small and medium sized enterprises (SMEs) 9
SMART awards 115
soft analysis 11
soft information 87, 123, 128
software: *RiskMetrics* 163; SAGE forecasting
    49–50, 71, 117
sophistication of monitoring 24
SPSS software package 49–50, 71
staff morale 62, 80, 120, 126
startup investment 54, 68
statistical evidence 21
Summary statistics of investor conduct *137*
SWOT analysis 101

Taiwan 119
technology, bleeding edge 136

technopoles, correlations with investment in
    technopoles *148*
thermal imaging 101–3
tools, decision making 86–7
total company risk: determinants of **161**; main
    determinants of 160
trace gas detection 112
Transportation Safety Administration (TSA) 121
trials, pre-clinical 101
turnaround 55
turnaround investments 124
Turnbull Report 39, 84

ugly sectors 133
UK investors 131; conservatism of approach
    16–17; most desirable sectors 133
uncertainty: appraisal 28; and complexity 24;
    qualitative and quantitative 19–22; and risk
    18–34; and risk assessment 27–9
United Kingdom (UK) 99–121; Cambridge 105;
    Edinburgh 115–21; Glasgow 112; high-
    technology investing culture 85; London
    Stock Exchange 105; M4 corridor 8, 43;
    Newport 40; Patent Office 40; *Venture
    Capital Report Guide to Venture Capital in
    the UK* 99; *Venture Capital Report Guide to
    Venture Capital in the UK and Europe* 42;
    see also UK
United States 121–8; California 108;
    Massachusetts 123–6
University of Edinburgh 115–21

valuation information, requirement for **144**
valuation of intangible assets 133
Value at Risk (VaR) 6, 162
values, ethical and moral 93
variance analysis approach 20
venture capital 131; houses 47; investing 132;
    portfolio size 67
*Venture Capital Report Guide to Venture
    Capital in the UK* 99
*Venture Capital Report Guide to Venture
    Capital in the UK and Europe* 42
Venture Capital Report (VCR) 40–1
venture capitalists: attitudes to risk **54**; conduct
    53–64; difference from entrepreneurs 19;
    importance of features of innovation **60**;
    importance of non-financial factors **62**; most
    important factors in risk appraisal **56**;
    participating in fieldwork *41*; rankings of risk
    of investment stage by mean rank **68**

Watson, T.J. 21